Joan Robinson (1903–1983)
and
George Shackle (1903–1992)

Pioneers in Economics

Series Editor: Mark Blaug

Professor Emeritus, University of London
Consultant Professor, University of Buckingham
Visiting Professor, University of Exeter

This important series presents critical appraisals of influential economists from the 17th century to the present day. It focuses in particular on those economists who were influential in their own time and whose work has had an impact – often inadequately recognized – on the evolution and development of economic thought. The series will be indispensable for a clear understanding of the origin and development of economic ideas and the role played by the leading protagonists of the past.

A full list of published titles in this series is printed at the end of this volume.

Joan Robinson (1903–1983) and George Shackle (1903–1992)

Edited by

Mark Blaug

Professor Emeritus,
University of London

An Elgar Reference Collection

Published by
Edward Elgar Publishing Limited
Gower House
Croft Road
Aldershot
Hants GU11 3HR
England

Edward Elgar Publishing Company
Old Post Road
Brookfield
Vermont 05036
USA

A CIP catalogue record for this book is available from the British Library

Library of Congress Cataloguing in Publication Data
Joan Robinson (1903–1983) and George Shackle (1903–1992)/edited by
   Mark Blaug.
      p.   cm. – (An Elgar reference collection) (Pioneers in
economics: 45)
   Includes bibliographical references.
   1. Robinson, Joan, 1903–1983. 2. Shackle, G.L.S. (George Lennox
Sharman), 1903–1992. I. Blaug, Mark. II. Series. III. Series.
Pioneers in economics: 45.
HB103.R63J62   1992
330.15–dc20   92–16244
                                                                    CIP

ISBN 1 85278 509 8

Contents

Acknowledgements

The editor and publishers wish to thank the following who have kindly given permission for the use of copyright material.

Academic Press, Inc. for article: E.K. Hunt (1983), 'Joan Robinson and the Labour Theory of Value', *Cambridge Journal of Economics*, **7** (3/4), 331–42.

American Economic Association for article: Harvey Gram and Vivian Walsh (1983), 'Joan Robinson's Economics in Retrospect', *Journal of Economic Literature*, **XXI** (2), 518–50.

M.C.B. University Press for articles: J.L. Ford (1985), 'G.L.S. Shackle: A Brief Bio-Bibliographical Portrait', *Journal of Economic Studies*, **12** (1/2), 3–12; Andrew S. Skinner (1985), 'Smith and Shackle: History and Epistemics', *Journal of Economic Studies*, **12** (1/2), 13–20; Brian J. Loasby (1985), 'Profit, Expectations and Coherence in Economic Systems', *Journal of Economic Studies*, **12** (1/2), 21–33; Peter E. Earl and Neil M. Kay (1985), 'How Economists can Accept Shackle's Critique of Economic Doctrines without Arguing Themselves out of their Jobs', *Journal of Economic Studies*, **12** (1/2), 34–48; J.L. Ford (1985), 'Shackle's Theory of Decision Making under Uncertainty: Synopsis and Brief Appraisal', *Journal of Economic Studies*, **12** (1/2), 49–69; John D. Hey (1985), 'The Possibility of Possibility', *Journal of Economic Studies*, **12** (1/2), 70–88; Peter G. McGregor (1985), 'Professor Shackle and the Liquidity Preference Theory of Interest Rates', *Journal of Economic Studies*, **12** (1/2), 89–106.

M.E. Sharpe, Inc. for articles: G.C. Harcourt (1981), 'Notes on an Economic Querist: G.L.S. Shackle', *Journal of Post Keynesian Economics*, **IV** (1), 136–44; Fernando Carvalho (1983–84), 'On the Concept of Time in Shacklean and Sraffian Economics', *Journal of Post Keynesian Economics*, **VI** (2), 265–80.

Every effort has been made to trace all the copyright holders but if any have been inadvertently overlooked the publishers will be pleased to make the necessary arrangement at the first opportunity.

In addition the publishers wish to thank the library of the London School of Economics and Political Science and The Alfred Marshall Library, Cambridge University for their assistance in obtaining these articles.

Introduction

Joan Robinson was the only woman ever to have achieved outstanding eminence in economic theory (which, no doubt, tells us more about economic theory than about women). Her *Economics of Imperfect Competition* (Macmillan, 1933; 2nd edn, 1969) taught an entire generation of economists the microeconomics that now figures so heavily in elementary textbooks. A stalwart defender of Keynes and a leading popularizer of Keynesian economics in the 1930s, she went on after the war to convert Keynesian short-period analysis into a Keynesian-type theory of economic growth, thus laying the foundation of a currently thriving school of Post Keynesian economics. Later she attacked the neoclassical theory of distribution in a classic article, 'The Production Function and the Theory of Capital', *Review of Economic Studies*, **2**, 1954, thereby launching the so-called 'Cambridge Controversies' – Cambridge, England, versus Cambridge, USA – one of the most acrimonious theoretical debates to have disfigured the face of modern economics. Convinced that she had discovered a fatal flaw in standard economic theory – capital cannot be measured independently of the rate of interest and the rate of interest is not uniquely related to the marginal productivity of capital – she moved steadily away on almost all economic questions towards a unique heterodox position of her own. Her entire professional life seemed to refute the old adage that everyone becomes more conservative as they get older.

Joan Robinson was born in 1903 into a middle-class, academic English family, descended on her father's side from F.D. Maurice, the great nineteenth-century Christian Socialist. She graduated from Girton College, Cambridge in 1925 and shortly thereafter married Austin Robinson, soon to become a Cambridge economist in his own right. After a spell in India the Robinsons returned to Cambridge where Joan joined the Cambridge faculty as an assistant lecturer in economics; she became a university lecturer in 1937, reader in 1949 and, finally, a full professor in 1965, retiring in 1971.

Her *Economics of Imperfect Competition* appeared in the same year as Edward Chamberlin's *Theory of Monopolistic Competition* (1933) and both authors independently explored the implications of advertising and product differentiation for the traditional theory of the competitive firm. The long debate about the subtle differences between Robinson's and Chamberlin's treatments occupied microeconomists for many years. Joan Robinson eventually repudiated her book as symptomatic of the kind of static equilibrium analysis she now deplored. Chamberlin, on the other hand, stuck to his guns and in the final analysis won the argument, in so far as there was any real argument. As a member alongside Harrod, Kahn, Meade, Austin Robinson, and Sraffa of the so-called 'circus' of Cambridge and Oxford economists who argued out Keynes' *Treatise* and helped him to formulate what was to become the *General Theory*, Joan Robinson played a key role in the story of the Keynesian Revolution. Her little book *Introduction to the Theory of Employment* (Macmillan, 1937; 2nd edn, 1969) was one of the most widely read prewar introductions to the Keynesian system. A few years later, she performed the same function for Marx in *An Essay on Marxian Economics* (Macmillan, 1942; 2nd edn, 1966), a sparkling, heretical, no-nonsense attempt to give Marx his due as a sort of early Keynesian, which remains to this day one of the best books ever written on Marxian economics. *The Rate of Interest and Other Essays* (Macmillan, 1953) but particularly *The Accumulation of Capital* (Macmillan, Richard D. Irwin, 1956; 3rd edn, 1969) announced a new phase in her work, the attempt to dynamize Keynes and to establish a new analysis of long-run growth under capitalism.

Exercises in Economic Analysis (Macmillan, 1960), *Economic Philosophy* (Watts, 1962; Penguin, 1969), *Essays in the Theory of Economic Growth* (Macmillan, 1962), *Economics – An Awkward Corner* (Allen & Unwin, 1966) and *Economic Heresies* (Macmillan, 1971) confirmed and extended her new departure into a wholesale rejection of the prevailing economic orthodoxy. Weaving together the ideas of such seemingly contradictory authors as Keynes, Kalecki and Sraffa, she struggled hard in her later years to provide an alternative economics that would not depend, as orthodox economics clearly does, on the purely hypothetical comparison of two or more equilibrium positions: since historical time is irreversible, she argued, comparative static analysis is almost irrelevant. *An Introduction to Modern Economics* (McGraw-Hill, 1973), co-authored with J. Eatwell, was to be the fountainhead of this 'new' economics; however, the book was not well received and is generally judged to be a failure as an introductory textbook for first-year students.

A glance at Joan Robinson's five volumes of *Collected Papers* (Basil Blackwell, 1951, 1964, 1965, 1973, 1979) shows that she is one of the best counter-examples of the generalization that all economists write badly: her style, marked by the frequent use of colloquialisms, rhetorical barbs, and a peculiar but intoxicating type of verbal algebra is a sheer delight to read. On the other hand, her admiration of Mao's China and Kim-Sung's North Korea was a continual embarrassment to her friends and foes alike.

The name George Shackle immediately conjures up the words 'expectations' and 'uncertainty' because his entire career has been tirelessly devoted to preaching the doctrine that economic activity is ruled by expectations of future events but that all future events are inherently uncertain and, therefore, more or less unpredictable. Stated like this, few economists would quarrel with the proposition: quarrelling only begins when we ask ourselves whether, in the light of this proposition, we can say anything about the formation of economic expectations; if future events are totally unpredictable, there is in fact little an economist can say about economic activity. Even Frank Knight, who insisted long before Shackle that a great many economic events are 'uncertain' in the sense of being non-repeatable, made room for future events that are simply 'risky', in which case the probability of their occurrence is in fact calculable.

In his earlier books, *Expectations, Investment and Income* (Cambridge University Press, 1938) and *Expectations in Economics* (Cambridge University Press, 1949; 2nd edn, 1952), Shackle avoided the extreme implications of his doctrine and offered a theory of 'the surprise function' as a way out of the dilemma of foresight in the presence of uncertainty: economic agents do have definite expectations about future events, at least in the negative sense of being 'surprised' by certain improbable outcomes, including the surprise of a totally unexpected event; 'the surprise function' is a special sort of non-probabilistic function of the expected values of future outcomes, and Shackle was able to formulate some general propositions about the shape of these surprise functions. However, Shackle's theory of surprise functions was not well received by the rest of the economics profession. Keynes had argued that investment is a volatile and unpredictable variable, precisely because of the unstable expectations of private investors, and this much was generally accepted by macroeconomists. But microeconomists nevertheless continued to operate with the working assumption that economic agents have perfect and hence correct foresight. In recent years, the theory of 'rational expectations' has indeed addressed itself to the manner in which economic expectations are formed but with little attention to Shackle's earlier work in the area.

Shackle himself has virtually abandoned his own technical contributions to the analysis of expectations and has increasingly broadened his argument into a fundamental criticism of the whole of received economic theory for ignoring the problem of pervasive uncertainty. In books like *Decision, Order and Time in Human Affairs* (Cambridge University Press, 1961; 2nd edn, 1969), *Epistemics and Economics: A Critique of Economic Doctrines* (Cambridge University Press, 1972), and particularly *The Years of High Theory, Invention and Tradition in Economic Thought 1926-1939* (Cambridge University Press, 1967), he has traced the precise points at which the economics of the interwar years went wrong, leaving little doubt that what is now needed is a total reconstruction of economic theory. The difficulty is to know how to set about this task and here Shackle is almost deliberately unhelpful. His vehement insistence that absolutely anything can happen tomorrow, and that economic expectations have literally no foundation on which to stand, is so destructive of all possibilities of economic theorizing that his writings virtually amount to the proposal to put a stop to the subject called 'economics'. His literary style, which has always read more like poetry than prose, has in recent years achieved an extraordinary rapturous intensity, which is better calculated to inflame the reader than to enlighten him. Nevertheless, his books leave an indelible impression and are a perfect antidote to the belief that there is absolutely nothing wrong with modern economics.

Shackle was born in Cambridge, England in 1903. He received his BA in 1931 and his PhD in 1937, both from the University of London. He began teaching at the London School of Economics in the 1930s and was deeply involved in the great debates of Keynesian Revolution, which divided the department of economics at LSE as it divided economics departments all over the British Isles. He left in 1951 to become Professor of Economics at the University of Liverpool, where he remained until his retirement in 1969. A Council Member of the Royal Economic Society from 1955-69, President of Section F of the British Association for the Advancement of Science in 1966, and the recipient of several honorary degrees, Shackle was even more active in the years of his retirement from academic life than he had been before: his output of books and articles showed a marked rise in the 1970s.

Note

Several paragraphs in this Introduction were borrowed from my *Great Economists Since Keynes* (Wheatsheaf Books, 1985).

[1]

POST KEYNESIAN PORTRAITS

Notes on an economic querist:
G. L. S. Shackle

G. C. HARCOURT

G. L. S. Shackle is the quintessential English Christian gentleman—courteous, modest, unassuming, considerate, speaking no ill of anyone, and not wishing to hear any, either. He has always been an exceptionally hard worker, and retirement—he is now 77—has made no difference: currently he is writing a paper for this year's meeting of the British Association (the 150th) at York and a biographical essay on Harrod. He writes for three hours each morning. Three hundred and fifty words—a page and a half—is his daily output, written in a beautiful hand in pencil, with an eraser near by so that, considerate as ever, his typist will have a perfect copy. (Shackle's mother said of him that he practiced the three Rs—reading, writing, and rubbing out.)

Shackle was born on July 14, 1903, in Cambridge, the only child of elderly parents (his father was fifty-one when he was born). The family moved to the nearby village of Great Shelford when Shackle was two, and he lived there until 1930. His father was a mathematician, had been a Wrangler, and coached the young Maynard Keynes for the scholarship examination for Eton. Shackle went to the Perse Preparatory School and then, by scholarship, to the Senior School. His distinctive writing style, for which he is justly praised, owes much, he says, to the disciplined and often inspiring teaching he received in his earlier years at the Perse. Shackle was accepted by St. Catharine's (his father's old college) in 1920, but

The author is Professor of Economics at the University of Adelaide. The article is taken from notes based on a visit to George and Catherine Shackle at their Aldeburgh, Suffolk, home, December 17-18, 1980. The author is grateful to Paul Davidson for comments on a draft of the paper.

the family finances were such that he was not able to take up the offer. So he worked for the next fourteen years before going to the L.S.E., first in a bank (where a kindly bank manager helped him to take his first step toward achieving his then goal of obtaining a Commerce degree externally at the University of London, by giving him an extra hour off at lunch time for reading); next, an unhappy year in a London tobacco firm; and then nine years or so as a prep school master at three schools (two in Wales).

While a prep school master, he decided again to take an external degree at the University of London (the hours at the bank had been too long for him to see it through before). He chose Latin, French, economics (he had started economics while at the bank, reading Sir Sidney Chapman's *Outline of Political Economy*, which he still reckons is an excellent book), and modern European history. What to the detached observer appears now as a small hurdle for such a first-rate intelligence appeared at the time to Shackle as the need to break the high jump record. He obtained the degree, and it rekindled in him his interest in economics, already set alight by Chapman and, later, by J. A. Hobson's books, which he found fascinating—"like a detective story, you chased the ideas through the argument." So he read for himself, first, *The Treatise on Money* and Hayek's *Prices and Production*. The result was an article in the first ever issue of *The Review of Economic Studies*, comparing and contrasting the themes in the two books (to which he added distinctively Shacklean touches). Shackle met the research students and younger teachers who had started *R. E. Studs* and from them learned of the Leverhulme research studentship at the L.S.E. They persuaded him to apply. He was interviewed by a committee which included Beveridge, Robbins, and Lucy Mair. He told them how he had read the three or four pages of Vol. 2 of the *Treatise*, in which Keynes sets out his understanding of Austrian capital theory. Shackle turned the argument into a diagram, only to find when he read *Prices and Production*, that Hayek had drawn the same diagram. "That must have been a thrill," they said. "It was," said Shackle. After the interview he went to tea, and Hayek, with the first of many kindnesses to Shackle, said in a loud whisper, "You made a great impression!" Naturally he was awarded the studentship, but he delayed starting at the L.S.E. until January 1935, so as to not let his headmaster down. Virtue was immediately rewarded—"a great stroke of luck"—for it enabled him to attend two exciting sets of lectures: Brinley Thomas on Myrdal and Lindahl

and the Swedish school (Thomas had just returned from a year in
Sweden); Hicks on what were to become the production plan chap-
ters of *Value and Capital*. Shackle was "thrilled to the marrow" by
Thomas who, he says, had real Welsh charisma. His lectures started
Shackle thinking on his own ideas on uncertainty and expectations.

Hicks's production plan, whereby the employer looks forward, shifts resources around in time, *all in thought*, was "a tremendously illuminating idea."

Hayek was appointed Shackle's supervisor; he told him he could work on "anything he liked." Shackle tried to apply the model of *Prices and Production* to an explanation of the business cycle. He found he could not get inside the model of *Prices and Production* —Shackle thinks it "reasonable to have found it difficult"—in order to make it work properly.

Then, in October of 1935, Shackle went to Cambridge (it was the first meeting of the joint London, Cambridge, and Oxford research students' seminar). He heard Joan Robinson give a superb account of what was to be in the *General Theory*. It was "an illumination," it cut Shackle free from the framework of *Prices and Production*, and it enabled him to anticipate both answers to the paradoxes which Richard Kahn posed in a provocative talk at the same meeting and, then, what was in the *General Theory*.

Shackle returned to London "alight" and asked Hayek if he could be released from working on Hayek's themes in order to work instead on Keynes', interpreting Keynes' work in the light of the *ex ante, ex post* distinction to which Shackle had been introduced in Thomas's lectures.[1] Showing tremendous magnanimity, Hayek told Shackle "of course, he could [work on Keynes]." It is one of the ironies of our profession that a most illustrious Keynesian should have started work with Keynes' most profound intellectual opponent.

---

[1] Shackle still thinks that Keynes himself never understood *ex ante* and *ex post*, getting them all mixed up together in both the *Treatise* (the widow's cruse argument) and the *General Theory*. Thus, says Shackle, in the *Treatise* "profits can be reinvested and still not used up." Keynes' profits are windfalls, *ex post* amounts, whereas investment decisions are *ex ante*. Similarly, in the *General Theory* Keynes would appeal to the identical equality of *S* and *I ex post*, yet treat it as if it could be a condition at the same time. Shackle added that Harrod was always against *ex ante* and *ex post*; he recalls the Econometric meeting in Oxford in the long vacation of 1936, at which three papers on the *General Theory* were read, by Harrod, Hicks ("Mr. Keynes and the Classics"), and Meade. Afterward there was a general discussion in which Harrod explained the nature of dynamic theory. Harrod said: "Suppose that output is growing. . . ." Questioner: "Do you mean *has* been or *is* going to grow?" Harrod: "I mean it *is* growing." This insight from the author himself sadly has been lost in the voluminous literature which has since grown up around Harrod's contributions to dynamic theory, with the honorable exceptions of the expositions of Kregel and Shackle himself.

Throughout his life Shackle has made substantial contributions within the Keynesian scheme and, at the same time, has remained an ardent admirer and friend of Hayek. There is to be published soon—it was written in 1978—what Shackle regards as his definitive view of Hayek, in which he feels that he has put Hayek's contributions in *Prices and Production* and *The Pure Theory of Capital* correctly into focus, the culmination of a lifetime of pondering on Hayek's schemes and theories.

Shackle wrote in a year and a bit as a London Ph.D. dissertation what was to become his first book, *Expectations, Investment and Income* (1938). He was examined by Hayek and Redvers Opie (of Magdalen College, Oxford). Opie carried news of the rising young star (well not *that* young) to Oxford, and Shackle received in quick succession letters from Marschak (then a Fellow of All Souls and Director of the Oxford Institute of Statistics) and Henry Phelps Brown at New College, each asking him to be *their* research assistant. Shackle thought that his lack of formal statistical know-how would be less of a handicap to Phelps Brown, so he accepted his offer and spent two years from March 1937 working very hard on British financial statistics. A number of joint papers plus one of his own emerged, and they formed the basis of a dissertation for his second doctorate, an Oxford D. Phil., then, as now, a *very* stiff qualification to obtain. (The youngster who thought that an external degree was the high jump was really in the clouds now.) His examiners, this time, were Harrod and Hitch. They gave him a stiff viva—the candidate thought that some of the questions were beside the point—but he sailed through this one as well.

During his formative period as a post-graduate student, Shackle was not only influenced by Hayek and Keynes but also by Kalecki. When Kalecki arrived in England, intending to write, in effect, his version of the main propositions of the *General Theory*, he asked the research students in the *R. E. Studs* group whether there was someone who could help him to polish up the English of the papers he had with him and that he intended subsequently to write. Shackle went to his room six or so times to do this and received a superb education, he says, as Kalecki paced about the room arguing out loud points of theory with himself. No doubt Shackle's great command of the English language, which would have imprinted itself on Kalecki's papers, was a suitable *quid pro quo*.

On the *General Theory* itself, in Shackle's view, the 1937 *Quar-*

terly Journal of Economics article, in which Keynes replied to his
critics, especially Viner, and also set out his views concisely, says
virtually all that needs to be said. Certainly it is what inspired
Shackle in his own subsequent work because of the emphasis on
investment as the linchpin of activity in a capitalist economy and
expectations about uncertain future events providing the vehicle
through which investment itself is determined. Thus

> investment is a highly hazardous business, a gambling question, for the
> businessman at the time of his decision does not know whether he will
> make profits or not, especially in future years. In these circumstances,
> businessmen are swayed by the current state of the news and can lose
> their nerve, keep their money in the bank and so unemployment starts
> —it's as simple as that.

Just before the war, following his exhausting two years at Oxford, Shackle was appointed by Nisbet to the Economics Department of St. Andrews University—he became one of three in the
department. Shackle, newly married, experienced a short idyll during that glorious northern summer before the start of World War
II, the sort of summer that St. Andrews experiences only once in
thirty years. He had a light teaching load, and there were picnics
every afternoon. When war broke out, he applied for a commission;
but before anything could be done, a telegram arrived from
Harrod, telling him to report to the Admiralty next morning. So,
during World War II, Shackle worked for Lindemann (later Lord
Cherwell, Churchill's special scientific adviser), in S Branch,
Churchill's private circus of economists. Harrod, at Cherwell's request, had found Churchill the economists he wanted from among
the several research assistants at the Oxford Institute—MacDougall,
Shackle himself, Helen Makower. Later on, Champernowne and
Bensusan Butt joined the group as well. Shackle worked there answering questions on all sorts of things, according to Churchill's
needs, until the 1945 election, at which S Branch disappeared even
quicker than its founder, the outgoing P.M. Shackle next worked
with James Meade (who took over from Robbins in the Economics Section of the Cabinet Secretariat), and then with Sir Robert
Hall, until A. J. Brown appointed him to a personal Readership at
the University of Leeds in 1950. During this period Shackle wrote
Expectation in Economics. The manuscript was sent to Austin
Robinson (then a Syndic of the Cambridge University Press); he
was enthusiastic—Shackle names him as its "god-parent" in the

142   JOURNAL OF POST KEYNESIAN ECONOMICS

preface—and the press accepted the first of a series of books that Shackle would publish with Cambridge. He stayed at Leeds for four terms before his appointment to the Brunner Chair at the University of Liverpool, which he held with distinction until his retirement in 1969.

While at Liverpool, Shackle had two spells of leave, one as stand-in for A. G. Hart at Columbia in 1957. The other spell was at Pittsburgh in 1966, through the auspices of Mark Perlman, now an old friend who has appreciated Shackle's work and contributions as much as anyone. At Pittsburgh, Shackle tried out on an enthusiastic graduate class the manuscript of *The Years of High Theory*, one of his greatest books. This is the story of how he came to think of writing it. He had been holidaying briefly in Ireland, and it was while he was sitting down to breakfast on the ship back to Liverpool that he suddenly thought of writing on innovations in economic theory, 1926 (Sraffa, *E. J.*, D. H. Robertson, *Banking Policy and the Price Level*) to 1939 (Keynes' afterthoughts on the *General Theory*). He especially wished to include the contributions of Hugh Townshend—he thought that Townshend understood Keynes better than Keynes understood himself, and Shackle especially liked Townshend's 1937 *Economic Journal* paper, "Liquidity-Premium and the Theory of Value."[2] Shackle also thought that Townshend's review of Shackle's first book showed the greatest insight of all the reviewers and gave the author his greatest pleasure.

Now followed a steady stream of books and articles, some collected as books. They centered around themes that were associated with Keynes' theoretical contributions, but which also reflected his first mentor's—Hayek's—preoccupation with the nature of knowledge in economics and the problems of coordination in a free society. The troubled and confused economic conditions of the 1970s have brought attention to Shackle's contributions to the theory of decision-making under uncertainty; but for a long time, he confesses, he wondered whether he was talking to himself alone. Because of Shackle's view on what constitutes originality—the person who, though not necessarily the first to think of an idea or an approach, nevertheless is the first to make a quantum jump—Shackle sees Keynes' preoccupation with expectations and uncer-

---

[2] Shackle thinks that liquidity preference is Keynes' greatest *theoretical* innovation, perhaps not a surprising judgment, as his own theoretical contributions are concentrated in the area of uncertainty and decision-making, utilizing his concepts of potential surprise and focus gains and losses.

tainty, their link with investment and the essential properties of
money, and the role of financial intermediaries and banks (a legacy
of Shackle's time working in a bank) as Keynes' greatest contribution—hence his liking for the 1937 *Q.J.E.* paper. Most of Shackle's
original work has been in these areas, exploiting the idea that *if*
the future is uncertain and unknowable, because most important
economic events are unrepeatable, so that the frequency-distribu-
tion interpretation of probability cannot be applied, and if a whole
spectrum of events is equally probable *ex ante*, the rational person
will concentrate on the outer bounds within which the events are
to happen—the best and the worst—when making decisions. Ever
mindful also of the microeconomic foundations of macroeconomics (long before such a preoccupation became the rage), Shackle
kicked off Charles Carter's series, *Studies in Economics*, for Allen
and Unwin with an unusual book on the theory of the firm, *Expectation, Enterprise and Profit* (1970). It is probably the best
place from which to obtain a concise and exceptionally clear account of Shackle's distinctive inventions. His exemplary writing
style has allowed him to write a number of more general textbooks, of which *Economics for Pleasure* (1959) has been the greatest commercial success.[3]

Apart from the two years with Phelps Brown in Oxford, his only
other venture into empirical work arose from a meeting he had in
Liverpool with, mostly, small businessmen. He set them some questions and answers, each to be regarded as independent, concerning
what economists would like to know about the behavior of businessmen—how they set prices, quantities, employment, decided
on investment—and asked them to mark the supplied answers
from 0 to 10. They responded eagerly, and the results were embodied in an article, "Business Men on Business Decisions," in *The
Scottish Journal of Political Economy* (February 1955).

Shackle himself does not think that his major ideas are suitable
for empirical testing. He discourages students from attempting
purely theoretical Ph.D. dissertations—if the ideas do not come,
or blow up, there is nothing to fall back on, whereas an empirical
study will always see you through in the end.[4] Though not a nov-

---

[3] It has been translated into seven languages, and its author tells me it nearly
got into double figures.

[4] Moreover, at Liverpool, because the well-stocked archives of the great business houses in this city were made open to the department, there has always
been a strong economic history tradition in its research.

ice at math—his father's genes show through—he nevertheless believes that theory in the social sciences is best done in language. It is a richer, more dimensional and evocative thought form and means of communication. Moreover, Shackle agrees that it is better to be vaguely right than precisely wrong! He particularly admired the way in which Keynes could gather up a whole set of ideas in one word—"sentiment," as used in the *Treatise*, is a favorite example. Like Marshall, Shackle thinks that diagrams can come in later as an aid; he himself is very partial to indifference curves and has made splendid use of them in his works on uncertainty, expectations, risk-taking, and so on. He does not remember when he read Knight's *Risk, Uncertainty and Profit*, but he does remember reading the Hayek–Knight exchanges on capital theory in the 1930s (he thinks Knight published essentially the same article in four or five different places!), and saying to an interviewing committee that he had little trouble in understanding the arguments of both authors but that he felt as he read that *both* were correct at the time—a not uncommon experience, but few of us have the candor to say so.

When Shackle retired from Liverpool, he taught for a number of years in Belfast, and his interest in Northern Ireland was marked by the receipt of his first Honorary Degree, at the New University of Ulster at Coleraine. Shackle takes a simple pride in these honors, also in giving the 1957 De Vries lectures, *Time in Economics*, his election to the British Academy, and his spell as President of Section F of the British Association. Today Shackle is happily retired in one of the nicest parts of Southern England (Aldeburgh). Living in a house the graciousness of which matches that of his own use of the English language, still happily beavering away at his books, enjoying his wife's company (and cooking), reading aloud the classics of English literature, still a rather solitary, reserved, but lovable figure whose contributions to our discipline are such as to ensure him an honorable place in the history of thought.

Journal of Economic Literature
Vol. XXI (June 1983), pp. 518–550

Joan Robinson's Economics in Retrospect[✿]

By

HARVEY GRAM, *Queens College*

and

VIVIAN WALSH, *University of Denver*

I meditate upon a swallow's flight,
Upon an aged woman and her house,
A sycamore and lime-tree lost in night
Although that western cloud is luminous,
Great works constructed there in nature's spite
For scholars and for poets after us . . .

William Butler Yeats

Introduction

FOR OVER FIFTY YEARS Joan Robinson's prolific flow of books and articles have been a source of controversy. For some of her readers, her theoretical writings have provided a basis for policy-oriented analysis and for perceptive criticism of traditional theory. Others have seen in many of the same writings arguments which they regard as neither analytically sound nor justified in their attribution to neoclas-

sical economics of an unconscious ideological bias. In three important respects, however, Robinson belongs to the mainstream of economic theorists. She extended the Marshallian tradition in which she was brought up; she participated first hand in the Keynesian Revolution; and she contributed to the development of the modern theory of capital and growth. Many of the theories she helped to construct are now part of the standard curriculum.

The questions raised by all economists are no doubt motivated, on the one hand, by an interest in the political aspects of market versus non-market (and policy induced) solutions to various economic problems, and, on the other hand, by a desire to extend and to generalize the logical structure of existing formal theories. For Joan Robinson, it is the political aspects of economic problems which have always motivated her interest in formal theory. Thus, although many of the famous questions associated with her name

* The occasion for this review of Joan Robinson's writings is the republication of her *Collected Economic Papers*, Vols. I–V. Cambridge, MA: The M.I.T. Press, 1980, but we have not entirely restricted our survey to the essays in that collection. We wish to thank anonymous referees and the following friends and colleagues for their many detailed comments on various drafts of this paper: William Baumol, Krishna Bharadwaj, Paul Davidson, Geoffrey Harcourt, Donald Harris, David Levine, Richard Roud, Roy Weintraub, and Sidney Weintraub. Their suggestions have greatly improved the paper, but none is responsible for any of the opinions here expressed. We also wish to acknowledge the permission given by Macmillan to quote the passage from Yeats.

Gram and Walsh: Joan Robinson's Economics in Retrospect   519

(such as the problem of measuring capital) were debated in highly abstract terms, the purpose of her argument was often to bring into the open those political, social, and moral dimensions of the economic issues under discussion which she felt were being systematically ignored. This lends to her literary style its great power and at the same time can cause great frustration. The young intellectual, weary of dry technical articles, finds her prose a heady mixture; the mathematical economist, trying to state the exact formal structure of her argument within a theory of consistent, optimizing behavior, may give up in despair. And yet her questions force one to rethink the deepest issues as to what economic theory should be about.

Looking back over the last three hundred years of economic theorizing, we submit that two broad types of questions have dominated discussion. The first to emerge dealt with growth and development; the second, with the efficient allocation of given resources. Certainly, the second type of question has yielded more readily to formal analysis and has thus attracted wide attention. Robinson has long been more interested in the first type of question which, while older, is still less well understood. Although no short list can ever pin down her wide range of interests, the following are among the broad questions she considers most important: (1) What are the forces that govern the size of the social surplus, the rate of its accumulation, and the nature of technical change? (2) In the course of accumulation, what determines the distribution of the surplus between income from work and income from property? (3) What characteristics of the process of accumulation under capitalism cause periodic, widespread unemployment? (4) Is there a systematic relationship between inflation, the business cycle, and the long run development of capitalism? (5) What would be the political-institutional prerequisites for a suc-

cessful, non-inflationary full employment policy under capitalism?

Robinson's analytical approach to these questions is Marshallian and Keynesian in spirit and is therefore likely to be misunderstood by those for whom the overall consistency of Walrasian general equilibrium theory is the touchstone of acceptable theory. Her method turns, in fact, on a crucial distinction between short-period partial equilibrium analysis and long-period general equilibrium analysis. Thus, the theorist who would fairly appraise Joan Robinson's work must immediately come to terms with the correct interpretation of her many attacks upon general equilibrium theory and comparative static analysis. She means by general equilibrium theory the static and intertemporal models of supply and demand equilibrium in the post-Walrasian tradition, as opposed to the modern classical models of production of commodities by means of commodities inspired by the work of John von Neumann, Piero Sraffa, and Wassily Leontief. Now, on the one hand, Robinson has certainly made important contributions to the modern revival of various classical themes, but it must be insisted that the most useful modern statements of these classical theories are in strictly general equilibrium terms.[1] Thus, it is only because of the identification she makes between "neo-neoclassical" economics[2]— the object of many of her attacks—and post-Walrasian general equilibrium theory, that she has not seemed to appreciate that many results of modern classical theory, of which she herself makes use, are

---

[1] We mean by general equilibrium theory any theory linking quantities and prices by means of the principle of duality. Our earlier joint work (Walsh and Gram, 1980) elucidated the differences between classical and neoclassical theories of general equilibrium using the concept of duality.

[2] Robinson uses the adjective "neo-neoclassical" to distinguish the (largely American) tradition of post-Walrasian neoclassical theory from the earlier (Scandinavian and English) school.

the product of the analytical power of general equilibrium methods.

There is, on the other hand, a legitimate and more and more widely appreciated element in Robinson's attack on general equilibrium theory. This concerns what she describes as the problem of "getting into equilibrium." Here one must distinguish between what C. J. Bliss describes as "two approaches that have been adopted with regard to economic equilibrium" (Bliss, 1975, p. 27). One approach, formalized in terms of Samuelson's correspondence principle (Samuelson, 1947, pp. 257–76), treats equilibrium as the outcome of a dynamic process. This is what Robinson has long rejected and what others are now questioning within the context of orthodox theory.[3] The other approach regards equilibrium "as no more than an analytical stepping stone . . . in an otherwise hopelessly difficult analytical endeavor" (Bliss, 1975, p. 27). This is Robinson's own use of the concept throughout her analysis of long-period problems: because the system she is analyzing is already in equilibrium, she insists that the results of such analysis can tell us nothing about the effects of unanticipated *changes* taking place in actual historical time.

A related aspect of Robinson's criticism of illegitimate uses of general equilibrium theory concerns the attempts to embed Keynes in Arrow-Debreu-McKenzie models, however modified or extended. Such attempts are based on the view that general equilibrium is the outcome of a dynamic process. Keynesian effective demand problems are then interpreted as the consequence of some deficiency or incompleteness in the operation of markets. Robinson's objection to this view of the

Keynesian problem, in addition to its dependence on the unsolved problem of "getting into equilibrium," is that it emasculates the role of uncertainty in Keynes.

I. *The Marshallian Influence*

"When I came up to Cambridge, in 1922, and started reading economics, Marshall's *Principles* was the Bible, and we knew little beyond it. . . . We heard of 'Pareto's Law,' but nothing of the general equilibrium system. . . . Marshall was economics" (Vol. I, p. vii).[4]

To appreciate the influence of Marshall on Joan Robinson, it is vital to understand first what Marshall himself did with the classical concepts of the long- and short-period which he inherited from Smith and Ricardo. The interpretation of Marshall as a *partial* equilibrium theorist suggests that a consistent version of his short-period analysis would entail all the properties of a timeless Walrasian *general* equilibrium of supply and demand. But this is to misinterpret Marshall. His analysis is partial in the more interesting sense that firms are managed by entrepreneurs operating in a short slice of *historical* time— they make decisions under conditions of uncertainty (as distinct from calculable risk). To subject the Marshallian model to a rigorous formulation within a coherent system of general equilibrium would suppress precisely what Marshall wanted short-period analysis for: the study of the choices of a particular entrepreneur, possessed of an historically given productive capacity, and making decisions which may turn out to be wrong, but which nevertheless result in the firm being in equilibrium

---

[3] In this connection, Frank Hahn reminds us: "The first important point to understand about [the Arrow-Debreu] construction is that it makes no formal or explicit causal claims at all. For instance it contains no presumption that a sequence of actual economic states will terminate in an equilibrium state" (Hahn, 1973, p. 7).

[4] The 1980 edition of Joan Robinson's *Collected Economic Papers,* to which all our references are made, is published by the M.I.T. Press. For brevity, only volume and page numbers will be indicated in parentheses following quotations and elsewhere. The pagination in the 1980 edition is the same as in the edition published by Basil Blackwell, Oxford, beginning in 1951.

(given the expectations guiding its conduct) for a short period of time. Such decisions may be inconsistent with the actions (of which the entrepreneur is not aware) being taken by other firms. This is a sort of equilibrium of a rough and ready, *partial* kind and it enabled Marshall to conduct a richly informative analysis of the short-period behavior of individual agents and of particular markets. It is not at all the timeless, or momentary, *general* equilibrium of neo-Walrasian theory in which all agents make mutually consistent decisions.

The strength of Marshall's method, mirrored in much of Robinson's work, is that it highlights those partial and ultimately inconsistent equilibria which may be the nearest we can come to depicting certain aspects of real life—the *formation* of short-run relative prices, for example. The analytical perfection of a general equilibrium model evades this problem, concerning itself instead with the *existence* of prices compatible with given conditions of static or intertemporal supply and demand. Even if Marshall's method is bound to be wrong to some extent, it gives an invaluable picture of an aspect of economic reality which general equilibrium models cannot offer. Were this not so, it would be impossible to explain the eternal youthfulness and survival of essentially Marshallian treatments of microtheory now that we have systems of general equilibrium which exhibit rigorously those properties of an economy with which they can properly be expected to deal. There would appear to be a terrain from which Marshall is extremely difficult to dislodge.

At the same time, the great weakness in Marshall's thought, from Joan Robinson's point of view, is his belief that an economy would get into a position of long-run classical equilibrium if the conditions of economic life "were stationary for a run of time long enough to enable them all to work out their full effect" (Marshall,

1961, p. 347). It should be noted that this commonsense interpretation of a long run as literally a period of time sufficient for economic forces to work out their effects was the concept developed by the original classical economists, and that Marshall refers with approval to Adam Smith in the passage just cited. For Robinson, however, "long-period equilibrium is not at some date in the future; it is an imaginary state of affairs in which there are no incompatibilities in the existing situation, here and now" (Vol. III, p. 101). This difference is fundamental and to some extent it separates Robinson from Smith and Ricardo. It also separates her from some modern neoclassics such as Samuelson who have felt it essential to offer a formal solution to the problem of getting into equilibrium (albeit in a Walrasian context). And, finally, it explains part of the controversy between Robinson and those modern classical economists who regard Sraffa prices as "centers of gravity" to which short-run prices are continually attracted. This idea, entirely consistent with the original classical tradition and with the spirit of Marshall's analysis, is rejected by Robinson on Keynesian grounds. For her, the key insight of Keynes is that an unregulated economy contains no dynamic process that would tend, if left alone, to get it into a position of general equilibrium.

Thus, an element of Marshall's thought survives in all of Robinson's later work; namely, the idea of a short-period equilibrium containing inherent contradictions, as distinct from the momentary multimarket equilibrium of Walras.[5] Of course,

[5] One of our referees called Robinson the "last Marshallian." In doing so, he brought to our attention a fascinating paper by Axel Leijonhufvud (1976), the last footnote of which bears particularly on our argument:

Neo-Walrasian closed system models have so far been inadequate—or, at best, grotesquely cumbersome—vehicles for representing the role of ignorance and the passage of time in human affairs. This has so far stood in the way of satisfactory modelling of the 'disequilibrium' motion of ongoing systems. Both problems are,

Marshall did not emphasize the contradictions, apart from noting what Robinson pointed out as nothing more than a passing remark about the effects of a failure of confidence (Marshall, 1961, p. 710–11). Rather, it was Keynes who exploded the compromises upon which Marshall's "fudge" was based, i.e., his notion that over time an economic system gradually moves of its own accord towards a position of long-run equilibrium.

II. *Lord Keynes and the Short Period*

As Robinson remarks, "The very essence of [Keynes'] problem was uncertainty. He started from a Marshallian short-period . . . [in which] decisions are being taken today on the basis of expectations about the future" (Vol. IV, p. 96). The genius of Keynes' ideas calls out for a short slice of historical time, but the difficulties inherent in handling uncertainty are so great that there existed from the beginning the almost irresistible temptation to freeze his concepts into equilibrium. Yet, it must be resisted. "For a world that is always in equilibrium there is no difference between the future and the past, there is no history and there is no need for Keynes" (Vol. V, p. 173). Robinson remarks that "J. R. Hicks was one of the first, with his IS/LM, to try to reduce the *General Theory* to a system of equilibrium. This had a wide success and has distorted teaching for many generations of

students" (Vol. V, p. 211). Later, Sir John Hicks (1976, 1980–1981) made important concessions to her point of view, arguing that Keynes' analysis was only half in time and half in equilibrium. She will accept no such compromise, insisting that *The General Theory* is set in a strictly short-period situation where "a state of expectations, controlling a given level of effective demand, is given only momentarily and is always in course of bringing itself to an end" (Vol. V, p. 211). Here we have one of Robinson's key contributions: the insistence on an interpretation of Keynes in terms of the Marshallian short-period, characterized by uncertainty, incompatible decisions, and unrealizable expectations.[6]

If one takes seriously the idea of a short period of historical time as Keynes' true domain, it becomes possible to see what, in contrast, were some of the essential properties of those theories which Robinson describes as pre-Keynesian or "bastard Keynesian" (Vol. III, pp. 56–69; Vol. V, pp. 127–28). In all cases, Keynesian concepts are embedded in general equilibrium models of the type in which equilibrium is the outcome of a dynamic process. The process involves logical, not historical, time and can therefore represent only calculable risk as opposed to the uncertainty upon which Keynes always insisted. This, in turn, trivializes the role of money, which serves only as a *numéraire* in models of intertemporal equilibrium and not as the essential link between the present and an uncertain future in a short-period Keynesian model. As has recently been remarked by Roy Weintraub, concerning arguments of Paul Davidson (1978, pp. 388–89) about the role of money in

---

it would appear, rooted in the hard-core heuristic routine of modelling the behavior of each individual agent so as to portray his every action as part of a comprehensively planned 'optimal' time-path.

· Marshall's theory did not insist on representing all action as part of an optimal plan. The behavior of individuals in his models is to be characterized rather as 'satisficing converging on maximizing.' A theory cast in such a form provides escape from most of the embarrassing riddles of time and ignorance met with in current 'neoclassical' (growth) models. These matters, . . . my *Maximization and Marshall* harps upon . . . at great length [Leijonhufvud, 1976, p. 107, n. 66; the work referred to is not yet published].

[6] It must never be forgotten that, as a member of the little group (known as the Circus) who worked with Keynes on manuscripts of *The General Theory* at Cambridge, she is in an excellent position to know what his ideas really were.

Gram and Walsh: Joan Robinson's Economics in Retrospect   523

Keynes, "These arguments force the conclusion that the kind of *numéraire* 'money' so easily introduced into the extended [Arrow-Debreu-McKenzie] model is intrinsically different from the 'money' which is the stuff of Keynes' economics" (Weintraub, 1979, p. 96). On the other hand, Kenneth Arrow and Frank Hahn have considered what they call the existence of Keynesian temporary equilibrium, in the context of a one good economy. They conclude that "if we take the Keynesian construction seriously, that is, as of a world with a past as well as a future and in which contracts are made in terms of money, no equilibrium may exist" (Arrow and Hahn, 1971, p. 361).

Weintraub, having carefully surveyed the relevant literature, recognizes the invalidity of the "neo-Walrasian synthesis" insofar as it has attempted to encompass Keynes. He points out, however, that certain critics, including Robinson, directed their attacks to early uses of an Arrow-Debreu-McKenzie model. His task, on the contrary, is to "show how recent work has attempted to rekindle interest in 'Chapter 12' Keynesianism and to provide a set of sophisticated models capable of dealing, in an integrated fashion, with the variety of insights and innovations that Keynes introduced when 'macroeconomics' was created" (Weintraub, 1979, p. 53). What he has in mind is a sequence of generalized, or incomplete, Arrow-Debreu-McKenzie models where the incompleteness refers to an absence of futures markets. For more than a decade, analysis of such models has been under way. Weintraub therefore remarks that, "The criticism of these new developments should be based on the developments themselves, and not on the fact they did not exist ten years earlier" (Weintraub, 1979, pp. 97–98). This point is clearly pertinent—does Robinson's critique of the neo-neoclassics still hold against these newer developments? Weintraub concludes his scholarly survey by stating that, despite positive accomplishments, "general equilibrium theory must be wary of claiming too much. There is not any model which successfully integrates micro and macro theory" (Weintraub, 1979, pp. 159–60). What does appear from recent work by general equilibrium theorists is an increasing awareness of just how much their predecessors had been emasculating Keynes. In this sense, Robinson's critique holds.

III. *The Long Period and the Meaning of Capital*

As the dust of the Keynesian Revolution began to settle, Joan Robinson's writings showed an increasing interest in long-run problems. Marshall's concept of the long period as a length of time sufficient for economic forces to establish a full employment equilibrium was now, in the light of her interpretation of Keynes, unacceptable to Robinson. But there was no theory to replace it. In 1949 she remarked that Keynes had "scarcely developed any theory of long-run development. Mr. Kalecki's pioneering work has been very little followed up . . . we have no systematic body of long-run dynamic theory to supplement the short-period analysis of the General Theory and to swallow up, as a special case, the long-run static theory in which the present generation of academic economists was educated" (Vol. I, p. 155). The long-run theory to which she refers had come down from the classics, but in Marshall certain of its important characteristics were lost.

In the classics, long-run prices and profits reflected the generation of surplus and the accumulation of capital, but in Marshall this is not easily seen. Robinson describes how this had come about: "Marshall's view of wages, profits and accumulation cannot be so clearly seen, partly because he concentrates attention on the details of relative prices, the fortunes of individual firms and supply and demand of particular commodities, while leaving the main outline into which these details fit extremely hazy" (Vol. II, p. 2). Thus, it is necessary to go back to the classics to understand the relations among surplus, accumulation, and a uniform rate of profit in the long run. Ultimately, the classic to whom Robinson would turn would be David Ricardo, but this did not begin until the appearance of Piero Sraffa's famous "Introduction" to his edition (with Maurice Dobb) of Ricardo's *Works and Correspondence* (1951, Vol. I, pp. xiii–lxii), and was not fully developed until the publication of Sraffa's *Production of Commodities by Means of Commodities* (1960). In the meantime, it was Michal Kalecki who led her back to the classics and, of course, to Marx.

Kalecki, as she has often said, approached the problems of investment, demand deficiency, and accumulation through Marx' schema of reproduction, which Robinson has always regarded as the most valuable part of Marx' theory. As she puts it, "the schema of expanding reproduction provide a very simple and quite indispensable approach to the problem of saving and investment and the balance between production of capital goods and demand for consumer goods. It was rediscovered and made the basis for the treatment of Keynes' problem by Kalecki and reinvented by Roy Harrod and Evsey Domar as the basis for the theory of long-run development. If Marx had been studied as a serious economist, instead of being treated on the one hand as an infallible oracle and on the other as a butt for cheap epigrams, it would have saved us all a great deal of time" (Vol. II, p. 7).

In attempting to generalize *The General Theory* in the light of her interpreta-

tion of Marx, i.e., to give it a long-run dimension, Robinson saw immediately that the first question to be faced concerned the nature of capital. In "Essays 1953," a selection of her early papers, she writes, "The short period means that capital is fixed in kind. You do not have to ask: When is capital not capital? because there is a specific list of blast furnaces and rolling stock and other hard objects, and for Marshall a given number of trawlers. In the long period capital equipment changes in quantity and in design. So you come slap up to the question: What is the quantity of capital?" (Vol. IV, p. 261). This was written in the year of her famous bombshell, "The Production Function and the Theory of Capital," in which she asked the same question and, as she later remarked, "was met, not only with incomprehension, but with ridicule and indignation" (Vol. II, p. vi).

It is easy to see nowadays why Sraffa's treatment of Ricardo was so inspiring to Robinson, for it caused her "to see that the concept of the rate of profit on capital is essentially the same in Ricardo, Marx, Marshall and Keynes" (Vol. IV, p. 247). In a neo-Walrasian model of the short run, there is a specific list of blast furnaces, trawlers, etc.—the given resources. They are parameters of the model. In any model of classical theory, as Sraffa made clear, there is a reproduction structure: capital is a stock of produced means of production whose items are continually being replaced, and whose conditions of reproduction are the very core of the model.[7] Inputs are treated as variables of the model, and every different composition of outputs entails a different composition of inputs.

"Prelude to a Critique of Economic Theory" (Vol. III, pp. 7–14) was one of

---

[7] The necessary condition for reproducibility in simple linear models has come to be known as the "Hawkins-Simon condition" (D. Hawkins and H. Simon, 1949). See note 9, below.

Gram and Walsh: Joan Robinson's Economics in Retrospect   525

the earliest reviews of Sraffa's famous book to show real insight into its nature and purpose.[8] Robinson begins with Ricardo's corn model, as seen through Sraffian eyes. This is still the simplest context in which to introduce the fundamental concepts of a classical reproduction structure. First, viability: In the corn model, the annual corn output must be at least sufficient to replace necessary corn input (seed plus subsistence). If the corn produced is more than enough for replacement of inputs, the economy is more than just viable— there is a surplus. In any classical model, if there is a positive surplus in the quantity system, this is reflected in a positive rate of profit in the dual price system, but here the rate of profit and the rate of surplus are identical: the ratio of corn surplus to the stock of corn used up. Robinson also describes a second fundamental property of the corn model with a subsistence wage: the independence of the rate of profit from the allocation of surplus output to luxury consumption and accumulation. She then asks: "Can the propositions derived from this model survive the removal of the postulate that only corn is required to produce corn?" (Vol. III, p. 8). In effect, we are being introduced to the fundamental category of commodities—those used directly or indirectly in the production of every commodity—called "necessaries" by Ricardo and "basics" by Sraffa. She allows the subsistence wage to become a vector of basics. As the mathematical methods of general equilibrium analysis have shown, "The same argument applies as before. The commodities reproduce themselves with a physical surplus. The condition that the rate of profit is uniform throughout the economy settles their relative prices" (Vol. III, p. 8). Here the uniform rate of profit appears as the equilibrium condition of long-run classical prices.

Adam Smith was the first to understand fully this property of classical prices (see Walsh and Gram, 1980, Chapters 1–4), and his long-run *natural* prices, which explicitly embody the uniform rate of profit, were accepted by Ricardo as they were later by Marx under the term *prices of production*. For all of these writers the positive rate of profit is the reflection in the dual price system of positive surplus being generated throughout industry in the primal quantity system.

In Marshall, where classical long-period prices with a positive uniform rate of profit in equilibrium survive, the important property of their being dual to the quantity relations (in which the surplus appears in physical terms) fades from view. The reason is that, in concentrating on the analysis of short-period pricing, Marshall correctly emphasizes supply and demand and treats the wages in particular trades as determined for the moment by these forces. It is the essence of his short-run analysis that relative wages and prices do not reflect the long-run equilibrium condition of a uniform rate of profit. But Marshall's wages measure marginal *net* products (net, that is, of the additional costs of equipping an additional worker, including profit on the additional wage fund), and so he requires a theory of the rate of profit. Profits, when explained at all, however, tend to be treated as a reward to a "factor service" called "waiting." Robinson argues that, in Marshall, "waiting" is just the willingness to own a stock of capital, i.e., to refrain from consuming it, and, as an explanation of the rate of profit it is not at all convincing, while, in his dynamic story, Marshall is always referring to the prospective rate of profit on investment which is a quite different, short-period concept. Thus, Marshall saw the long period as through a glass darkly, whereas Robinson is face to face with it now.

Consider the simplest two-sector model

[8] See also Peter Newman (1962), Krishna Bharadwaj (1963), and Ronald Meek (1961).

that will illustrate the problem of measuring capital and determining the rate of profit: a model where corn and iron are produced by means of corn and iron with a physical surplus being generated in each sector.[9] The stock of capital is then a heterogeneous bundle of commodities which cannot simply be added up. So, if we wish to represent profit as a return to capital, we have to ask: what is the value of the stock of capital? We can use either corn or iron as *numéraire*, as Robinson points

[9] Such a model is developed at length in our earlier joint work (Walsh and Gram, 1980). Briefly, in a model with non-joint production and circulating capital, quantity equations incorporate a matrix of input-output coefficients, a_{ij}, measuring requirements of commodity i per unit of output of commodity j where $i,j = C,I$ indicate corn and iron.

$$(a_{CC}Y_C + a_{CI}Y_I)(1 + g) = (1 - \lambda_C)Y_C$$
$$(a_{IC}Y_C + a_{II}Y_I)(1 + g) = (1 - \lambda_I)Y_I$$

Gross output of commodity i is Y_i, the uniform rate of growth of stocks of corn and iron in each sector is g, and the proportion of the gross output of each commodity consumed is λ_i, $i = C,I$. Formally, this system can be written:

$$b_{CC}Y_C + b_{CI}Y_I = X_C$$
$$b_{IC}Y_C + b_{II}Y_I = X_I$$

where $X_i \equiv \lambda_i Y_i$, $b_{ii} \equiv 1 - a_{ii}(1 + g)$, and $b_{ij} \equiv -a_{ij}(1 + g) \leq 0$, $i \neq j$. The famous equivalence theorem can then be applied· "For any $X_i \geq 0$, $i = C,I$, there is a solution $Y_j \geq 0$, $j = C,I$, if and only if the Hawkins-Simon condition (that all upper left-corner principle minors of $\|b_{ij}\|$ are positive) holds true" (Hukukane Nikaido, 1972, pp. 13–19). This restriction places a maximum value on g which, in any case, must be non-negative. For growth rates less than this maximum, part of the surplus in each sector, $Y_i - \Sigma_j a_{ij}Y_j$, may be consumed thus allowing for strictly positive X_i and λ_i. In Walsh and Gram we solved the quantity equations of the corn and iron model, eliminating Y_C and Y_I, to obtain a functional relationship among the three variables: g, λ_C, and λ_I (1980, pp. 284–85). The corn and iron economy is more than just viable, i.e., it produces a surplus, if and only if at least one of these variables is positive. Of course, different values for g, λ_C, and λ_I imply different solutions for gross and net outputs. A labor constraint can be appended to the two quantity equations to indicate the relationship between the allocations of labor, total employment E, and the labor force L:

$$a_{LC}Y_C + a_{LI}Y_I = E \leq L$$

out, but once we have solved the price equations we know not only the relative price of corn in terms of iron, but also the rate of profit.[10] It is for this reason—

[10] Continuing with the formal model set forth in the preceding note, price equations (dual to the quantity equations) have the form:

$$(p_C a_{CC} + p_I a_{IC})(1 + r) + w a_{LC} = p_C$$
$$(p_C a_{CI} + p_I a_{II})(1 + r) + w a_{LI} = p_I$$

where p_j, is the price of good j, $j = C,I$; w is the wage rate; and r is the (uniform) rate of profit on the value of (circulating) capital per unit of output in each sector, $\Sigma_i p_i a_{ij}$, $j = C,I$. As in the case of the quantity equations, the price equations can be written in the form:

$$p_C d_{CC} + p_I d_{IC} = q_C$$
$$p_C d_{CI} + p_I d_{II} = q_I$$

where $q_j \equiv w a_{Lj}$, $j = C,I$; $d_{ii} \equiv 1 - a_{ii}(1 + r)$; and $d_{ij} \equiv -a_{ij}(1 + r) \leq 0$, $i \neq j$. Thus, for any $q_j \geq 0$, $j = C,I$, there is a solution $p_i \geq 0$, $i = C,I$ if and only if the Hawkins-Simon condition applies to the matrix $\|d_{ij}\|$. This result indicates the duality between g and r—each has the same maximum value associated in the one case with zero consumption of the surplus, and in the other case with zero wages. When r is less than its maximum value there is room for positive wages. The solution for w in terms of r, eliminating p_j, $j = C,I$ from the price equations is the wage-rate/profit-rate trade-off associated with the technique matrix $\|a_{ij}\|$. Thus, given r, the wage rate in terms of each commodity and the relative price of one commodity in terms of the other are determined (Walsh and Gram, 1980, p. 328). Of course, there is one degree of freedom here, but it would be wrong to conclude simply from that fact that criticisms of neoclassical distribution theory based on analytical models of this type are pointless. In *any* general equilibrium model, special cases aside, prices (on which the value of capital depends, for example) and distribution are mutually determined. The whole point of the model of production of commodities by means of commodities (and labor) is that quantities can vary without necessarily affecting the solution, whatever it may be, for prices and distribution. In a Walrasian model of production of commodities by means of given factors, on the other hand, this is generally not the case (except along flat facets of a production possibilities surface where only one resource constraint is binding). Indeed, it is a hallmark of such neoclassical models that differences in the composition of output entail differences in the relative scarcity of the given factors of production and that, under competitive pricing, these differences are reflected in income distribution.

It may also be noted here that in models of produc-

that relative prices and the rate of profit are simultaneously determined in general equilibrium—that no meaning can be attached to the *value* of capital independent of a particular rate of profit. In her famous paper, "The Production Function and the Theory of Capital," which started the capital theory controversy (G. C. Harcourt, 1969, p. 369), we find Robinson making this point: "the value of the stock of concrete capital goods is affected by [the] rate of profit and the amount of 'capital' that we started with cannot be defined independently of it" (Vol. II, p. 127). Of course, she also had a good deal to say in that paper about time and uncertainty, about the heavy weight put upon the assumption of equilibrium, which "emphasizes the impossibility of valuing capital in an uncertain world" (Vol. II, p. 126). But, as became evident from Sraffa's work, uncertainty is beside the point since, in any case, the Sraffa system is in logical time and therefore has no place for uncertainty. Thus, as she rightly points out in her review, "What he demonstrates decisively (though doubtless the deaf adders will take no notice) is that there is no such thing as a 'quantity of capital' which exists independently of the rate of profit" (Vol. III, p. 13).

---

tion of commodities by means of commodities, the technique matrix in, for example, the two sector model:

$$\begin{bmatrix} a_{cc} & a_{ic} & a_{Lc} \\ a_{ci} & a_{ii} & a_{Li} \end{bmatrix}$$

which is associated with a maximum w, for any given r, need not be the matrix (supposing there is more than one) associated with, say, a maximum $\lambda_c = \lambda = \lambda_i$, for any given g (see Walsh and Gram, 1980, pp. 371–96). It follows that equilibrium prices in a model of this type are not necessarily associated with an efficient choice of technique (Harris, 1978, pp. 167–72). This is not to say that the interpretation of relative prices as measures of opportunity cost and of relative factor scarcity is false within the analytical framework of certain neoclassical models whose structure differs in a fundamental way from modern classical models of the production of commodities by means of commodities.

In the ensuing controversy concerning the meaning of capital and the nature of the process of accumulation, numerous models were presented in the defense of various points of view. We shall confine our discussion to certain general aspects of the debate. What the critics of neoclassical theory were attacking was the notion that the rate of profit is determined by an equilibrium between supply and demand in the market for capital. Robinson began the debate by asking in what units capital is to be measured. She concluded that the value of capital can be established only in the context of a long-run equilibrium (Vol. II, p. 123). Then, comparing one position of long-run equilibrium with another, she found that where the profit rate is higher the value of capital per man may be higher or lower. Similarly, a more labor intensive technique may be associated with a higher or lower real wage. In the context of this discussion, the phenomenon of reswitching of techniques was discovered and given great prominence by, among others, P. Garegnani (1970). The significance of this for Robinson was its association with the unorthodox result that a relatively labor intensive technique could be associated with a relatively high real wage. "Thus double switching is associated with perversity. The interesting point, however, is the perversity, not the duplicity" (Vol. IV, p. 75).

The reaction to Robinson's question about the meaning of capital took several forms. The importance attached by the critics of neoclassical theory to the heterogeneity of capital goods, i.e., to the fact that different methods of production embody *physically distinct* capital goods, led Paul Samuelson (1962) to offer his "surrogate production function" model as a particular case in which the existence of heterogeneous capital goods does not destroy the steady state relationships exhibited in Robert Solow's (1956) one-sec-

528   *Journal of Economic Literature, Vol. XXI (June 1983)*

tor growth model. Another aspect of the heterogeneity of capital, namely, the fact that capital goods of a given type may enter into the production of various commodities in different proportions, was considered by Hirofumi Uzawa (1961, 1963) in his articles on the two-sector neoclassical growth model. And Hahn (1966) presented a model in which capital goods were not only physically distinct but also entered into the production of various goods in different proportions. It is a common feature of such growth models that (even supposing all production functions to be "well-behaved") technology must be restricted in certain ways in order to establish the stability of an equilibrium growth path. The most famous such restriction is Uzawa's capital intensity condition: the capital goods sector must be labor intensive in production relative to the consumption goods sector. (This sufficient condition can be weakened as shown by E. M. Drandakis, 1963 and Taichi Ezawa, 1970.) In proving the existence of stable equilibrium growth paths, Hahn also assumed particular (Cobb-Douglas) forms for the production functions in his model. The need for such assumptions indicates that outside the confines of the one-commodity model, a possibly wide range of technologies and initial conditions must be excluded in order to show that stable solutions exist for certain neoclassical growth models (Hahn, 1966, p. 644).

It is important to note that in neoclassical growth models more general than the one-commodity model, an inverse relationship between capital per worker and the rate of profit arises only at the sectoral level. In Uzawa's model, for example, it is the physical capital/labor ratio in the capital goods sector which varies inversely with the rate of profit—not the overall value of capital per worker in the economy as a whole. The latter may increase or decrease with the profit rate (Gram, 1976) and this is also true of fully disaggre-

gated neoclassical growth models (Bliss, 1975, pp. 84ff.). Now, it is true that Robinson has often remarked that Sraffa's analysis was completely successful in "knocking out the 'marginal productivity of capital' as the determinant of the rate of profit" (Vol. V, p. 214). Her pseudo-production function (equivalent as a representation of choice of technique to an envelope of Sraffa wage-profit curves) shows that there is no basis for postulating an inverse relation between the value of capital per worker and the rate of profit, and, for Robinson, this "killed off the doctrine of 'marginal productivity of capital' associated with the [aggregate] production function (though it has refused to get buried)" (Vol. V, p. 21). The fact remains, however, that she has not based her recent criticisms of neoclassical theory on this argument. Indeed, to the dismay of other critics who have continued to insist on the importance of showing that no inverse relationship exists between the value of capital per worker and the rate of profit, Robinson has taken her stand on a different ground. Her position is that, regardless of the complexities one might wish to consider concerning the structure of technology, neoclassical theory suffers from the fatal flaw that, having construed general equilibrium as the end result of a dynamic process, it has nevertheless failed to produce a satisfactory theory of how an economy can "get into equilibrium."[11] She has

---

[11] We would submit that Hahn's 1966 argument supports Robinson's position at least indirectly and is, in fact, far more damaging to Solow- and Uzawa-type growth models—insofar as they are intended, as Leijonhufvud suggests (1976, p. 106), to provide simplified macroeconomic structures corresponding to the Walrasian general equilibrium system—than any results concerning the shape of the relationship between the value of capital per worker and the rate of profit based on a comparison of steady states. Indeed, the problem of "getting into equilibrium" is exactly what Hahn was bringing to the fore in his 1966 paper and has been discussing in other contexts ever since (1973, 1977). What is surprising is that neither he nor others who have taken up this question in recent years have seemed to notice that

Gram and Walsh: Joan Robinson's Economics in Retrospect   529

set aside issues like reswitching (which, in any case, have already been incorporated within the standard structure of neoclassical intertemporal equilibrium theory; see Edwin Burmeister, 1980, pp. 196, 205–06), and has concentrated instead on the main theoretical issue which has always remained open for her. It is, in effect, Marshall's "fudge"—moving from the short-period to a position of long-run equilibrium—revisited in another form.

It was Samuelson's answer to Robinson's question about the meaning of capital, namely, his "surrogate production function" model, which crystallized her views on the defects of neoclassical methodology. Samuelson's model is, in Robinson's terminology, a special case of the pseudo-production function corresponding to straight line wage-profit curves in Sraffa's analysis. "As an answer to Sraffa, it was a mere evasion but, at this time of day, I think it is rather useful; it enables us to see very clearly where neoclassical fallacies lie" (Robinson, 1980b, p. 127). Samuelson's analysis is, from Robinson's point of view, illegitimate because there can be no *movement* along his surrogate production function, however well-behaved it may appear. She claims that Samuelson is arguing that movements are possible. What he actually wrote was only that two separate points on the pseudo-production function correspond to two different steady states. Each one is a stable equilibrium and there is an infinite set of *non*-steady state *equilibrium* paths between them. This is not a movement *along* the pseudo-production function, but it does presume, as Samuelson readily admits, that "a competitive market system will

have the 'foresight' or the perfect-futures markets to *approximate* in real life such warranted paths that have the property that, if everyone knew in advance they would occur, each will be motivated to do just that which gives rise to them" (Samuelson, 1975, p. 45).

Here then is the disagreement—and it is just another manifestation of the problem of "getting into equilibrium." What Robinson rejects is the notion that in the face of *change*—which means that expectations are falsified—equilibrium can be maintained. Samuelson and others are much more willing to entertain the possibility that "avaricious speculators in forward markets" can be counted on to generate an outcome tolerably close to a general equilibrium of supply and demand (Samuelson, 1975, p. 45, n. 7). Whatever the empirical foundation for this belief may be, it is certainly true that neoclassical analysis is constructed on the assumption that equilibrium is maintained in order to find out if adjustment paths compatible with equilibrium exist; and, in theory, there are many such paths.[12] Again, Robinson's objection is that in the face of *change*, which falsifies expecta-

---

Robinson has been insisting for decades that this unanswered question vitiates, from a theoretical standpoint, the entire neoclassical research program. No doubt, the reason for this is that Robinson's position is based on a deep, intuitive understanding of Keynes rather than on a formal "non-existence" theorem structured within the framework of neo-Walrasian general equilibrium analysis.

[12] In this connection, it should be noted that, well before the capital theory controversy heated up, Dorfman, Samuelson, and Solow had written of "efficient program[s] of capital accumulation [that they presume] no uncertainty so that *ex ante* expected prices or rates of change of prices—which each competitor knows but cannot himself affect—will correspond exactly to *ex post* observed prices. Under these strong assumptions of perfect certainty, where the *ex ante* future must agree with the *ex post* past, the whole future pattern of prices is knowable but each small competitor need know with certainty only the present instantaneous rate of change of prices" (Dorfman, Samuelson, and Solow, 1958, pp. 319–20). Under the assumptions of the theory, myopic behavior is thus shown to lead the system along an equilibrium path. Robinson, of course, would answer that under conditions of uncertainty, the price-forming process typical of capitalism does not maintain equilibrium; a model which shows how equilibrium could be maintained, given perfect foresight, is nothing more than an idle amusement: e.g., "Accumulation and the Production Function" (Vol. II, pp. 132–44).

tions, there is no basis for assuming that the independent behavior of firms—their price setting rules, their investment decisions, their policies concerning dividends, etc.—will be compatible with equilibrium.

As opposing positions in the capital controversy solidified, Robinson decided that one American had been right all along, although the rest had either ignored or forgotten his answer. In 1979, she wrote:

> I only recently discovered that Thorstein Veblen had made my point, much better than I did, in 1908. [He wrote,] 'Much is made of the doctrine that the two facts of "capital" and "capital goods" are conceptually distinct, though substantially identical. . . . The continuum in which the "abiding entity" of capital resides is a continuity of ownership, not a physical fact. The continuity, in fact, is of an immaterial nature, a matter of legal rights, of contract, of purchase and sale. Just why this patent state of the case is overlooked, as it somewhat elaborately is, is not easily seen' [Vol. V, p. 116].

And, again, in criticizing what she sees as the essential idea behind Samuelson's surrogate production function model, namely, the "productivity of . . . extra 'capital'," she once more cites Veblen who "pointed out long ago [that] productivity is a function of the technology in use, not of the instruments needed to apply it. Technical knowledge is the possession of society as a whole but because of the great cost of modern installations, capitalist businesses can 'corner the wisdom of the ancients' and extract profits from it" (Robinson, 1980b, p. 127). Thus, the *meaning* of capital, and hence the basis for the distinction between income from work and income from property which is essential to Robinson's own analysis[13] and to her

critique of neoclassical theory, is, in her view, quite simply the *monopoly* by firms on the technology of production. Where such monopoly is abolished, at least in principle by state ownership under socialism, capitalism ceases to exist, but capital goods exist and continue to enhance the productivity of labor. In this sense, *capital under capitalism is perhaps the most important element in the economics of imperfect competition.*

IV. *Robinson's Analytical Method*

To learn from Robinson's constructive arguments, one must understand the significance of a position of long-run equilibrium in her scheme of ideas as opposed to its role in neoclassical theory. In neoclassical theory, long-run equilibrium is significant only insofar as it is the outcome of a process: a sequence of momentary equilibria in which all markets clear in every period. In "getting into" a position of long-run equilibrium, each "period" inherits from the past its endowment of factors and their ownership among consumers, its technology, and its tastes. In some models all prices are set at the beginning in a complete set of futures markets under conditions of correct foresight—if some of these markets are absent it may be impossible to prove that a sequence of equilibria exists. Given certain assumptions about underlying stochastic processes, it may be possible to replace the hypothesis that futures markets exist by the hypothesis of rational expectations in a model in which probability distributions of expected future prices gradually converge to their

---

[13] No reader of Joan Robinson can miss the point that for her there is a fundamental distinction between income from work and income from property which she regards as having clear moral implications. It could be argued, of course, that some small property incomes might be less morally objectionable than the huge incomes earned in modern societies by doing "questionable" kinds of work. This dilemma is evident in Robinson's own writings when she finds herself compelled to treat the high incomes of top executives as property income. The assumption is analytically arbitrary—where, precisely, should the line be drawn? One may or may not have sympathy with Robinson's moral views, but her dilemma cannot be solved simply by assuming that there is a one-to-one mapping between extremely broad income categories and morally justified expenditure.

true equilibrium values. In any case, the structure of the neoclassical argument typically turns on the questions of existence and uniqueness of momentary equilibrium and the stability (local and global) of long-run equilibrium.

For Robinson, long run-equilibrium is significant, not as the outcome of a process of getting into equilibrium, but rather as a concept defining a class of models in which it is conceivable that expectations could be realized and therefore continually renewed as the driving force behind the behavior whose outcome the model depicts. Thus, in a steady state the future is sufficiently *simple*, relative to the past, to suppose that consistent, realizable expectations exist without assuming perfect foresight (or its stochastic counterpart) and "without being obliged to deprive [anyone] of Free Will" (Robinson, 1979, p. 129). A consequence of this approach is that the problem of stability, which is central to neoclassical theory, simply does not arise in the context of Robinson's equilibrium model since expectations are, by hypothesis, being realized. For her, *in*stability is a short-run phenomenon—a consequence of falsified expectations.

Robinson illustrates her point by referring to "the most familiar piece of economic analysis: on the plane surface of the page of a text-book two curves are drawn, representing the flow supply of a commodity per unit of time and the flow demand for it each as a function of price" (Robinson, 1962, p. 22; Vol. IV, pp. 254 ff.). She argues that the notion of a tendency to equilibrium is legitimate only if "there is a clear concept in the minds of dealers as to what the equilibrium position is . . . for in this case, dealers believe that profit is to be made by selling when price is above [equilibrium] and buying when it is below" (Robinson, 1962, p. 23). Her distinction between *logical* and *historical* time is thus intended to answer the question: "What meaning can we attach to the

conception of a position which is never reached at any particular moment of time but yet which exists only in virtue of the fact that the parties concerned believe, at each moment of time, that it will be reached in the future?" (Robinson, 1962, p. 23). To make her point, Robinson considers two types of economic argument. In the first, there is a general equilibrium system which is in equilibrium *ab initio*. Here, the procedure is to specify "a sufficient number of equations to determine its unknowns, and so [find] values for them that are compatible with each other" (Robinson, 1962, p. 23). Supply and demand curves define the simplest case, a Walrasian general equilibrium another (see her comments on the two-sector model for that theory, Vol. V, pp. 50–52), and the Sraffa system, a third. In the other type of argument, the procedure is to specify "a particular set of values [of the variables] obtaining at a moment of time which are not, in general, in equilibrium with each other, and [to show] how their interactions may be expected to play themselves out" (Robinson, 1962, p. 23). In such a disequilibrium context it is necessary to make assumptions about the formation of out-of-equilibrium expectations. The first type of model, if it moves at all, moves in logical time: the effect of *differences* in the underlying data can be analyzed, but *change* cannot. The second type of model moves in historical time since, she argues, it is capable of getting out of equilibrium and can therefore be used to analyze the effect of change taking place in a given short-period situation. What this distinction denies therefore is any role for general equilibrium methods in the context of the short period.

It is important to see that, on the basis of this methodology, standard stability arguments find no place in Robinson's canon. Robinson rejects stability theory because it is "based on a mechanical analogy, [which] is inappropriate in economic analysis. For mechanical movements in space, there is no distinction between approaching equilibrium from an arbitrary initial position and a perturbation due to displacement from an equilibrium that has long been established. In economic life, in which decisions are guided by expectations about the future, these two types of movement are totally different" (Vol. V, p. 49). Thus, in general, whenever a *change* occurs, "the position is no longer one of equilibrium . . . [and] to find a new equilibrium (if there is one) we have to fill in a whole story about the behaviour of the economy when it is out of equilibrium, including the effect of disappointed expectations on decisions being taken by its inhabitants. The Walrasian system is no more capable of dealing with changes in demand than the system of Sraffa or von Neumann" (Vol. V, p. 52). And so, when Robinson sets up a steady state model, she considers it "a nonsense question to ask: Is such a path stable, so that if the economy were displaced by some chance event, it would return to the path again?" (Robinson, 1962, p. 25). For her, the concept of general equilibrium *implies* "sufficient foresight to pick in advance the forms in which investment will be embodied suitably to the market situations that will be met with in the relevant 'future'. . . . A world in which expectations are liable to be falsified *cannot be described by the simple equations of the equilibrium path*" (Robinson, 1962, p. 25, our italics).

These points are essential to an understanding of Robinson's arguments. In *The Accumulation of Capital* (1956) and its companion guide, *Essays in the Theory of Economic Growth* (1962), she begins with the steady state because, for her, it is the only legitimate general equilibrium model, and then, as she puts it, "descends" into the short period in order to face problems of disequilibrium, i.e., falsified expectations. This is, in a sense, precisely opposite to the neoclassical method of argument which "moves" (with the aid of perfect foresight or its probabilistic counterpart, rational expectations) through a sequence of momentary equilibria "towards" a position of long-run equilibrium. Given this fundamental difference in methodology, it is no wonder that Joan Robinson's contributions to the capital theory controversy were widely misunderstood—they simply found no place within the structure of neo-Walrasian theory.

A. *Long-run equilibrium*

There are numerous places where Robinson discusses the determinants of long-run equilibrium (e.g., Vol. II, pp. 99–106). "A Model of Accumulation" (Robinson, 1962, pp. 22–87) is particularly useful, however, because it specifies a list of six determinants of equilibrium which she regards as largely independent of each other; namely, (1) technical conditions, (2) investment policy, (3) thriftiness conditions, (4) competitive conditions, (5) the wage bargain, and (6) financial conditions.

Robinson puts under the heading of "technical conditions" all possible input-output relationships specifying how commodities are reproduced by means of commodities, labor, and natural resources. Because the initial purpose of the model is to analyze a process of accumulation, scarcities of natural resources are ruled out; labor is treated as mobile in the sense that, whatever the composition of output, it is assumed to have the training suitable for different occupations; and capital goods are likewise assumed to embody whatever the profit maximizing technique of production may be. The case in which "factors" are given in the Walrasian sense, as a specific list of particular machines already in place together with a particular distribution of workers already

Gram and Walsh: Joan Robinson's Economics in Retrospect   533

attached to different industries, is appropriate in her scheme only to a short-period *dis*equilibrium analysis.

Under "investment policy," Robinson builds in the main institutional characteristic of an uncontrolled capitalist economy, namely, the fact that firms control investment and that they have an *inherent desire to grow*. The desired rate of growth of productive capacity increases with the expected rate of profit, but because faster accumulation of capital increases risks in a world of uncertainty, Robinson assumes that successive increments in the expected rate of profit are associated with progressively smaller increases in the desired rate of growth.

The manner in which she specifies "thriftiness conditions" reflects the uncertainty surrounding investment decisions. If firms were simply agents of households facilitating (through production) intertemporal consumption choices, it would be appropriate to treat saving as "whatever proportion of total net income individuals, taking one with another, desire to make it" (Robinson, 1962, p. 38). But in an uncertain world, in which capital markets are necessarily imperfect, it is important for growth-oriented firms to retain a portion of net profits over and above depreciation charges (calculated on a generally conservative basis) and interest obligations (determined by the given structure of their indebtedness). The remaining profit is paid out as dividends, part of which will be saved by rentier households. (Workers, as a whole, consume the earnings of those who are employed; there is no net saving out of wages.) As a proportion of profits, dividends are largely a matter of convention in Robinson's model (capital gains and losses bringing yields on shares into line with interest rates on bonds). Thus, the proportion of profits saved in excess of depreciation allowances depends on the share of profits distributed by firms and

on the proportion of dividends and interest payments that rentiers save. Given this, "the ratio of saving to total net income depends upon the ratio of total profits to total income" (Robinson, 1962, pp. 39–40).

The state of competition is important as a factor determining the equilibrium distribution of income. Robinson argues that higher profit margins, by reducing the purchasing power of real wages, reduce sales and therefore employment and the overall utilization of plant. Higher margins are not therefore associated with higher profits. And, similarly, lower margins (associated with more competitive pricing) do not reduce profits. Instead, real wages are higher so that expenditure, employment, and the utilization of plant are also higher. Therefore the same profits are earned on a higher volume.

The level of money wages responds to excess demand in Robinson's scheme when "plant is available to carry out the investment decisions of firms and to meet the demand for commodities that investment is generating, but there are not enough hands to man it" (Robinson, 1962, p. 42). There is also a floor to the level of real wages so that when the price level rises following an increase in investment or rentier consumption, a point comes (the "inflation barrier") at which money wages irresistibly rise.

Finally, the importance of "financial conditions" again reflects the view that capital markets cannot be perfect in a world of uncertainty. Robinson includes the "relation between the distribution of the urge to accumulate of firms and the distribution of borrowing power" (Robinson, 1962, p. 43) as part of the economy's propensity to accumulate. Thus, a closer match between borrowing power and the desire to undertake accumulation would raise the propensity to accumulate. The power of the banking system to restrict lending in the face of a sharp rise in the demand for money associated with a rise in costs (higher money wages or material costs) comes into the argument "as a stopper to inflation" (Robinson, 1962, p. 44).

In describing the interlocking relationships which define a position of long-run equilibrium, Robinson emphasizes that the driving force in her model is the rate of accumulation that firms are together bringing about.[14] The requirements of equilibrium are expressed in terms of the realization of expectations of firms carrying out investment. Thus, gross investment, increasing at a steady rate, must bring about a balanced increase in all components of the stock of capital, the initial stocks being such as to allow this to happen. The level of prices in relation to money wages must be such that expenditure out of wages and distributed profits generates a level of demand corresponding to the normal capacity operation of plant and equipment. Otherwise, realized profits would fall short of the expected profits which provide the motive for in-

---

[14] It is easy enough, at this stage in the development of dynamic models of capital accumulation, to write down the equations characterizing a steady state growth path. Notes 9 and 10 above provide the basic structure for a simple two sector model which can be closed by postulating linear Engel curves and a saving-investment balance linking profit rate and growth rate (Walsh and Gram, 1980, pp. 332–36). But one hesitates to cast Robinson's golden age models in this mold, for there is more in her verbal descriptions than such formal structures adequately portray (which is not to say that we eschew or denigrate formal analysis). Perhaps the best one can do is to say that, even in a golden age, *decisions* in Robinson's argument are being taken (as one of our referees put it) in a state of Marshallian confusion (owing to Keynesian uncertainty). It just happens to be the case that events are unfolding in such a way as to be consistent with what are, in any case, only the rather sketchy outlines of steady state growth paths offered by formal growth theory. Marshallian firms, as it were, are leaving behind steady state growth tracks, but those tracks do not in any very adequate way tell us why they are behaving in a manner consistent with the requirements of a golden age, and they are certainly not to be enshrined as a complete description of what is going on (J. A. Kregel, 1975, p. 74).

vestment. Moreover, the pattern of prices must be such that "each output [pays] for the labour that it requires, the intermediate products which enter into it (including amortization of plant) and interest on the capital employed in producing and selling it. When the stock of capital is valued at normal prices, the rate of profit on capital is then equal to the rate of profit on investment" (Robinson, 1962, pp. 44–45). Because there is no saving out of wages, profit is equal to investment plus rentier consumption, while the rate of profit is equal to the rate of accumulation divided by the proportion of profits saved. The real wage is then determined in Robinson's model by "technical conditions" and the rate of profit. The level of money wages, to which the level of prices is adjusted, is arbitrary. The stock of money, given the level of prices, is adjusted to establish a rate of interest "arbitrarily determined by the banking system" (Robinson, 1962, p. 45). Such a rate of interest must, however, be below the rate of profit in order to allow for dividends and retained earnings.

There is no mechanism in Robinson's description of equilibrium which would cause an economy, starting from some arbitrary initial position, to approach a path of steady proportional growth. Robinson sets forth the conditions for balanced growth only to show that although such an equilibrium path is not inconceivable, its main theoretical interest lies in revealing certain inherent contradictions in the process of accumulation. Some of these contradictions would develop even if the requirements of long-period equilibrium were initially established.

The simplest example is that of a "limping golden age" described by Robinson as a situation in which the initial stock of physical plant, although appropriate in its internal structure to the desired rate of growth, is insufficient to provide for full employment. (In a true "golden age" full

Gram and Walsh: Joan Robinson's Economics in Retrospect   535

employment is maintained.) The "limp" gradually disappears if the rate of accumulation causes output to rise at a faster rate than the combined rate of increase in output per head and the supply of labor. Assuming a constant or growing labor force, the "limp" gets worse if output per head grows at a faster rate than total output. In the latter case, growing unemployment reduces the standard of living of the work force as a whole, because Robinson assumes that the unemployed are supported by the employed. If, as a result, the rate of growth of population falls off, "a situation might be reached in which the rate of accumulation and the rate of growth of the labour force were equal, the ratio of non-employment being great enough to keep the latter down to equality with the former" (Robinson, 1962, p. 54). This is a "leaden age."

The argument that unemployment in a "limping golden age" could be cured by a drop in money wages is answered by Robinson in both short- and long-period terms. In the short run, a drop in money wages without a drop in prices would reduce sales and precipitate a slump. Expenditure out of the higher profits on those goods which *are* sold is too little (because of the high propensity to save out of profits) and comes too late (because dividends are a function of last period's profits) to make up for the drop in expenditure caused by lower real wages. If the drop in money wages *is* accompanied by a drop in prices, the consequent drop in interest rates will never be enough to offset the pessimism associated with lower expected profits and the burden of fixed interest obligations. Investment is reduced, not increased. And finally, even if we could ignore these short-run problems, Robinson argues that there is no reason to suppose that in long-period equilibrium a lower real wage is necessarily associated with a less mechanized technique (Vol. IV, p. 75). In any case, an entirely different

stock of capital would be required by the profit maximizing technique associated with a lower real wage.

Robinson's analysis of "limping golden ages" provides the first and most important lesson to be learned from the method of long-period analysis; namely, that when the realized rate of growth is limited only by the desired rate of growth (and is therefore less than the possible rate), there is no automatic mechanism that will guarantee full employment. Thus, the central message of Keynes is extended to the long period: employment in the long run depends primarily on the accumulation of capital and the accumulation of capital depends primarily on the uncertain expectations of profit held by capitalist firms (as opposed to the intertemporal consumption choices of independent households in a dynamic model of neo-Walrasian general equilibrium).

A second lesson that Robinson draws from the method of long-period analysis concerns the situation in which the desired rate of growth exceeds the possible rate. The basic problem is a scarcity of labor not offset by a sufficient increase in output per head. If, as a result, money wages rise, pushing up costs and thereby creating a credit squeeze, credit rationing will make the situation worse by causing firms to choose less mechanized techniques with each round of investment. Robinson regards it as highly unlikely that, in place of credit rationing, the monetary authorities could bring about a rise in interest rates just sufficient to bring the desired rate of growth into line with the possible rate, while creating just the margin of unemployment which would be sufficient to hold money wages constant. In any case, such a policy would involve considerable waste if the required margin of unemployment were significant. The best way out is probably the most difficult to manage: a careful use of monopsony power in the labor market "so that each firm has its own group of workers and does not attempt to recruit any more" (Robinson, 1962, p. 56). The advantage of this form of restraint is that "the techniques chosen [with each round of investment] are likely to be more mechanized than [those] which would maximise profits [in the absence of restraint], and the rate of profit on capital is pushed down to such a level as to reduce the desired rate of growth to fit the actual rate that is being realised" (Robinson, 1962, p. 56).

Finally, Robinson introduces the "inflation barrier" as a limit upon the rate of accumulation. As in the case of a "limping golden age," the stock of capital is insufficient to employ the whole work force. Any attempt to increase the stock requires, at least temporarily, a drop in consumption per employed worker. But if labor is sufficiently well organized to prevent a fall in the real wage rate, "any attempt to increase the rate of accumulation, unless it is accompanied by a sufficient reduction in consumption out of profits, is then frustrated by an inflationary rise in money-wage rates" (Robinson, 1962, p. 59). The situation is described as a "bastard golden age," in which "every scrap of consumption out of profits is directly at the expense of accumulation" (Robinson, 1962, p. 63). It may occur not only at a high level of real wages (in an economy with well organized unions) but also at a low level of real wages such that no further reduction is tolerable. In the latter case, a low standard of life holds down the rate of growth.

Robinson has also used long-period equilibrium analysis as a framework within which to discuss the problem of technical change. There are numerous discussions in her *Collected Papers* (Vol. I, pp. 157–58; Vol. II, pp. 76–77, 159–84; Vol. V, pp. 24–25, 214–16) and a more lengthy treatment in *Essays in the Theory of Economic Growth* (1962, pp. 88–119). Space considerations prevent us from discussing these arguments at length. Robinson's defini-

tions of labor-saving and capital-saving innovations are well known (Vol. II, pp. 164–66), as is her discussion of biased versus neutral technical change (Vol. II, pp. 171–72). Suffice it to say that Robinson's primary concern is to analyze the effects of technical progress on wage and profit *shares* under the assumption that the rate of profit remains unchanged. The motivation for this assumption is the idea that to maintain a steady rate of accumulation requires the maintenance of a steady rate of profit. Thus, the purpose of her analysis is to show, first of all, how real incomes (mainly real wages, but in some models the real value of rentier incomes as well) would have to change, given neutral or biased progress, in order to maintain effective demand and so maintain profits. Secondly, in the face of neutral or biased technical change, the investment policy of firms must, in Robinson's analysis, follow a particular course if labor is to be allocated between sectors in such a way as to maintain employment. Throughout her analysis Robinson is always concerned with the problems of structural imbalance and the possible failure of incomes to grow in just the way required to maintain the conditions of long-run equilibrium. Thus, her analysis is best seen as the basis for identifying causes of short-period disequilibrium.

B. *Short-Period Disequilibrium*

To construct a short-period model, it is necessary to "escape from the requirement of an equilibrium past" (Vol. II, p. 142). Thus, as Robinson often writes, "let us descend into a short-period equilibrium, and postulate that there is a specific stock of capital goods, that just happens to be whatever it is" (Vol. II, p. 142). "The structure of the capital stock embodies the consequences of misguided investments made in the past; its age-composition is all higgledy-piggledy, and its division between sectors is never exactly appropriate

Gram and Walsh: Joan Robinson's Economics in Retrospect   537

to the investment now being planned" (Robinson, 1962, p. 69). These mistakes of the past mean that expectations held in the past have not been realized, and so "there is no warrant for postulating that the expectations to-day guiding investment plans will turn out to be correct in their turn" (Vol. II, p. 143). Here then are the two sources of disequilibrium in Robinson's short-period model: neither the stock of capital goods nor the state of ex- pectations formed by past experience are consistent with equilibrium, i.e., with the realization of expectations guiding current decisions.

The determinants of a short-period "equilibrium"[15] include the rate of gross investment already going on, the level of money wage rates already negotiated, and the incomes of rentier households already determined by the most recent payments of interest and dividends. Employment depends on the level of investment and the volume of sales of consumption goods which in turn depends on the flow of money demand and the pricing policy of firms.

Because of imperfect competition in the selling of manufactured goods, Robinson regards prices as being set by adding a gross margin to prime costs.[16] In her model, this convention breaks down, temporarily, only in conditions of a strong seller's or buyer's market. Since prime costs are mainly wages, it is the level of money wages which is the main determinant of the level of prices. Gross margins "are set by the rule that, at the expected rate of output, receipts should cover the total

costs of producing and selling the goods, including whatever seems [in view of the *degree of monopoly*] a reasonable level of profits" (Vol. IV, p. 64). Thus, profits to individual firms are abnormally high or low depending on whether sales are higher or lower than expected. If, in this argument, "expected" output is replaced by the "normal" output for which equipment is designed, the hypothesis that gross margins are determined by the *degree of monopoly* "admits a long-period element into the process [of price formation] in the sense that firms are assumed to take account of average costs for a standard output" (Vol. V, p. 189). Realized net profit then varies directly with the ratio of actual to standard output.

Taking profit margins and money wage rates as given, the flow of gross profits on the sale of consumption goods will be "equal to the wage bill for investment *plus* the excess of expenditure out of profits [including realized capital gains] over saving out of wages" (Vol. IV, pp. 64, 72). In the simplest case, there is no saving out of wages, and "the flow of gross profits is equal to the expenditure of capitalists upon investment and their own consumption" (Robinson, 1980b, p. 200).[17]

This short-period, partial equilibrium (in Marshall's sense) contains inconsistencies and is therefore always disrupting

---

[15] We use the word "equilibrium" only in the sense in which Robinson uses it. It is not intended to refer to a situation which is self-sustaining. The short period is, by definition, a situation containing internal contradictions which will soon assert themselves, but which, within a given short period, are not apparent.

[16] For critical comments on the mark-up hypothesis, see Lorie Tarshis (1980) and Janet L. Yellen (1980). In using this hypothesis, Robinson regards it as a natural response to uncertainty about future market conditions. See also note 17 below.

[17] Samuelson has remarked that he cannot find "in Professor Robinson's voluminous writings a clear statement of exactly what, outside steady states, her theory of income distribution is" (Samuelson, 1975, p. 46, n. 8). Certainly, there is an indeterminate element in Robinson's short-run theory of distribution, for what are "reasonable" profits? But she does not regard this as a serious drawback. For Robinson, there are many elements in a short-period disequilibrium situation which are conventional, or rule-determined. Such conventions could be interpreted as rational responses to uncertainty. In any case, she does not claim to have said the last word on the pricing policy of firms. Indeed, for her, it represents "the border-line between long- and short-period theory of prices, which has been very inadequately explored" (Vol. V, p. 19). "The question of the formation of profit margins still needs more investigation" (Vol. V, p. 189).

itself.[18] In particular, the planned level of investment is constantly changing in the light of revised expectations of future profits generated by the current situation. (It is only in a long-run equilibrium that the expectations guiding investment are being realized and therefore renewed so as to generate a steady forward advance.) Robinson analyzes these inherent changes using two relations linking the rate of profit to the rate of growth. One shows the realized rate of profit as a function of the actual rate of growth that gives rise to it. The other shows the planned rate of growth as a function of the expected rate of profit that brings it about. However, as neither the rate of profit nor the rate of growth is well-defined in a short-period situation, we must regard her argument as no more than a first step towards a satisfactory analysis of short-period disequilibrium.

As Robinson herself remarks, "Both the realised rate of profit and the expected rate are vague and complex entities. The realised rate of profit is vague because there are various conventions that can be used to assess it. The expected rate is vague because of uncertainty. Both are complex because each is an amalgam of the variegated experience of a large number of firms" (Robinson, 1962, p. 30). She nevertheless proceeds to summarize a short-period situation in terms of her two "relations." It is an ingenious, but not

an entirely successful argument (Harris, 1978, pp. 186–92).

To begin with, firms are assumed to calculate, using conventional accounting procedures, a current realized rate of profit on past investments. This must involve a conventional allowance for depreciation which presumably takes inflation into account; it is also net of interest obligations on accumulated debt. Against the realized rate of profit, Robinson plots in a diagram (Robinson, 1962, p. 48) the rate of accumulation which has given rise to it. The rate of accumulation is also a net figure so that depreciation, on some conventional basis, must first be subtracted from gross investment; the resulting net addition to capital must be transformed into a rate of growth by comparing it to the value of the stock of capital. Capital, in turn, is valued by projecting current prices and sales into the future and then discounting the associated flow of net receipts by the previously calculated rate of profit. The experience of all the various firms is then aggregated. In this way, all the problems associated with "descending into the short-period" are collapsed into one opaque relationship.

Robinson's next step is to introduce a behavioral relationship already referred to in our discussion of "investment policy" under long-period equilibrium conditions. In a short-period model this relationship is plausible because it is based on the hypothesis that a higher rate of accumulation for the system as a whole entails greater risks for individual firms and therefore requires greater inducement in the form of a higher expected rate of profit. In Robinson's diagram, the desired rate of growth therefore increases with the expected rate of profit, but at a decreasing rate. Finally, setting the expected rate of profit equal to the realized rate, the entire short-period situation is summed up in terms of "a double-sided relationship between the rate of profit and the rate of accumula-

---

[18] Here, again, we draw attention to Leijonhufvud's argument. In a Marshallian short period (as opposed to a neo-Walrasian momentary equilibrium), an economic system may be characterized by increasing disorganization—it is as if a country were occupied only by "foreigners" none of whom knows the market situation and "where no one can have a very confident notion of what equilibrium prices will eventually emerge" (Leijonhufvud, 1976, p. 103). Information feedback from the marketplace is not resulting in coordinated behavior and is, in fact, precipitating uncoordinated, chaotic behavior. This picture is at the opposite pole to that offered by the theory of rational expectations in which accumulated experience causes price expectations to converge on their (Walrasian) equilibrium values.

Gram and Walsh: Joan Robinson's Economics in Retrospect   539

tion. . . . The accumulation going on in a particular situation determines the level of profits obtainable in it, and thus (on the basis of the type of expectations which we have postulated) determines the rate of profit expected on investment. The [expected] rate of profit in turn influences the rate of accumulation" (Robinson, 1962, p. 47).

In Robinson's model, the rate of accumulation may be so low that it does not generate a rate of profit sufficiently high to cause firms to maintain the rate of growth: there is a minimum rate of profit below which the "engine of growth" stalls and the economy ceases to expand. A rate of growth just above this "stalling speed" generates a rate of profit sufficient to raise the expected rate of profit so that the system feeds upon itself and begins to expand at an increasing rate. Because the desired rate of growth rises in a smaller proportion than the expected rate of profit to which it gives rise, the actual rate of growth will tend to stabilize at such a value that the associated profit rate is just sufficient to maintain the growth rate.

Robinson cites several reasons why a rate of growth which appears to be an equilibrium rate, given short-period conditions, is unlikely to be maintained unless it has already been established for some time. One set of problems is associated with those time lags in the distribution of profits which affect the realized rate of profit through the expenditures of rentier incomes. This has a stabilizing effect in the face of a *change* in investment; given a level of investment, however, it is "liable to cause wobbles in the relation between the current rate of accumulation and the current proceeds from the sale of consumption goods" (Robinson, 1962, p. 50). A second source of endogenous instability is associated with an erratic flow of investment which leaves the age-composition of the physical stock of capital inappropriate to a steady rate of growth.

"From one short-period to the next, the relation between current gross investment and net accumulation is then liable to be upset by a larger or smaller quantity of renewals falling due. Thus, having attained the desired rate of accumulation at one moment, the firms may be tipped off it at the next" (Robinson, 1962, p. 50). And, finally, the more uneven the past history of accumulation, the more uncertain the present situation so that a chance rise (or fall) in the rate of profit may set up the expectation of a further rise (or fall). Then the rate of accumulation depends on the rate of change of the profit rate, rather than its level, and the model becomes inherently unstable (Robinson, 1962, pp. 67–69).

What are we to conclude about an analysis of the short period which is based in part on a relationship so vague as the one linking a short-period overall rate of accumulation to an average realized rate of profit? One answer is to confront the underlying conception of her analysis, however incomplete the analysis itself may be, with traditional short-period macroeconomic theory as expressed in the textbook version of the *IS/LM* model or its extension to aggregate supply and demand curves. In the traditional analysis there is a desired stock of capital (measured in terms of productive capacity) which bears a proportional relationship to the expected flow of sales. The lower the rate of interest, the higher the desired stock. The resulting flexible accelerator model, when combined with the multiplier mechanism, generates a downward sloping *IS* curve. In conjunction with the *LM* curve, the model yields a downward sloping aggregate demand curve: a lower price level (or rate of inflation) increases the real value of the stock of money, puts downward pressure on interest rates, and so increases the desired stock of capital leading to increased net investment and increased consumption (via the multiplier). Output therefore rises. Robinson has always felt that it is *this* analysis which is vague, and that it totally misrepresents Keynesian ideas.

In her discussion (and Keynes'), it is a *fall* in the rate of interest in the face of *given* expectations of profits (not a low rate of interest) which encourages investment in the short run. The *IS/LM* model does not include the expected rate of profit as an explanatory variable separate from the rate of interest; and it assumes that, when the economy has adjusted to a lower rate of interest, the equilibrium stock of capital will necessarily be larger. But this adjustment is necessarily a long-period adjustment and long-period analysis (outside the context of the one-commodity model) shows that there is no basis for assuming that the value of the stock of capital will necessarily be higher when the interest rate is lower. Moreover, when the argument is used to derive a downward sloping aggregate demand curve, it leads to what is for Robinson a fundamental error. A *fall* in the price level (or the rate of inflation) in the face of previously negotiated money-wage contracts and a given structure of indebtedness, is far more likely to result in a fall in investment (because of the associated fall in expected profits) than to an increase (because credit conditions have eased somewhat).

We conclude from this—and it should be noted that Hicks himself now has serious reservations about the *IS/LM* framework as a representation of Keynesian short-period problems[19]—that Robinson has at least focused on the proper question: the relationship in the short run between changes in planned investment and changes in expected profits caused by the

outcome of a short-period, *partial* equilibrium. It is this question, central to Robinson's view of the short period, which gets lost in standard treatments of macroeconomic theory.

Perhaps the most useful part of Robinson's short-period analysis concerns inflation. In an equilibrium context, a "bastard golden age" is one in which the desired rate of growth is high enough to require a lower real wage than organized labor will tolerate. Financial controls hold the rate of accumulation in check just inside the "inflation barrier," although, to succeed, such controls must create a margin of unemployment compatible with stable money wages. As a consequence, high interest rates dampen "animal spirits," thereby reducing the rate of technical progress. This makes the underlying situation worse by reducing the rate of increase in output per man. When financial controls fail to keep money wages from rising at a faster rate than productivity, firms are assumed, in the simplest case, to maintain margins, and so an inflationary spiral begins. The inflation itself generates arbitrary redistributions of wealth and increases the costs of managing a portfolio of assets because money is now a less satisfactory vehicle for carrying purchasing power forward through time.

Robinson considers it native to attempt to solve the problem of inflation by asking the unions to keep money wages from rising at a faster rate than productivity (Vol. IV, pp. 64–66). This is to ask them to "recognize the justice of keeping gross margins constant." But what do gross margins cover? She draws up a list: salaries of overhead staff, amortization, promotion and advertising, direct and indirect taxes paid by firms, net retained earnings, and distributed profits. The first two are "necessary costs," leaving aside "the high salaries of top executives" which she likens to selling costs insofar as they are a consequence of imperfect competition. (They might

[19] See Hicks (1980–1981) where it is argued that in the *IS/LM* model it must be assumed that stock and flow equilibrium are continuously maintained *within* a short period. Thus, uncertain expectations are always realized. Hicks deals with this anomaly by suggesting (tentatively) that expectations be regarded as multi-valued (Hicks, 1980–1981, p. 152).

also be compared to the "rents" of top professionals in all fields.) The third item is "not much to get your teeth into," even though the creation of a market entails, for the individual firm, a cost "as necessary as prime costs." The fourth and fifth items raise basic questions about "whether the objects of government outlay are well chosen" and about whether "the content of outlays on investment" are in the best interests of society as a whole. Robinson sets these issues aside except to make the point that "expenditure of profits on investment which increases the productivity of industry [can be distinguished] from expenditure on take-overs" (Vol. IV, p. 66) which will in all likelihood redistribute finance in such a way as to reduce overall liquidity (Vol. III, p. 137). Thus, it is the sixth and final item—distributed profits—which is the real sticking point for her. "For the firm it is necessary to pay dividends to keep up its credit, but what do the workers gain from it? . . . Workers, managers and research teams bring about technical progress and accumulation, and the capital falls into the lap of shareholders who are not making the smallest contribution to the process which is bringing it into being. Income from property is not the reward of waiting, it is the reward of employing a good stockbroker" (Vol. IV, pp. 65–66). Thus, because profit margins cannot be entirely justified, inflation is, for Robinson, a political problem insofar as it is the outcome of collective bargaining within a system in which firms set prices by marking up prime costs.

Even without the political issue associated with consumption out of income from property, Robinson observes an inherent bias towards inflation under capitalism. Progressive industries, instead of lowering prices as output per head rises, may simply increase selling costs in an effort to expand their now more profitable markets. Higher margins become "necessary" for the technical leaders in a field

who cannot then lower prices whereas "the less progressive find it necessary to raise them" (Vol. IV, p. 66) whenever their unit costs rise. On an international scale the same problem arises when one nation gets a jump on the others by taking advantage of the latest technological advances. Output per worker rises so that firms in the progressive nation are in a position to grant some increase in wages without bringing financial checks into operation. Supposing unit costs to fall, this nation enjoys the advantage of expanding exports and a strong currency which further eases the pressure on money wages because wages are partly spent on imports. Less progressive countries find that the pressure on money wages is exacerbated by a weak currency which raises the prices of imported wage goods. The authorities then restrict credit in an effort to defend the currency. This reduces investment, lowers the rate of technological advance, and increases the international imbalance of trade.

V. *The Theory of International Trade*

Starting from a Marshallian base, Joan Robinson made significant contributions to foreign trade theory at each stage of her work. She begins with the reappraisal and critique of conventional neoclassical trade theory, in the light of Keynes, and ends with a post-Sraffian critique of the neoclassical interpretation of Ricardo's foreign trade theory and of the meaning and role of international capital movements.

In the thirties Robinson was working out the implications of Keynesian analysis for the foreign trade theory she had inherited from Marshall. Her famous essays, "The Foreign Exchanges" and "Beggar-my-Neighbour Remedies for Unemployment" (Vol. IV, pp. 212–40) "were written while Keynes' *General Theory* was going through the press" (Vol. IV, p. 174),

Keynes read her drafts and she cut out anything which she could not persuade him was correct—these papers clearly represent the first impact of Keynesian thought in their field.

In "The Pure Theory of International Trade" (Vol. I, pp. 182–205), which originally appeared in 1946, Robinson begins her first systematic criticism of foreign trade theory, taking her lead from Marshall's *Pure Theory of Foreign Trade* (1879). It is interesting to note that she calls this Marshallian model the "classical model." As her main purpose is to discuss the effects of the gold flow mechanism on the level of employment, it is not misleading to put Ricardo and Marshall in the same category since neither had an explicit theory of the failure of effective demand (though Marshall gave hints that it could arise). Her argument is entirely Keynesian in spirit. As gold flows out in the face of a deficit, "it is the fall in real income, in the first instance, which reduces imports and staunches the outflow of gold. But this equilibrium in the balance of payments is maintained only on condition that incomes remain at their reduced level" (Vol. I, p. 184). The fall in prices postulated by the price-specie flow mechanism is simply postponed until a sufficiently long stretch of unemployment forces a reduction in money wages and hence "costs relatively to the world level (which at the same time may be rising because of the contrary effects produced in countries gaining gold)" (Vol. I, p. 184). The burden of the argument is that relative changes in costs, rather than interest rates, provide the more plausible mechanism by which imports can be brought into line with exports. She concludes: "From a formal point of view, the classical analysis (on its own assumptions) can thus be vindicated. It is to be observed, however, that there is nothing in the argument to show that balance can necessarily be established for a deficit country with

its existing population. If it is densely populated (relative to the fertility rather than the extent of its soil) and depends upon imports of food, the process just described, by which a fall in home money incomes relatively to world prices reduces the physical volume of imports, will involve extreme distress. . . . The hidden hand will always do its work, but it may work by strangulation" (Vol. I, pp. 188–89).

Turning to the doctrine of comparative costs, Robinson notes that the advocates of free trade have generally admitted that one country can gain from tariffs at the expense of the rest of the world, barring retaliation. The most cogent argument in favor of free trade would therefore simply be "that it is immoral for one country to [attempt to] gain an advantage at the expense of the rest" (Vol. I, p. 199). Her rejoinder is that when a country's position is comfortable the argument has great weight, but when a country's position is miserable then "the establishment of equilibrium under classical free trade conditions requires an intolerable sacrifice in her terms of trade" (Vol. I, p. 199). Finally, she observes that even with international lending introduced, "the whole analysis is based upon the arbitrary assumption that world full employment is always preserved. When that assumption is not fulfilled there is no one pattern of trade which can be described as equilibrium" (Vol. I, p. 204). For this reason, she concludes, "the classical model for the analysis of international trade is reduced to wreckage . . . and, for better or worse, international trade must be directed by conscious policy" (Vol. I, p. 205).

In her inaugural address, "The New Mercantilism," Robinson highlights the international aspects of the Keynesian problem. The thrust of her argument turns on the "deflationary kink in a financial system in which every country likes to gain reserves and hates to lose them. . . . The most important benefit of a surplus on in-

Gram and Walsh: Joan Robinson's Economics in Retrospect 543

come account, which affects the whole economy, is that, provided that there are energetic enterprises and thrifty capitalists to take advantage of it, it permits home investment to go full steam ahead, while a deficit country is nervously pulling on the brake for fear of excessive imports" (Vol. IV, pp. 7–8). Given a general tendency to rising money wages, the competitive position of the deficit country is made all the weaker as a result of sluggish investment, "while the strong country can afford a greater rise [in money wages], because output per head is increasing faster, and yet is subject to less pressure, because its workers' real earnings are visibly growing" (Vol. IV, p. 9).

The effects of Sraffa on her writings in foreign trade appear for the first time in the second paper in Volume IV, "The Need for a Reconsideration of the Theory of International Trade." Here, she is attempting to map out new territory, for as she remarks in her final sentence, "Once we have seen through the neo-neoclassical fallacy that 'capital' is a factor of production there is a great deal of rethinking to be done" (Vol. IV, p. 24). Thus, a passage appears which pinpoints what Ricardo was really writing about wherever he was concerned with foreign trade:

> For Ricardo, the rate of profit on capital depends upon the labour-cost of producing the necessary real wage. Where the imported commodity is a wage good, trade tends to raise the rate of profit. (This was a point of great importance in his campaign against the corn laws.) [Vol. IV, pp. 16–17].

This is where the modern classical reinterpretation of Ricardo's foreign trade theory must begin. It is a research program which must deal with the contrast between the neoclassical timeless model of trade between countries producing commodities by means of labor and malleable capital (or at best a job lot of given resources), and the classical, post-Sraffian

model of trade between countries endowed with given reproduction structures. In these classical models trade affects the capital stock and the rate of profit, unlike the neoclassical models which focus instead on the international mechanism by which consumers' preferences are satisfied within the context of a given international distribution of resources.

In "Reflections on the Theory of International Trade" (Vol. V, pp. 130–45), Robinson goes on to point out that "Ricardo's theory of profits was not well understood until Piero Sraffa disinterred the simple 'corn' model. . . . Ricardo never quite succeeded in reformulating his theory of profits when the real wage consists of a number of different commodities, produced by various techniques, but we know from Sraffa and von Neumann that there is no difficulty in doing so" (Vol. V, p. 132). What does Ricardo's theory of profits have to do with his theory of foreign trade? Everything. "A lower real cost of procuring wine in England does not affect the rate of profit on capital . . . the whole advantage goes to the drinkers of wine. What Ricardo was really concerned about was to abolish the Corn Laws so as to lower the real cost of wage goods and raise the rate of profit. . . . An increase in profits leads to an increase in the rate of accumulation and so of the growth of employment, national income and wealth. This was the desideratum of the whole argument" (Vol. V, p. 134).[20] Indeed it was. As one of the present authors has pointed out (Walsh, 1979), everything Ricardo wrote on foreign trade except the two pages on comparative cost is concerned with the absolute advantage of England

---

[20] In countries like France or Italy, wine was long an item of working class consumption. In Ricardo's England, on the contrary, it was not. Hence, Ricardo uses "wine" to designate a luxury commodity—what Sraffa calls a non-basic commodity. The question of what commodities are or are not basics in any given society is a matter for empirical investigation.

544   *Journal of Economic Literature, Vol. XXI (June 1983)*

in manufacturing and her absolute disadvantage in corn, and with the effect of cheap imported corn in raising the rate of profit. Ricardo devoted numerous letters, several pamphlets, and four chapters of his *Principles* to this question. More than a reinterpretation of what is essential in Ricardo's trade theory is involved, however, for what Robinson's argument points to are the salient features of a modern classical foreign trade theory. The implications of such theories are now being explored (Oscar Morgenstern and G. L. Thompson, 1976; Ian Steedman, 1979a,b).

VI. *Marx after Robinson*

Among the more striking consequences of the revival of classical theory has been the reinterpretation and reevaluation of Marxian economics. On the one hand, the analytically best elements in Marx (e.g., the schema of reproduction) came to be much more sympathetically understood and accurately appraised than they had ever been by the orthodox economics profession. Robinson was an early contributor to this reappraisal. On the other hand, it became increasingly clear that certain pieces of analysis previously thought to be the exclusive property of Marxian theory could, in fact, be presented without their traditional Marxian garb, in terms of concepts which developed out of the general tradition of classical theory. And one can find early instances of this in Robinson's work. She had lived through days when *any* favorable remark about Marx could cause scandal—and she could never resist saying "boo!" to a goose. This probably obscured the fact that she never accepted from Marx any piece of analysis which was not consistent with the ancient tradition of classical economics and its modern developments. The orthodox, pious Marxists, unlike the orthodox neoclassics, saw this from the beginning. They were warned, of course. In "An Open Letter from a

Keynesian to a Marxist," she tells the Marxists, "I understand Marx better than you . . . I have Marx in my bones and you have him in your mouth" (Vol. IV, p. 265). And, in "Who is a Marxist?" she takes the orthodox Marxists to task for merely reiterating "the slogan that only labour produces value. . . . This left the theory of the productivity of 'capital' in possession of the field" (Vol. V, pp. 248–49). The orthodox neoclassical economics profession, she suggests, ought to be grateful: "Indeed the verbal Marxists are doing them a good turn by helping to shield them from Sraffa's logic" (Vol. V, p. 253).

Both aspects of Robinson's reaction to Marx—her willingness to take his economics seriously and her insistence that it pass muster *as economics,* appear as constant themes throughout her writings. In a passage first published in 1941, she argues that "the relationship between Marxist and academic economists has changed in recent years. . . . The circumstances of the times have forced them to concentrate on two problems, monopoly and unemployment, which naturally raise doubts as to whether all is for the best in the best of all possible economic systems . . . and the view is gaining ground that it is misleading to treat capital itself as a factor of production, on the same footing as labour" (Vol. I, p. 133). And, in the 1948 paper "Marx and Keynes," she tells us that Keynesian theory "has implications, not yet fully worked out, which undermine the traditional academic theory of the long-run supply of capital and of the distribution of the product of industry between labour and capital. Academic theory, by a path of its own, has thus arrived at a position which bears considerable resemblance to Marx's system" (Vol. I, pp. 136–37). She is taking Marx seriously, but he is being tested to see how far he measures up to Keynes.

From the beginning, Robinson regarded the labor theory of value as an un-

Gram and Walsh: Joan Robinson's Economics in Retrospect   545

necessary and confusing detour. Marx' prices of production are the same as Marshall's long-period supply prices. Stick to this and there need be no disagreement (cf. Vol. I, pp. 133–51). The appearance of Sraffa's *Production of Commodities by Means of Commodities* was crucial: the Sraffa system shed light on the labor theory of value, illuminating both its character and its problems. Thus, the question arose as to whether adding a system of value relations enabled one to say anything which could not be said in terms of the ordinary modern classical quantity system and its price system dual. A number of writings in this spirit began to appear, of which Arun Bose (1975) and Ian Steedman (1977) may serve as examples. Bose goes further in a later work (1980), arguing that labor values do not even exist, in principle. His formal proof concerns the impossibility of reducing capital to a quantity of dated labor which, if it could be done, would establish "the existence of capital as a 'factor,' whose 'quantities' would be unambiguously determined and measured *independently* of the level of wages and profits" (Bose, 1980, p. 63). On the basis of his "impossibility theorem" Bose rejects the labor value approach to the Marxian theory of capitalist exploitation. Robinson would obviously agree. In her article on "The Badly Behaved Production Function" (with K. A. Naqvi), she writes, "The main point of the argument [in Chapter Six of Sraffa's *Production of commodities*] . . . is to show that capital *cannot* be reduced to dated labour. Sraffa is here demonstrating that, even if it could be, there is no such thing as a quantity of capital independent of the rate of profit, elaborating a point that Wicksell had already conceded" (Vol. IV, p. 74).

In "The Relevance of Economic Theory," Robinson brings the full force of her wit to bear on Marxists and others who merely dismiss orthodox neoclassical economics, instead of destroying it by using

"the new criticism, inspired by Piero Sraffa" (Vol. IV, p. 114). She uses the same criticism with equal ruthlessness against neoclassical concepts of capital *and* against labor values. In "Who Is a Marxist?" she aims specifically at "a certain group of professed Marxists" (Vol. V, p. 250) who have refused to accept Sraffa's analysis. Elsewhere, she criticizes the Marxists, not so much for rejecting Sraffa as for getting the concept of the organic composition of capital mixed up with the neoclassical concept of the ratio of capital to labor, remarking that the latter had been "pulverized by Sraffa's critique" (Vol. V, p. 262). She concludes her argument by saying that "when Marxian analysis is disentangled from its false association with the neoclassical production function, it is seen to be all the more cogent" (Vol. V, p. 274). Finally, in her review of Ian Steedman's *Marx after Sraffa* (1977), Robinson remarks:

> Steedman points out that when we have a description of capitalist production and distribution in terms of physical processes and flows of payments, a description in terms of *value* adds nothing at all. (The present reviewer pointed this out in 1942 and has been treated as an enemy by the professed Marxists ever since. It will be interesting to see if Steedman meets with the same fate.) [Vol. V, p. 276].

Robinson attacked the labor theory of value because she saw it as standing in the way of an appreciation of what was important to Marx. "What divides Marx's theory from others is not at all the question of relative prices of commodities, but the question of the *total* supply of capital and the rate of profit on capital *as a whole*. On this question there is a sharp difference between Marx and the pre-Keynesian academics" (Vol. I, p. 139). This question is common to Marx and his predecessors, Ricardo and Smith, and emerges again in modern classical general equilibrium theory at the hands of Neumann, Sraffa, and others. It is not a ques-

546   *Journal of Economic Literature, Vol. XXI (June 1983)*

tion which can be posed in terms of the analytical categories of post-Walrasian general equilibrium theory. This goes a long way to explaining why the capital theory controversy was left unresolved— important analytical categories which had meaning in one conceptual system were without meaning in the other.

VII. *Conclusion*

In an age in which precision of thought is often vulgarly confused with mathematical formalism, Robinson's deliberate avoidance of mathematics and her declaration that she *has* a clear ideological position (Vol. II, p. iv) has sometimes led the naive to dismiss her work as *all* ideology. The brief answer to this is brilliantly set forth in her own paper "Marx, Marshall and Keynes" (Vol. II, pp. 1–17) where she points out that, although these three great economists had strong ideological positions which were profoundly different, each can be shown to have made scientific contributions which can be used by someone of the opposite ideological position. "To learn from the economists regarded as scientists it is necessary to separate what is valid in their description of the system from the propaganda that they make, overtly or unconsciously, each for his own ideology. The best way to separate out scientific ideas from ideology is to stand the ideology on its head and see how the ideas look the other way up. If they disintegrate with the ideology, they have no validity of their own. If they still make sense as a description of reality, then there is something to be learned from them, whether we like the ideology or not" (Vol. II, p. 12).

Joan Robinson describes herself as a left-wing Keynesian. "You might almost say that I am the archetypal left-wing Keynesian. I was drawing pinkish rather than bluish conclusions from *The General Theory* long before it was published. (I was in the privileged position of being one of a group of friends who worked with

Keynes while it was being written.) Thus I was the very first drop that ever got into the jar labelled 'Left-wing Keynesian'. Moreover, I am quite a large percentage of the contents of the jar today, because so much of the rest has seeped out of it meanwhile" (Vol. IV, p. 264). The content of left-wing Keynesianism can be inferred from numerous passages in Robinson's writings. Her first and most important point is that "the existence of unemployed resources should be regarded not as a troublesome problem but as a glorious opportunity—an opportunity to do something useful" (Vol. III, p. 109). But she doubts that capitalist firms can ever be counted upon to make good use of the opportunity: "Private enterprise is wonderfully flexible in jumping from one profitable market to another, but it is very rigid in resistance to social control. [When] the authorities want employment to revive, they can only push industry further down the grooves that it has worn for itself. There is no point in thinking of what we really want, such as abolishing poverty and restoring peace. All we can ask for is what they choose to give us. We must keep the show going or else they won't give us anything at all" (Vol. V, p. 129). Robinson would therefore give top priority to the socialization of investment, i.e., to the exercise of public control over the *content* of new investment ("The Second Crisis of Economic Theory," Vol. IV, pp. 100–05).

The second most important tenet of her left-wing Keynesianism is the belief that it is possible, in a democratic society, to exercise public control over the distribution of income from property. For Robinson, there is no justification for the consumption of income from private property: capital goods are the embodiment of technical knowledge, and therefore private ownership of capital is a form of monopoly over something which belongs to society as a whole—technical knowledge. But to control distribution of

Gram and Walsh: Joan Robinson's Economics in Retrospect   547

income from property, Robinson implies in many of her writings that public ownership of the means of production is a necessary condition—there is no other effective way to prevent consumption of "unearned" income.

Finally, on the international scene, she holds that there is no justification for the legacy of colonialism: the foreign ownership of natural resources in Third World countries. "If the wealthy countries were genuinely anxious to put the new nations on their feet they would . . . compensate the capitalists at home, and present the developing countries with the equity in their own resources" (Vol. IV, p. 13).

Robinson has argued that it is difficult to disentangle economic theory from political opinion, but in the case of her own writings, she makes the task easier by being clear about her own ideology. It is neoclassical theory, she insists, which contains a hidden ideology. In an address, she remarked: "I want to speak about the philosophy of economics. It is an extremely important element in the view of life and the conceptions which prevail in this country [the United States]. Freedom is the great ideal. Along with the concept of freedom goes freedom of the market, and the philosophy of economics is that the pursuit of self-interest will lead to the benefit of society. By this means the moral problem is abolished. The moral problem is concerned with the conflict between individual interest and the interest of society. And since this doctrine tells us that there is no conflict, we can all pursue our self-interest with a good conscience" (Vol. V, p. 43). But, is this the message of neoclassical economics? Insofar as that theory is based on the formal system first set forth by Walras, it would certainly be wrong to impute this ideological bias to its author (Walsh and Gram, 1980, pp. 142–45, 155). And nothing in twentieth century developments of that system of thought can be interpreted as having *introduced* political opinion into its formal structure. More-

over, the solutions to models of general equilibrium in the neoclassical tradition say nothing about the desirability, on social or political grounds, of the resulting income distribution, for example. Rather, these models simply elude most of the politically motivated questions Robinson would like to see economists addressing, or at least recognizing.

In commenting on the capital theory controversy, which he described as "the muddle we have got into in recent years," Frank Hahn wrote that "social class is not an explanatory variable in neo-classical theory" (Hahn, 1972, p. 2). But this is not because social class—and hence, for Robinson, the fundamental distinction between income from work and income from poverty—is left out on purpose in order to make neoclassical theory "value-free." Rather, it is left out because it cannot be included in a formal theory which takes the distribution of ownership of pre-existing factors of production as parametric to its structure. In another comment on that same controversy (described as "The Great Charade"), Hahn accuses participants on the Cambridge, England side of "a habit of thinking [sic] elevating and grand-sounding questions or sentences as constituting humane and penetrating thought" (Hahn, 1975, pp. 363–64). Is the question of the relationship between the process of accumulation and the division of income between work and property a "grand-sounding question"? One can agree with Hahn that, within the framework of an intertemporal Arrow-Debreu-McKenzie general equilibrium model, it is not a well-formulated question. But, within an analytical framework in which a dual relationship is established between surplus and profits, questions of this type can be perfectly well-formulated.

Robinson's other great questions were Keynesian and these, it is becoming increasingly clear, cannot be well-formulated within an Arrow-Debreu-McKenzie model. Leijonhufvud describes the effort to embed Keynes within a general equilibrium theory this way: "The notion of what is to be done is thus one of shoving the firm axiomatic neo-Walrasian microfoundations in under the ramshackle 'Keynesian' macro-superstructure which, once safely propped up on that basis, might then be reconstructed without risk to the life, limb and good repute (for formal competence) of those engaged in the task" (Leijonhufvud, 1976, p. 104). He then remarks that "the results of this work have been of a character that should be rather unexpected to anyone who naively embraced the presumptions just outlined. For, in the main, the lessons learned have been about the *limitations* of inherited neo-Walrasian theory—about what cannot be done with it as it now stands. And 'what cannot be done with it' includes, most specifically, of course, analysis of 'Keynesian' macro-processes" (Leijonhufvud, 1976, pp. 104–05). Particular credit is given to the 'new Cambridge' economists[21] for "being out far ahead of the pack in arguing the fundamental irrelevance of neo-

Walrasian general equilibrium theory to Keynesian economics" (Leijonhufvud, 1976, p. 107, n. 65). Thus, as Hahn himself remarked, "We have . . . reached the point where the rather grandiose Arrow-Debreu notion gives way to the more 'feet on the ground' Keynesian one" (Hahn, 1973, p. 16).

Robinson, of course, was never seduced by the analytical beauty of general equilibrium theory. Her "feet on the ground" approach to economics is, self-consciously, to start from a political position insofar as it dictates the questions which first capture her interest. (And this, of course, provides an excuse for some to ignore her arguments.) Once engaged, however, she has always ruthlessly pursued the analytical implications of a question, albeit in the tradition of Marshall and Keynes. In the work of all three of these great economists, time is of the essence. Thus, Robinson is most assuredly a Keynesian in her insistence on the importance of irreducible uncertainty in economic affairs, but in this she is also following Marshall whose arguments are always haunted by the irreversible direction in which time passes. Indeed, it may be fairly concluded that the great bulk of Robinson's work represents a sometimes lone stand against the hegemony of the neo-Walrasian Counter-Revolution in economic theory of the last several decades. As the inadequacies of that theoretical framework become increasingly apparent, Robinson's arguments and criticisms will, no doubt, appear increasingly cogent.

[21] That Leijonhufvud should describe as "new" a group of economists of which Joan Robinson is obviously a member, is perhaps a symptom of what is, for her, the great tragedy of modern economic theorizing; namely, the fact that Keynesian ideas must be continually "rediscovered" after each new wave of general equilibrium theory smothers them over. At the end of her *Economic Heresies* (1971), she wrote: "We can surely agree to start again where Keynes left off. Who wants to deny that the future is uncertain; that investment decisions, in a private-enterprise economy, are made by firms rather than by households; that wage rates are offered in terms of money, or that prices of manufactures are not formed by the higgling of a perfectly competitive market?" (Robinson, 1971, p. 142). And then, after predicting that the 1970s might prove to be "a testing time for modern capitalism," and listing a series of problems which, in fact, materialized, she concluded, "It should be the duty of economists to do their best to enlighten the public about the economic aspects of these menacing problems. They are impeded by a theoretical scheme which (with whatever reservations and exceptions) represents the capitalist world as a kibbutz operated in a perfectly enlightened manner to maximize the welfare of all its members" (Robinson, 1971, p. 144).

REFERENCES

ARROW, KENNETH J. AND DEBREU, GERARD. "Existence of an Equilibrium for a Competitive Economy." *Econometrica*, July 1954, 22(3), pp. 265–90.
_____ AND HAHN, FRANK. *General competitive analysis.* San Francisco, CA: Holden-Day, 1971.
BHARADWAJ, KRISHNA. "Value through Exogenous Distribution," *Econ. Weekly* (Bombay), Aug. 24, 1963, pp. 1450–55; reprinted with changes in *Capital and growth.* Eds.: G. C. HARCOURT AND

Gram and Walsh: Joan Robinson's Economics in Retrospect 549

N. F. LAING. Harmondsworth: Penguin Books, 1971, pp. 183–95.

BLISS, C. J. *Capital theory and the distribution of income*. Amsterdam: North-Holland, 1975.

BOSE, ARUN. *Marxian and post-Marxian political economy, An Introduction*. Harmondsworth: Penguin Books, 1975.

——. *Marx on exploitation and inequality: An essay in Marxian analytical economics*. Delhi: Oxford U. Press, 1980.

BURMEISTER, EDWIN. *Capital theory and dynamics*. Cambridge: Cambridge U. Press, 1980.

DAVIDSON, PAUL. *Money and the real world*. 2nd ed. NY: John Wiley, 1978.

DEBREU, GERARD. *The theory of value*. NY: John Wiley, 1959.

DORFMAN, ROBERT; SAMUELSON, PAUL A. AND SOLOW, ROBERT M. *Linear programming and economic analysis*. NY: McGraw-Hill, 1958.

DRANDAKIS, E. M. "Factor Substitution in the Two-sector Growth Model," *Rev. Econ. Stud.*, Oct. 1963, *30*(3), No. 84, pp. 217–28.

EZAWA, TAICHI. "On the Uniqueness and Stability Conditions of a Balanced Growth Path in Neoclassical Two-Sector Models," *J. Econ. Theory.*, Dec. 1970, *2*(4), pp. 427–36.

GAREGNANI, P. "Heterogeneous Capital, the Production Function and the Theory of Distribution," *Rev. Econ. Stud.*, July 1970, *37*(3), No. 111, pp. 407–36.

GRAM, HARVEY. "Two-Sector Models in the Theory of Capital and Growth," *Amer. Econ. Rev.*, Dec. 1976, *66*(5), pp. 891–903.

HAHN, FRANK. "Equilibrium Dynamics with Heterogeneous Capital Goods," *Quart. J. Econ.*, Nov. 1966, *80*(4), pp. 633–46.

——. *The share of wages in the national income, An enquiry into the theory of distribution*. London: Weidenfeld & Nicolson, 1972.

——. *On the notion of equilibrium in economics*. Cambridge: Cambridge U. Press, 1973.

——. "Revival of Political Economy: The Wrong Issues and the Wrong Argument," *Econ. Rec.*, Sept. 1975, *51*(3), pp. 360–64.

——. "Keynesian Economics and General Equilibrium Theory: Reflections on Some Current Debates," in *The microeconomic foundations of macroeconomics*. Ed.: G. C. HARCOURT. Boulder, CO: Westview Press, 1977.

HARCOURT, G. C. "Some Cambridge Controversies in the Theory of Capital," *J. Econ. Lit.*, June 1969, *7*(2), pp. 369–405.

HARRIS, DONALD J. *Capital accumulation and income distribution*. Stanford, CA: Stanford U. Press, 1978.

HAWKINS, D. AND SIMON, H. "Note: Some Conditions of Macroeconomic Stability," *Econometrica*, July–Oct. 1949, *17*(3–4), pp. 245–48.

HICKS, JOHN R. "Some Questions of Time in Economics," in *Evolution, welfare, and time in economics: Essays in honor of Nicholas Georgescu-Roegen*. Eds.: ANTHONY M. TANG, FRED M. WESTFIELD AND JAMES S. WORLEY. Lexington, MA: Lexington Books, 1976, pp. 135–51.

——. "IS-LM: an explanation," *J. Post-Keynesian Econ.*, Winter 1980–81, *3*(2), pp. 139–54.

KEYNES, JOHN M. *The general theory of employment, interest and money*. London: Macmillan, 1936.

KREGEL, J. A. *The reconstruction of political economy: An introduction to post-Keynesian economics*. London: Macmillan, 1973, 1975.

LEIJONHUFVUD, AXEL. "Schools, 'revolutions', and research programmes in economic theory," in *Method and appraisal in economics*. Ed.: SPIRO J. LATSIS. Cambridge: Cambridge U. Press, 1976.

LEONTIEF, W. W. *The structure of the American economy, 1919–1939*. NY: Oxford U. Press, 1951.

MARSHALL, ALFRED. *The pure theory of foreign trade*. Rare tracts No. 1, London: London School of Economics, [1879] 1930; Reprints of Economic Classics, NY: Kelley, 1974.

——. *Principles of economics*. 9th ed. (variorum). London: Macmillan for the Royal Economic Society, [1920] 1961.

McKENZIE, LIONEL W. "On the Existence of General Equilibrium for a Competitive Market," *Econometrica*, Jan. 1959, *27*(1), pp. 54–71.

MEEK, RONALD. "Mr. Sraffa's Rehabilitation of Classical Economics," *Scot. J. Polit. Econ.*, June 1961, *8*(2), pp. 119–36; reprinted in *Science and society*, Spring 1961, *25*(2), pp. 139–56; and in *Economics and ideology and other essays: Studies in the development of economic thought*. By R. L. MEEK. London: Chapman & Hall, 1967.

MORGENSTERN, OSKAR AND THOMPSON, G. L. *Mathematical theory of expanding and contracting economies*. Lexington MA: Lexington Books, 1976.

NEUMANN, JOHN VON. "A Model of General Economic Equilibrium," *Rev. Econ. Stud.*, 1945–46, *13*(1), pp. 1–9.

NEWMAN, PETER. "Production of Commodities by Means of Commodities," *Schweiz. Z. Volkswirtsch. Statist.*, 1962, pp. 58–75.

NIKAIDO, HUKUKANE. *Introduction to sets and mappings in modern economics*. Amsterdam: North-Holland, 1972.

ROBINSON, JOAN. *The accumulation of capital*. London: Macmillan, 1956, 1965, 1969.

——. *Essays in the theory of economic growth*. London: Macmillan, 1962.

——. *Economic heresies, Some old-fashioned questions in economic theory*. NY: Basic Books, 1971.

——. *The generalization of the general theory and other essays*. London: Macmillan, 1979; originally published as *The rate of interest and other essays*. London: Macmillan, 1952.

——. *Collected economic papers*, Vols. I–V. Cambridge, MA: The M.I.T. Press, 1980a; Oxford: Basil Blackwell, 1951–1979.

——. *What are the questions? and other essays, Further contributions to modern economics*. Armonk, NY: M. E. Sharpe, 1980b.

SAMUELSON, PAUL. *Foundations of economic analysis*. NY: Atheneum, [1947] 1965.

——. "Parable and Realism in Capital Theory: The

Surrogate Production Function," *Rev. Econ. Stud.,* June 1962, *29*(3), No. 80, pp. 193–206.

———. "Steady-State and Transient Relations: A Reply on Switching," *Quart. J. Econ.,* Feb. 1975, *89*(1), pp. 40–47; reprinted in part in *Collected economic papers.* By JOAN ROBINSON Vol. V, pp. 83–87.

SOLOW, ROBERT. "A Contribution to the Theory of Economic Growth," *Quart. J. Econ.,* Feb. 1956, *70*(1), pp. 65–94.

SRAFFA, PIERO. "Introduction" to *Works and correspondence.* Vol. I. *On the principles of political economy and taxation.* By DAVID RICARDO. Ed.: PIERO SRAFFA with the collaboration of M. H. DOBB. Cambridge: Cambridge U. Press for the Royal Economic Society, [1817] 1951.

———. *Production of commodities by means of commodities: Prelude to a critique of economic theory.* Cambridge: Cambridge U. Press, 1960.

STEEDMAN, IAN. *Marx after Sraffa.* London: New Left Books, 1977.

———, ed. *Fundamental issues in trade theory.* NY: St. Martin's Press, 1979a.

———. *Trade amongst growing economies.* Cambridge: Cambridge U. Press, 1979b.

TARSHIS, LORIE. "Post-Keynesian Economics: A Promise that Bounced?" *Amer. Econ. Rev.,* May 1980, *70*(2), pp. 10–14.

UZAWA, HIROFUMI. "On a Two-Sector Model of Economic Growth," *Rev. Econ. Stud.,* Oct. 1961, *29*(1), No. 78, pp. 40–47.

———. "On a Two-Sector Model of Economic Growth, II," *Rev. Econ. Stud.,* June 1963, *30*(2), No. 83, pp. 105–18.

WALSH, VIVIAN CHARLES. "Ricardian Foreign Trade Theory in the Light of the Classical Revival," *Eastern Econ. J.,* Oct. 1979, *5*(3), pp. 421–27.

——— AND GRAM, HARVEY. *Classical and neoclassical theories of general equilibrium, Historical origins and mathematical structure.* NY: Oxford U. Press, 1980.

WEINTRAUB, E. ROY. *Microfoundations: The compatibility of microeconomics and macroeconomics.* Cambridge: Cambridge U. Press, 1979.

YEATS, WILLIAM BUTLER. "Coole Park, 1929," *The variorum edition of the poems of W. B. Yeats.* Eds.: P. ALLT AND R. K. ALSPACH. NY: Macmillan, 1957, pp. 488–89.

YELLEN, JANET L. "On Keynesian Economics and the Economics of the Post-Keynesians," *Amer. Econ. Rev.,* May 1980, *70*(2), pp. 15–19.

[3]

Cambridge Journal of Economics 1983, 7, 331–342

Joan Robinson and the labour theory of value

E. K. Hunt*

The 'metaphysical' nature of value theory is an issue that has been discussed recurringly in Joan Robinson's writings. In these writings one finds a consistent and profound ambiguity. Her most strikingly negative statements about the labour theory of value were written in *An Essay on Marxian Economics*:

The awkwardness of reckoning in terms of *value* . . . accounts for much of the obscurity of Marx's exposition, and none of the important ideas which he expresses in terms of the concept of *value* cannot be better expressed without it (Robinson, 1966, p. 20).
...[N]o point of substance in Marx's argument depends upon the labor theory of value. Voltaire remarked that it is possible to kill a flock of sheep by witchcraft if you give them plenty of arsenic at the same time . . . Marx's penetrating insight and bitter hatred of oppression supply the arsenic, while the labour theory of value provides the incantations (Robinson, 1966, p. 22).

Similarly in *Economic Philosophy*, Robinson wrote:

One of the great metaphysical ideas in economics is expressed by the word 'value' . . . It does not mean market prices, which vary from time to time under the influence of casual accidents; nor is it just an historical average of actual prices. Indeed, it is not simply a price; it is something which will explain how prices come to be what they are. What is it? Where shall we find it? Like all metaphysical concepts, when you try to pin it down it turns out to be just a word (Robinson, 1962, p. 26).

At the risk of needless repetition the full impact of Robinson's view must be starkly and unequivocally highlighted: Marx's argument for the labour theory of value (in *Capital*, Vol. I) was 'a purely dogmatic statement' which never was 'intended to be an original contribution to science. It was simply an orthodox dogma' (Robinson, 1962, pp. 36–37). Moreover, when Marx attempted to explain exploitation on the basis of value theory 'the whole argument appears to be metaphysical. . . . Logically it is a mere rigmarole of words ...' (*ibid.*, p. 37). And finally, 'a metaphysical belief, as in the law of value, cannot be wrong and this is the sign that there is nothing to be learned from it' (*ibid.*, p. 39).

Marx regarded (and most of his contemporary disciples regard) the labour theory of value as the heart of his intellectual system. Therefore it is not surprising that many Marxists, though recognising both the greatness of Robinson's intellectual achievements and the undoubted emotional, moral and ideological sympathy she has had for many of the ideas as well as some of the political institutions of contemporary Marxism, consider Robinson to be fundamentally a critic. Roman Rosdolsky, for example, believes that Robinson is a 'striking example' of a 'gulf' between the academic and Marxist schools of political economy, a gulf that has 'grown so large that the adherents of one school can

*University of Utah.

0309–166X/83/030331 + 12 $03.00/0

scarcely understand the language of the other' (Rosdolsky, 1977, p. 530). He concludes his discussion of Robinson's critique of Marx by asserting that 'she might, perhaps, understand what Marx said literally, but never "what he really meant" ' (*ibid.*).

But despite the devastatingly negative implications of Robinson's dismissal of the labour theory of value, she shows decidedly mixed feelings on the matter. She writes that 'the concept of value seems to me to be a remarkable example of how a metaphysical notion *can inspire* original thought, though in itself it is quite devoid of operational meaning' (Robinson, 1966, p. xi). The labour theory, it would seem, while utterly devoid of any real meaning ('rigmarole of words' from which 'there is nothing to be learned') is somehow the source of important theoretical insights. Indeed, she argues that 'metaphysical propositions . . . provide a quarry from which hypotheses can be drawn' and are 'necessary' to science (Robinson, 1962, p. 3).

Clearly there is a profound ambiguity in her attitude toward the labour theory of value. This ambiguity probably accounts for the divergent attitudes toward Robinson's writings that one finds in the Marxist literature. One finds her referred to as both an antagonistic critic and an ally. As a self-professed Marxist, it is my view that she is much more of an ally than an antagonist. indeed, in this paper I shall argue that

(1) Robinson's argument that Marx treats the labour theory of value as definitionally true is a correct argument and

(2) that her suggestions that it is an important 'source' or 'inspiration' of scientific insight is fundamentally sound even though she never adequately explains how an empty 'rigmarole of words' from which 'nothing . . . [can] be learned' can be such a source.

The difficulty, I submit, is her apparent reliance on the positivist notion that all definitions are either (a) lexical or (b) stipulative and that in neither event can we learn more from them than (a) how words are generally used or (b) how a specific person is using a word. It is not my intention in this paper to enter into epistomological debates but merely to note that the rationalist tradition in science (in contrast to the empiricist or positivist position) is built on the belief that whether a definition is lexical or stipulative it may, in either case, be true or false.

This claim for the truth or falsity of definitions reflects the rationalist's distinction between the qualities of the 'thing' that are 'essential' to its being the kind of thing it is and the qualities that are accidental and could have been otherwise without altering the kind of thing it is. If a definition includes all of the essential qualities or features of a thing it is a true definition. If it omits some essential qualities or includes some accidental qualities it is (to some degree) untrue. An important part of science, in this tradition, is the working out of all of the implications of true definitions.

Without defending this rationalist approach to science, I would like to argue that both neoclassical and Marxist value theories are based on propositions that are, implicitly or explicitly, assumed to be *true by definition.* (I have argued this at length elsewhere: Hunt, 1977, pp. 11–25.) Indeed, Robinson has treated this as a serious flaw in each of these theories. I shall argue that this is not a flaw at all, but simply not a legitimate criterion, by itself, for accepting or rejecting either theory. As will become obvious in my argument, I believe that there are good grounds on which to choose between these theories and I think the labour theory is superior to the utility theory. I shall end the paper by indicating very briefly why I believe that the ideas of Keynes and Sraffa must be assimilated into either the labour theory of value or the utility theory of value or face historical extinction.

Since the time of Adam Smith (if not earlier), economists' interest in prices have taken two very separate (even though not entirely unrelated) forms. First is the interest in describing and understanding the actual, immediate process of price formation in which prices come to assume their general, habitual, customary or normal magnitudes. Second is the interest in understanding the social and moral meaning or importance of prices, i.e., in understanding the role of prices in human development, in social, economic and political processes and, most generally, in the quest for a well-ordered good life for the individual and/or for the society.

In the actual writings of nearly all significant economic theorists these two concerns have not been separated—and it is my opinion that they are not completely and entirely separable. Nevertheless, I believe that we can increase our understanding of economic theory by separating mentally the two concerns. The concern with the process of price formation or the quantitative determination of actual price levels I shall call price theory. The concern with the social nature of prices I shall call value theory. (Given the relevant texts in the history of economic doctrines this particular labelling of the two concerns is definitely not arbitrary. With more space I believe I could show that the labeling has definite historical as well as analytical justification.)

When this distinction is made, it is most interesting to note that the two most important intellectual traditions in economics—the neoclassical and the Marxian—yield (at least at a sufficiently high level of generalisation) nearly identical price theories despite their profoundly different value theories. Both traditions see capitalist entrepreneurs as the setters of prices. Both see these entrepreneurs as generally endeavouring to maximise profits. Both see market competition as the most significant constraint within which the entrepreneurs' profit-maximising, price setting decisions are made. Although the neoclassical conceptions of 'pure' or 'perfect' competition differ from the conception of competition in the writings of the classical economists and Marx, competition need be neither 'pure' nor 'perfect' to get the result required by neoclassical price theory (the purity and perfection are needed only for their formulation of welfare economics, about which more will be said later). For the price theory of the neoclassical, classical and Marxian schools alike there must in general be enough competition so that the presence of prolonged, abnormally high profit rates will attract new competitors and thus tend to push all (or nearly all, since monopoly is treated as a special case in these approaches) profit rates toward the social average.

Thus, both schools see the process of price formulation as one in which the profit-maximising entrepreneur sums his costs of production and then—in equilibrium at least—adds the socially average rate of profit to these costs to arrive at the price. Any industry that is able to maintain barriers that prevent competition from pushing that industry's rate of profit toward the social average is treated as an exception to this 'normal' or usual process and is analysed on a separate or *ad hoc* basis.

This conception of price formulation is what I believe should be called price theory as distinguished from value theory. Using this terminology, the 'price theory' just described can be said to come close to being one of the very few genuine 'principles of economics' common to nearly all schools of theory. The theories of value of the various schools, however, differ markedly. In order to assess the significance of these differences I shall first discuss the general relation of value theory to price theory and then examine briefly the neoclassical utility theory of value and the Marxian labour theory of value.

In price theory, as I have defined it above, it is clear that because of the fact that the outputs of most industries serve as inputs to other industries—and all non-labour inputs in any given industry are outputs of other industries—the cost of production of any commodity (and hence its price) depends on the prices of other commodities. Therefore, price theory leaves us with a set of unknowns (prices) and a set of general functional relations between each price and all other prices. Clearly, by itself price theory is incomplete. In order to break the circularity in which each price simply depends on other prices we must have what Maurice Dobb has called a 'value constant' (Dobb, 1940, pp. 1–17). In purely analytical terms, a value constant is some principle or set of principles the knowledge of which enables the theorist to give specific and unique content to the general functional relation between each price and the other prices of the system. With the addition of this value constant price theory yields a specific set of equations the mathematical solution of which yields prices.

The set of principles from which we derive the value constant is a theory of value. Obviously price theory is analytically incomplete without a value theory and this, in part at least, explains why the two are generally held to be synonymous. The rationale for distinguishing between price and value theory comes from the fact that in addition to providing the value constant that renders price theory analytically complete, value theory plays another extremely important role in economic theory. It anchors price theory securely onto the intellectual foundation that Joseph Schumpeter labelled the theory's 'preanalytical vision'. It is this 'vision' that ultimately dictates our conception of what sort of entity prices are and hence our conception of the social and moral significance of the market allocation of resources. It is this vitally important role of value theory that accounts for the frequently polemical nature of debates on value theory.

Every economic theorist (indeed every theorist) begins theorising on the basis of an elaborate set of views (which may or may not have been consciously examined) about the ultimate nature of reality. These views include, of course, what philosophers label as principles of ontology or metaphysics. But they also include considerably more. What Aristotelian metaphysics is to physics, the Schumpeterian preanalytical vision is to social theory. It contains the theory's most fundamental conceptions of the nature of human beings and the nature of human society.

Neither metaphysics nor preanalytical visions are amenable to empirical or logical proof or disproof. If they were amenable to proof or disproof they would not be metaphysics or preanalytical visions but rather ordinary physics and social theory. This, of course, accounts for the desire of logical positivists in the 1930s to purge philosophy and science of all metaphysics, and contemptuously to label the elements of the preanalytical vision as either metaphysics, moral philosophy, or meaningless phrases. There is, however, a growing number of philosophers who hold that the logical positivists' quest was inherently impossible to carry out because all theorising absolutely requires first principles that are not amenable to empirical or logical proof or disproof. It is all such first principles of a social theory that I refer to as the preanalytical vision of the theory.

Because preanalytical visions are amenable to neither empirical nor logical disproof, Schumpeter explicitly chose to ignore them in his *History of Economic Analysis*—his assumption being that we have no intelligent means for a normative choice among competing preanalytical visions. I think that this assumption is wrong. Different preanalytical visions predispose us to focus on different social and economic problems and lead to entirely different attitudes toward our social setting and our actions within that setting. Thus, they have enormously important practical consequences in human social action and interaction. Therefore, I would propose that while empirical evidence and logical arguments ought to be important in our normative evaluation of competing propositions in the realm of economic theory proper, the relevant criteria for choosing among competing preanalytical visions are practical and ethical. And since the propositions of analytical economic theory are generally tied to one or another preanalytical vision by a theory of value, a normative assessment of rival theories of value becomes extraordinarily difficult because it must perforce be based upon not only logical and empirical criteria but practical and ethical criteria as well.

I shall argue that the acceptance of one or another preanalytical vision has definite and important ethical implications. This, I believe, can be clearly demonstrated. What is much more difficult to demonstrate, however, but is nevertheless assumed throughout the paper, is that there are good intellectual and ethical reasons for choosing one vision rather than another. Since one's theories of ethics and epistemology derive in part from one's preanalytical vision, one cannot use ordinary ethical, empirical or logical proofs to establish the superiority of one preanalytical vision over another. It does not follow, however, that the choice is ethically or intellectually arbitrary. I believe that there are good reasons for choosing between the different preanalytical visions, and very powerful arguments have been made for this general proposition (see, e.g., Putnam, 1981).

In the remainder of this paper I assume the validity of these arguments and also assume that the differing ethical implications of these two preanalytical visions are not unrelated to the ethical and rational choice between the two visions.

Having stated the general principles of my argument, I shall now examine briefly the neoclassical and Marxian theories of value within the general context of the preceeding discussion.

The neoclassical preanalytical conception of a human being is that of a single-minded seeker of a maximum of pleasure (or utility, or position on a preference ordering, or whatever other euphemism is used). The specific nature of the individual likes and dislikes (i.e., his utility function or preference map) is taken as given without any regard whatsoever for the social processes and institutions within which the likes and dislikes were formed. The individual's actions take place in an environment that again is taken as given and not generally investigated. This environment is conceived as an elaborate set of constraints within the confines of which the individual must conduct his perpetual, Sisyphean quest for the attainment of an endless succession of constrained optima. The individual begins each 'period' with an endowment that yields him relatively little utility. He gives up parts or all of this endowment in a series of exchanges that bring him temporarily to a constrained optimum. The 'optimum' is very brief, however, since the same process continues to recur endlessly.

One might imagine that I have described only 'consumption theory' and not 'production theory.' This is not the case. The more perceptive undergraduate economics student soon notices that there is a striking analytical symmetry between 'consumption theory' and 'production theory' in neoclassical economics. In fact, in the words of a leading neoclassical text, the individual begins with an 'initial endowment', that is, 'a combination of goods that provides a starting point for optimising choice' (Hirschleifer, 1970, p. 2). The individual then exchanges with other isolated exchangers or he produces. But the analytical symmetry between utility functions and production functions is by no means accidental. The same text concludes that all economic theory is exchange theory because 'consumption theory' deals with exchange among individuals while 'production theory' reduces to the fact that 'production is "exchange" with nature' (*ibid.*, p. 12).

In fact, the preanalytical vision of neoclassical economics is so extremely individualistic that the only way in which human sociality appears at all is in the individual's need for other entities with whom to exchange. The theory applies different labels according to whether these entities are human or non-human. But a rose is a rose, and the asocial nature of the theory is strikingly clear when one sees that it does not matter either analytically or substantially whether these entities are human or not. The isolated Robinson Crusoe is, in this theory, absolutely no different than the participant in a social process. Indeed, differing social or cultural contexts make no difference whatsoever. Another widely used neoclassical text asserts that this theory is 'applicable to all economic systems and countries' (Alchian and Allen, 1964, p. 5).

This then is the core of the value theory that emerges from the utility theorists' pre-analytical vision of human beings. While many Marxists would argue that neoclassical economics is not concerned with a capitalist economy at all, but, rather with a competitive barter economy, this is beside the point. The theory is the basis of conclusions that neo-classical economists believe apply to a capitalist economy. It furnishes the context within which they see entrepreneurs as setting prices by summing costs and adding the socially average return on their capital. Clearly this context is very important because the only response these theorists have made to the innumerable devastating critiques of their concepts of utility functions (for a summary of these critiques see Hunt, 1981) and production functions (for a summary, see Harcourt, 1972) has been to devise more abstract and esoteric formulations that still retain the necessary analytical characteristics. Necessary for what? The answer to this question is utterly unequivocal: necessary intellectually in order to derive all the conditions of Pareto optimality from the analysis of pricing within a competitive capitalist society.

It is the aim of nearly all neoclassical value theory to culminate in a demonstration of how the competitive capitalist economy automatically attains Pareto optimality. Typical of nearly all orthodox microeconomic texts is the revised edition of *Microeconomic Theory* by C. E. Ferguson, which consists of 16 chapters. The last chapter is entitled 'Theory of Welfare Economics', and it is obvious that most of the first 15 chapters are designed to lay the analytical foundations for the last chapter on neoclassical welfare economics, which is the climax and *dénouement* of the entire book.

Early in the final chapter Ferguson wrote:

We now wish to show . . . that a perfectly competitive, free enterprise system guarantees the attain-ment of maximum social welfare. The proof rests upon the maximising behavior of producers and consumers. To recall the dictum of Adam Smith, each individual, in pursuing his own self interest, is led as if by an 'invisible hand' to a course of action that promotes the general welfare of all (Ferguson, 1969, pp. 444–445).

There follow nine pages of summary explanation outlining the deductive argument that culminates in the demonstration of the attainment of Pareto optimality. The most important aspect of these nine pages is this: Ferguson is able to tie together his demonstration of neoclassical welfare economics and the attainment of bliss in a coherent and brief manner because, with each point he makes, he is able to refer his readers to earlier chapters or sections of his book. His standard explanation of orthodox microeconomic theory has developed the ideas and analytical tools that inevitably lead to the conclusions of neoclassi-cal welfare economics. Indeed, in examining the previous 15 chapters, we can see very little else to which they do lead. The nine-page demonstration of welfare economics ties the entire book together and then concludes: 'This unique equilibrium . . . is called the point of 'constrained bliss' because it represents the unique organization of production, exchange and distribution that leads to the maximum attainable social welfare.'

The most significant point to note in neoclassical welfare economics is its conservative consensual character (see Hunt, 1981). Defined away are all situations of conflict. In a world of class conflicts, imperialism, exploitation, alienation, racism, sexism, and scores of other human conflicts, where are the changes that might make some better off without making others worse off? Improve the plight of the oppressed and you worsen the situation of the oppressor (as perceived by the oppressor, of course)! Important social, political, and economic situations where improving the lot of one social unit is not opposed by naturally antagonistic social units are indeed rare. The domain of this theory would, indeed, seem to be so restrictive as hardly to warrant serious investigation, were it not for the fact that the theory is considered important by the overwhelming majority of neoclassical economists.

Thus, a conservative social-economic philosophy rests on the foundations of the pre-analytical vision of the utility theorists and it is precisely the utility theory of value that anchors the concept of price determination that is common to both neoclassicism and Marxism to this conservative philosophy.

From the preanalytical vision underlying the utility theory the value constants are derived primarily from (a) the mathematical properties of preference maps or utility functions and (b) the mathematical properties 'of well-behaved' neoclassical production functions. With these, the set of price equations becomes determinate and the price theory is complete and logically consistent. Moreover, in addition to the necessary value constants the preanalytical vision supports a social philosophy that includes all the essential elements of bourgeois ideology. While this ideology is not identical to neoclassical economics, the utility theory of value ties neoclassical economics to this ideology. Thus, it is common to find neoclassical texts where the author claims merely to be stating scientific economic theory, but where many if not all of the following conclusions of bourgeois ideology are explicitly defended:

   (i) the market harmonises all interests so that social harmony and not conflict is the normal state of human affairs;
   (ii) since human beings are by nature maximising exchangers the present capitalist economic system is not essentially different from (only an improved or even perfected version of) earlier economic systems;
   (iii) the market tends automatically to create the most efficient allocation of resources (indeed, it automatically creates 'constrained bliss') such that no outside interference or reform could augment human welfare unambiguously; and
   (iv) there is a certain ethical logic in the income distribution that obtains in a market capitalist system since it is assumed that each factor of production will earn a reward that is equal to its marginal productivity.

In sharp contrast, the preanalytical vision that underlies the labour theory of value is almost the antithesis of that underlying the utility theory. Whereas the latter sees humans as essentially exchangers the former sees them as producers. The labour theory rests on a preanalytical vision that focuses on the fact that the 'crust' of the earth is an environment that is not immediately suitable for the sustenance of human life. The natural environment must be transformed if it is to support human life. Production is this transformation. And production has only one universally necessary social or human ingredient—labour. To be sure the natural environment must exist in order to be transformed—something cannot be made from nothing. But to say that 'land' (or natural resources) is a factor contributing to production in a manner analogous to the contribution of labour is seen as a form of fetishism, in which non-human material things are endowed with human qualities. A tree cannot be chopped down if no tree exists, but no one says that a tree is chopped down partly by a lumberjack and partly by itself simply because it exists. This is because production is purely a *social activity* of human beings, and value is a purely social phenomenon which Marx sees as having no inherent connection with the physical or chemical features of the commodities that have value. The sun is as essential to human productive activity as is the crust of the earth. But no one speaks of the sun being a factor of production on the same footing as labour. On examination, of course, this is because we cannot be excluded coercively from making use of the sun while we can be so excluded from making use of natural resources. But coercive exclusion is not an essential element of production and it is therefore difficult to see how it should be the defining feature of what constitutes a 'factor of production'. Within the labour theory tradition coercion does not play this role and labour is the only human or social ingredient in production (though labour theorists certainly accept the less than profound stipulation that human life and production cannot be sustained in an absolute void).

The second major difference between the two preanalytical visions is that whereas the utility theorists see humans in starkly individualistic terms (remembering that in neoclassical theory there is no important difference between exchanging with nature and exchanging with another human being) the labour theorists see humans as essentially and fundamentally social creatures (the historical roots of the word 'socialism' can be found in precisely this distinction between the two views). Production is seen as always being a social process of interdependent social beings transforming a given pre-existing natural environment.

The individualism of the utility tradition causes this productive interdependence among human beings to be seen by utility theorists as a dependence of the isolated individual on a non-human material thing—capital. Thus, for example, if we see a carpenter building a house, the utility theorist sees three factors of production at work: first, the carpenter, second the wood, land and other natural resources, and third, the saw, the hammer, and the other tools. Each of these three factors is doing its separate part in building a house. Each factor produces and each receives a return that is equal to its productivity. The labour theorist sees this as a social process of transforming nature to make it habitable for human life. The process (which, of course, could not occur in the void of outer space) requires a large number of socially interdependent human beings working. Some humans are extracting natural resources, some are fashioning them into lumber, hammers, saws and other tools and the carpenter is providing the last of these interdependent social exertions. Thus, when the utility theorists say that the lone carpenter depends on capital and that capital (in the forms of the hammer, saw and other tools) creates value just as the carpenter creates value, the labour theorists insist that this is again a form of fetishism in which a purely human form of interdependent productive activity is seen as the value-creating 'contribution' of a non-human, material thing.

Only within the context of the above-described 'labour' or 'social production' preanalytical vision can one understand the sense in which the labour theory of value is definitional. Value expresses what Marx takes to be an essential fact of capitalism—the fact that interdependent labour is only *indirectly* social and is not seen by the participants in the capitalist system as being a social relation at all.

To illustrate this, Marx described the *directly*-social labour of precapitalist society with which indirectly-social labour can be contrasted:

Under the rural patriarchal system of production, when spinner and weaver lived under the same roof—the women of the family spinning and the men weaving, say for the requirements of the family—yarn and linen were *social* products, and spinning and weaving *social* labour within the framework of the family. But their social character did not appear in the form of yarn becoming a universal character exchanged for linen as a universal equivalent, i.e., of the two products exchanging for each other as equal and equally valid expressions of the same universal labour time [as would be the case under capitalism]. On the contrary, the product of labour bore the specific social imprint of the family relationship with its naturally evolved division of labour. Or let us take the services and dues in kind of the Middle Ages. It was the distinct labour of the individual in its original form, the particular features of his labour and not its universal aspect that formed the social ties at that time. Or finally let us take communal labour in its spontaneously evolved form as we find it among all civilised nations at the dawn of their history. In this case the social character of labour is evidently not affected by the labour of the individual assuming the abstract form of universal labour ... The communal system on which this mode of production is based prevents the labour of an individual from becoming private labour and his product the private product of a separate individual; it causes individual labour to appear rather as the direct function of a member of the social organisation (Marx, 1970, pp. 33–34).

In capitalist commodity production Marx sees each individual producer as producing only for the market. One neither knows nor cares who will consume one's commodity or who will produce the commodities one consumes. Each person produces only in order to acquire exchange value. And the use values one acquires with one's exchange values are seen as merely the quantitative equivalents of one's own production, desired only to sustain one's own life.

As a general rule, articles of utility become commodities only because they are the products of the labour of private individuals or groups of individuals who carry on their work independently of each other. The sum total of all the labour of these private individuals forms the aggregate labour of society. Since the producers do not come into social contact with each other until they exchange their products, the specific social character of each producer's labour does not show itself except in the act of exchange. In other words, the labour of the individual asserts itself as a part of the labour of society, only by means of the relations which the act of exchange establishes directly between the products, and indirectly, through them, between the producers. To the latter, therefore, the relations connecting the labour of one individual with that of the rest appear, not as direct social relations between individuals at work, but as ... social relations between things (Marx, 1967, pp. 72–73).

Thus, value is a social attribute of (or a social abstraction symbolised by the physical existence or use value of) a commodity.

The important point here is that the foundation of the labour theory of value—the assertion that value is abstract labour congealed in a commodity—is *not* a theory in any usual sense in which we speak of theories. It is intended simply to be descriptive of what Marx considers to be one of the most important, essential facts of capitalism, namely, that the concrete, particular labour of the isolated individual 'becomes social labour by assuming the form of its direct opposite, of abstract universal labour' (Marx, 1970, p. 34).

Only as such a *universal* magnitude does it represent a social magnitude. The labour of an individual can produce exchange values only if it produces universal equivalents. ... The effect is the same as if the different individuals had amalgamated their labour-time and allocated different portions of the labour-time at their joint disposal to the various use values. The labour time of the individual is thus, in fact, the labour-time required by society to produce a particular use-value, that is, to satisfy a particular want (*ibid.*, pp. 85–86).

This foundation of the labour theory of value is, then, definitional. But the definition is not arbitrary. It is rather a name for a real process that Marx sees as the essential nature of social interdependence in capitalism. As such, it is amenable to neither proof nor dis-proof. Its persuasiveness depends upon whether after an in-depth investigation of the social labour process Marx is describing one concludes that the process really, *and essentially*, occurs as he says it does. And the labour theory's scientific merit rests entirely on the usefulness of the insights gained by looking at capitalism in this way. It is clear that Marx saw value in exactly this way. In the following quotation Marx explicitly acknowledges Robinson's charge that the labour theory of value is definitional:

> Since the exchange-value of commodities is indeed nothing but a mutual relation between various kinds of labour of individuals regarded as equal and universal labour, i.e., nothing but the material expression of a specific social form of labour, it is a tautology to say that labour is the *only* source of exchange value and accordingly of wealth insofar as this consists of exchange-value (*ibid.*, p. 35).

But while this conception of value is definitional, it represented, for Marx, a profound scientific discovery whereby one could go behind the superficial appearance of market exchange to discover the hidden essence of capitalism. It was, of course, not a lexical definition. It was emphatically not, however, merely an arbitrarily stipulative definition. Rather Marx believed it to be an accurate, descriptive definition of the real essence of the indirect sociality involved in capitalist commodity production. He realised that it is not an empirically obvious definition. Indeed, many of the descriptive, historical and institutional accounts in *Capital* are intended to show the reader that only with this definition in mind can one consistently comprehend the empirical facts of capitalism.

The labour theory of value, then, must be regarded as one of the most important elements in Marx's preanalytical vision of capitalism. Within the context of this vision Marx derives what we (following Dobb) have labelled his value constants with which his set of simultaneous equations for prices become determinate. Again, as in the utility theory, there are two general sources for these constants. First, the quantitative magnitudes of the various portions of the labour force socialy assigned to the various interdependent tasks, and second, the division of the values created in production between those who produce and those who own. With this information the price equations become solvable.

The differences from the utility tradition are inevitable and are clearly derivable from the two contrasting preanalytical visions. First, unlike the utility tradition the labour theory tradition sees capitalism as a historically unique mode of production. It is a mode in which an individual's labour appears to be private rather than social (and this gives rise to the illusion that land and tools produce in the same way that people produce). This appearance is caused by the fact that in a capitalist system individual producers produce in isolation and in ignorance of their social and technological interdependence. The social nature of the individual's labour appears only as a price in an exchange. Thus, neoclassical economics as a social science deals elaborately with prices, interest rates, wage rates, profit rates etc., and only very sparingly with human beings—and then only with humans as that rarified abstraction 'rational maximising exchangers'. Labour theorists, on the contrary, attempt to show that human behaviour, including exchange behaviour, is the outgrowth of sociality and is strikingly and importantly different from one socioeconomic system to another.

Second, since only labour produces, it follows that in a society in which labourers receive only a portion of what they produce and non-producers (usually through some system of ownership) receive the surplus there is a fundamental, antagonistic conflict between these social classes. Therefore, whereas harmony is the normal state of affairs in utility theory, conflict is seen as the normal state of affairs by the labour theory—normal, that is, until that historical point at which non-producers cease having social, political and economic control over producers.

Third, since the labour theory does not view individuals as social entities with metaphysically given desires, but rather sees desires as coming into being within the process of social interaction, it follows that labour theorists reject the ethical foundations of neoclassical efficiency analysis. The labour theorists generally deny the 'well-behaved' utility and production functions as well. Thus, neoclassical efficiency analysis is seen as almost entirely ideological and non-scientific.

Fourth, the denial of exogenous production functions is sufficient grounds for rejecting the ethical conclusions to which the neoclassical income distribution theory generally leads. More importantly, however, the view that value is a purely social phenomenon reflecting merely one historically particular form of social labour leads inevitably to the view that under capitalism property income is not only derived from parasitic exploitation of labour but is the inevitable outcome of a particular kind of alienated labour and ought ethically to be abolished. I have argued elsewhere (Hunt, 1982, pp. 7–25) that once the definitional basis of the labour theory of value is understood it can be shown that it is integrally related to Marx's early philosophical writings on the alienation of labour, and hence it becomes an integral part of the ethical condemnation of capitalism. But just as neoclassical economic theory is not identical to bourgeois ideology but leads to it through the utility theory of value, so the labour theory of value is not itself an evaluative theory. Like the utility theory, however, it links economic theory to a social philosophy that is evaluative. The labour theory of value intellectually connects an analysis of capitalism with an ethical outlook that inevitably condemns capitalism. Indeed, I believe that it can be convincingly argued that the marginal productivity theory of distribution was developed because of this implication of the labour theory perspective. One of the most important originators of the marginal productivity theory of distribution, John Bates Clark, wrote:

The welfare of the laboring classes depends on whether they get much or little; but their attitude toward the other classes—and therefore, the stability of the social state—depends chiefly on the question, whether the amount that they get, be it large or small, is what they produce. If they create a small amount of wealth and get the whole of it, they may not seek to revolutionise society; but if it were to appear that they produce an ample amount and get only a part of it, many of them would become revolutionists, and all would have the right to do so. The indictment that hangs over society is that of 'exploiting labor'. 'Workmen' it is said, 'are regularly robbed of what they produce. This is done within the forms of law, and by the natural working of competition'. If this charge were proved, every right-minded man should become a socialist; and his zeal in transforming the industrial system would then measure and express his sense of justice (Clark, 1965, p. 4).

It is clear that these contrasting preanalytical visions have most drastically conflicting practical and political implications. It is also clear that practical and ethical criteria are at least as important as empirical and logical criteria in choosing between the two theories of value.

Many neoclassical economists would argue that I have made an invalid comparison. They argue that their theorising is merely the working out of the logical implications of various sets of arbitrary assumptions. Since nearly all Marxists argue that their theory rests on abstractions of real processes, one might argue that I have attempted to compare the incomparable, that I have wrongly conflated the very different roles of assumptions and abstractions in economic theory. There are undoubtedly a few neoclassical economists interested solely in deductive logic. The Austrian School of neoclassical economics has,

342   E. K. Hunt

however, explicitly argued that their analysis rests on the foundations of abstractions that reflect the essential nature of the existing economic system, and I have argued elsewhere (Hunt, 1979, Ch. 15 and 18) that other important schools of neoclassical theorists arrive at conclusions that can only be defended on the assumption that their theory is based on essential abstractions. The issue can be decided, I submit, by opening nearly any elementary textbook written by an important neoclassical theorist. In every such textbook that I have examined, the conclusions of bourgeois ideology that I have outlined above are claimed to be (a) actually true of existing capitalist economies (with minor modifications and caveats) and (b) derived deductively from the scientific principles of economic theory. Therefore, I conclude that the theories are generally comparable and that the choice between them is, in part, practical and ethical.

I shall end this paper with one final assertion. It is my belief that very few people are attracted to the study of economics solely or even primarily by the desire to explain the immediate causes of the magnitudes of relative prices, or the process whereby a market in disequilibrium attains (or fails to attain) equilibrium. Rather most of us are interested in the social and moral meaning and significance of prices and the capitalist pricing system. This requires a well-developed philosophical system. Value theory ties the theory of price determination and the theory of market adjustment to such a philosophical system. If I am right about economists' motivations, then Keynes's theoretical insights into the processes of market adjustments and Sraffa's theoretical insights into the structural determinants of equilibrium prices will (since neither is anchored in what I have called value theory) either be assimilated into one or the other of the two great value theory traditions or will gradually disappear from contemporary intellectual currency. As Joan Robinson has written: 'Metaphysical propositions ... are necessary to ... the realm of science ... [because] without them we would not know what it is we want to know' (Robinson, 1964, p. 3).

Bibliography

Alchian, A. A. and Allen, W. R. 1964. *University Economics*, Belmont, Calif., Wadsworth
Clark, J. B. 1965. *The Distribution of Wealth*, New York, Augustus M. Kelley
Dobb, M. 1940. *Political Economy and Capitalism*, London, Routledge and Kegan Paul
Ferguson, C. E. 1969. *Microeconomic Theory*, Homewood, Ill., Irwin
Harcourt, G. C. 1972. *Some Cambridge Controversies in the Theory of Capital*, Cambridge, CUP
Hirschleifer, J. 1970. *Investment Interest and Capital*, Englewood Cliffs, N.J., Prentice-Hall
Hunt, E. K. 1977. Empiricism and Rationalism in Economic Theories of Value, *The Social Science Journal*, vol. 14, no. 3, October
Hunt, E. K. 1979. *History of Economic Thought, A Critical Perspective*, Belmont, Ca., Wadsworth
Hunt, E. K. 1981. A Radical Critique of Welfare Economics, in E. J. Nell (ed.), *Growth, Profits and Property*, Cambridge, CUP
Hunt, E. K. 1982. Marx's Concept of Human Nature and the Labor Theory of Value, *Review of Radical Political Economics*, vol. 14, no. 2, Summer
Marx, Karl 1967. *Capital, Vol. I*, New York, International Publishers
Marx, Karl 1970. *A Contribution to the Critique of Political Economy*, New York, International Publishers
Putnam, H. 1981. *Reason, Truth and History*, Cambridge, CUP
Robinson, J. 1962. *Economic Philosophy*, New York, Anchor Books
Robinson, J. 1966. *An Essay on Marxian Economics*, Second Edition, New York, St Martins Press
Rosdolsky, R. 1977. *The Making of Marx's Capital*, London, Pluto Press

[4]

FERNANDO CARVALHO

On the concept of time in Shacklean and Sraffian economics

Shackle has consistently criticized economists for not presenting the assumptions underlying the concept of "time" which they are using. "Time" is a concept that is usually neglected even in methodological discussions. Neoclassical economics, particularly, has treated this problem in a rather light way, approaching time as just another "space dimension."[1]

The importance of an unambiguous statement on the concept of time cannot be exaggerated. Until one deals explicitly with the concept of time one cannot analyze the concept of changes in the economic system.

Time is defined by what is possible for agents to do while it is passing away. Thus, it has to do with the perspective of the researcher, his starting points, and the preselection of processes considered as the most essential for the understanding of economic activity. The idea of an economic "process" itself is at stake. False ideas related to processes will inevitably entail pseudo-concepts of time and vice versa. Any theoretical proposition that involves processes of any nature has to allow "time" in some sense to flow. The concept of time employed depends in a crucial way on the idea of change. If nothing changed, time would not exist.[2] The reverse is also true: for things which do not change there is no time.[3]

The author is Assistant Professor of Economics, Universidade Federal Fluminense, Niteroi, RJ, Brazil. He is deeply indebted to Paul Davidson for his comments, criticisms, and patient editorial assistance. Discussions with Nina Shapiro were particularly fruitful. The author is also grateful to Johan Deprez, Alfred Eichner, Carmen Feijo, and Antonio Castro for their comments. A grant from the National Research Council of Brazil (CNPq) is thankfully acknowledged.

[1]Shackle (1968), p. 19, (1976), chap. 27. See also J. Robinson (1978), p. 12.

[2]"There could be no Time if nothing changed" is "a proposition hard to deny" (Georgescu-Roegen, 1971, p. 131).

[3]God, for instance, cannot get "older." His traditional representation as an old man

266   JOURNAL OF POST KEYNESIAN ECONOMICS

Although space allows for "change" (that is, locomotion), it differs from history (that is, changes in time) for the latter is not reversible. There are no ultimate "givens" in history. States engender states in the sense that the "parameters" of a certain situation change to transform themselves into new "parameters."[4] This means that history is not a collection of states associated with given parameters among which one can travel at will. To give birth to a new "state" it is necessary to destroy the old one and this means that it is impossible "to go back" to the original situation.

This conceptualization requires rejection of the mechanistic view of time, where time is conceived as being "absolute," something that flows independently of what is happening (and even of whether something is happening or not).[5] In this mechanistic approach the only form of motion that is defined is locomotion, that is, something that does not cause qualitative permanent changes.[6] In other words, one can go somewhere, know it, map it, and "come back" in time (as well as in space). If on the other hand time is irreversible, this "mapping" of the future is impossible and uncertainty emerges with full force.

Georgescu-Roegen conceives of two ways of defining time: as historical, irreversible, quality-changing "Time" or as mechanistic, locomotion-like "time."[7] It is Time with a capital T that is important in economic phenomena and a fundamental concept to the study of monetary economies.

Production takes Time: In monetary economies productive activity is always oriented toward a future market[8] undertaken by entrepreneurs with the objective of earning profits (and not necessarily to the "satisfaction" of consumers). The existence of money and liquidity in such systems makes it possible to "move" purchasing power through

certainly tries to grasp the wisdom associated with age but it is an obvious contradiction of the idea of eternality.

[4] Strictly speaking, in this situation they are no longer parameters.

[5] See Einstein and Infeld (1966), 177-192. Or, as it is put by Nordman: "In a word, if I dare use this image, time in classical science was similar to a stream carrying phenomena as well as ships but it does not flow less or differently when there are no ships" (1921, p. 16).

[6] "Mechanics only knows locomotion, and locomotion is both reversible and quality-less" (Georgescu-Roegen, 1971, p. 1).

[7] Georgescu-Roegen, 1971, pp. 134-140. Processes that are Timeless but not timeless are what P. Davidson (1982-83) calls ergodic processes: it is possible to allow for the flow of "time" in them but not of "Time"!

[8] Even production to order faces some degree of uncertainty. In times of crisis, for instance, contracts are broken.

time (Davidson, 1972, pp. 64-65). In monetary economies the connection between time, uncertainty, and money plays a fundamental part in the determination of the laws of historical motion.

Neoclassical views of time, on the other hand, clearly fall into the category of mechanistic time. If the Post Keynesian approach is to become a viable alternative to neoclassical economics, it must explicitly develop the importance of Time (as opposed to time) to economic processes. There are two significant currents of Post Keynesian thought that attempt to deal with the Time concept; one strand is strongly influenced by Shackle, the other by Sraffa. The limitations of neoclassical thought are seen differently by these branches and hence two alternative approaches have been constructed. In this paper we intend to discuss each of these in terms of the concept of time that is, implicitly or explicitly, employed. We will show that both of these branches of Post Keynesian thought, while providing significant insights, still have important limitations as historical approaches.

Shacklean theory

Classification of time

Shackle's lifelong concern with decision-making processes under non-probabilistic uncertainty led him to become one of the first interpreters of Keynes to stress that the "new economics" consisted mainly of the full acknowledgement of the fundamental ignorance that surrounds economic decisions which focus on future consequences.

To define the subject of economics as the study of decision making implies taking into account the modes through which agents construct hypothetical outcomes to choose among them. Shackle desired to show the conditions under which these decisions are not "empty," i.e., what makes a decision "creative." This required resolving the question of the Time concept at the outset of his analysis which relates *present* decisions and *future* outcomes. To develop his approach, Shackle created a four-way classification of Time (Shackle, 1968).

Firstly, we have *mechanical* time: this is the time of the external observer, who knows everything, the future as well as in the past. With this concept all moments become "co-valid" (1968, p. 3), in the sense that past, present, and future are just moments of a known sequence. Motion is conceived as the mechanistic interaction between force and acceleration, as in classical mechanics. Examples of this kind of approach are the models of business cycles of Kalecki, Samuelson, and

268   *JOURNAL OF POST KEYNESIAN ECONOMICS*

Hicks (Shackle, 1968, p. 223).

Secondly, there is the *evolutionary* time, whose paternity Shackle attributes to Marshall. This rather complex concept refers to "a segment of real history" (1968, p. 188). In this case, the outside observer is no longer omniscient. Historical approaches require this concept of Time.

Thirdly, we have *timeless* models, in which time does not flow in any significant sense. The best examples of this approach are General Equilibrium models, which assume prereconciliation of plans via instantaneous processes of information generation and diffusion.

The fourth concept is *expectational* time. This concept occupied most of Shackle's attention: it is a concept relevant to the agent, the decision-maker at the moment of decision (Shackle, 1969, Part 1). Decision-making processes are, by definition, future-oriented. The agent "knows" that the past is immutable and the future is to be created, as a result of the choices done *in the present*. "Expectational time is an aspect of a decision-maker's effort to choose a course of action in face of uncertainty about the outcome which would flow from this course or that" (1968, p. 67).

Expectational time, however, is not a reality, but a mental construct, a mode of organization of information about the past and an elaboration of hypotheses about the future. In this construct, from the point of view of the decision-maker, there is only the "solitary moment," the present during which the construction of hypotheses is done and actions are chosen. It is an existential experience where imagination performs the main role, creating alternative "scenarios" as Ariel created visions to the shipwrecked in Prospero's island. Seen as an existential experience, expectational time is in fact atemporal because it is always present: it does not flow. It allows for uncertainty in decision making, and for the possibility of sudden changes in the "state of expectations," but it does not allow for processes. If one is concerned with History, however, one has to go beyond expectational time and combine it with evolutionary time.

Expectational versus evolutionary time

Shackle realized the risks in using only expectational time. While Shackle correctly indicates that mechanical time (as well as timeless approaches) fails to consider phenomena resulting from decision making under uncertainty, he nevertheless does not always succeed in making it clear that the analysis of crises, liquidity preference, and unemployment cannot solely rely on the concept of expectation time.

These phenomena must be studied in evolutionary time. In particular, the role of money and finance in capitalist economies can be grasped only in terms of expectational time combined with evolutionary time. Alone, the expectational time approach can suggest *how* money can alleviate an individual's fears in his moment of decision; it cannot, however, by itself explain where money came from or even, really, *what* is money. The expectational time approach cannot explain why money alleviates fears nor can it deal with the consequences of money to the economic process as a whole. What is lost by focusing only on expectational time is the concepts both of process and of interactions.

These latter concepts, on the other hand, are at the core of evolutionary time. As Shackle indicates, the idea of *mechanism* is fundamental to a theory of evolution (1968, p. 188). Despite the common semantic root, however, a *mechanism* is not a *mechanistic* device whose motion would take place in mechanical time. Living bodies are mechanisms because they involve interactions between organs that limit the extent to which changes are possible. As biology illustrates (Foa, 1982), we can conceive of process that takes place in historical time, in which many individual parts are involved in a global fabric. The existence of limits does not preclude changes, not even radical changes. Evolutionary time in economics would find an analogue of living bodies in social bodies (Foa, 1982; Georgescu-Roegen, 1971, p. 11).

The Shacklean expectational time approach must face a difficult problem: the concept of mechanism, fundamental to the idea of evolution and evolutionary time, necessarily reduces the solitariness of individuals. There is a conflict between the order of the mechanism and the imagination of the solitary person which must be resolved.

Orderliness versus imagination

Shackle's main subject is the mediation exerted by active consciousness as a non-neutral connection between external stimuli and behavioral responses. His central proposition is: the future must be created by human action; the future is not (completely) determined by the past; the future exists only as a ''plan'' in the present; therefore, the freedom to ''create'' the future is the freedom to ''imagine'' it. Shackle's apparatus is mainly oriented to the study of important decisions (Kahn, 1972, p. 81n.), ''crucial experiments'' as Shackle would call them (cf. Davidson, 1982-83). In these decisions, the role of free imagination is more important than it is in routine matters. Yet, this distinction is often blurred by the general concept of decision as a choice among imagined outcomes.

As a theory of free imagination Shackle's approach is radically individualistic and subjectivistic. Those characteristics he shares with the "Austrian" School (see Dolan, 1976). The modern Austrian school denies any possibility of objective determinism in economic processes. Its starting point is a radical form of subjectivism. Since individuals are continuously gaining new knowledge their behavior is likely to be nonrepetitive and, therefore, unpredictable (Dolan, 1976, pp. 30, 40, 42). Austrians strongly emphasize uncertainty (and welcome Shackle's works for his views about it); they take the "freedom" of the agent to its ultimate consequences. The individual mind is the ultimate source of all action and this makes the future completely unpredictable.

It is remarkable therefore that, as critical of neoclassical equilibrium concepts as they are, Austrian economists cannot free themselves of the necessity of using the equilibrium apparatus. Lachman, for instance, despite his radical denial of the possibility or the usefulness of any notion of general equilibrium, when faced with the natural implication of his analysis, namely, the impossibility of "order" in economic life, can offer as the only alternative the idea of equilibrium of the individual (Dolan, 1976, p. 131). If, however, there is no order beyond the individual, decision is empty and powerless. The future then cannot be "created" except as a result of accidental interactions of otherwise unrelated individuals. Shackle's approach to some extent shares this limitation of the Austrian approach; it overemphasizes the freedom of the agent and underestimates the influence of conditions other than his own imagination. In this context, orderliness becomes an external necessity or constraint, something that cannot be explained *within* Shackle's theory.

Shackle does recognize that order is necessary to guarantee that a decision is not powerless (as it would be were the world entirely unpredictable). "Orderliness" means regularity, but regularity while dealing with more than one agent in an interdependent economic system. It is necessary, therefore, to go beyond expectational time and the unending moment of decision if order is to be assessed in the actual historical, evolutionary development of the economy. Moreover, order must be real (not imaginary), if we wish to avoid the concept of "accidental coincidence."[9]

Orderliness is a theoretical puzzle for any individualistic

---

[9]How could a great number of individuals imagine the same rules? It should be remembered that the whole group of questions studied as "macroeconomic theory" is intractable from the standpoint of the individual. Besides, the individual himself is posed, in this way, in an "empty" space, in social, political, or, broadly, institutional terms.

expectational approach. Shacklean economics will be increasingly en-
cumbered if it does not break out of its individualistic expectational
time premises. While emphasizing the creative individual's freedom to
create the future, Shackle does recognize constraints on individuals'
actions. These are vaguely identified as "natural laws," human nature,
and institutions (Shackle, 1969, p. 12).

Acknowledging the existence and importance of institutions, however, creates new problems for the Shacklean approach. Institutions
transcend individuals. They enforce constraints on actions and events
because they orient, constrain, and direct the behavior of individuals.
Yet, institutions are a datum to each individual: they cannot originate
from his solitary deliberations.

Institutions are at the same time the offspring and the guarantee of
order. Their existence implies the presence of a social fabric, a mechanism in which individuals perform their functions. The existence of
institutions therefore conflicts with the identification of the individual
as the ultimate explanation of all phenomena, as an "uncaused cause"
(Shackle, 1982-83, p. 180).

Institutional questions tend to be obscured by the Shacklean approach, losing place to a growing emphasis on the process of imagination. This creates a tension in his works between his adherence to the
Keynes and Myrdal approaches and his Austrian roots. Keynes, despite
his use of the concept of uncertainty, clearly believed that behavioral
uniformities existed.[10] Policy making would be a useless activity if
these uniformities did not exist and could not be played upon. Keynes
was of course very conscious that at times certain policies can obtain
unexpected results; nevertheless it is undeniable that he supposed that
wise policies would achieve good results. Shackle praises Myrdal for
the distinction he created between *ex ante* and *ex post* variables. Time is
explicitly introduced in this fashion (Shackle, 1973, p. 40). For
Myrdal, however, this is part of the Wicksellian theory of cumulative
process and monetary equilibrium. Consistent patterns of behavior are
an integral part of this latter theory.[11]

[10]As to Keynes in the *General Theory*, Shackle says that it is possible to find two
different propositions: the first, present in Books 3 and 4, would *totally* deny connections between periods; the second, in chapter 22, implicitly supposes these connections (Shackle, 1976, p. 447).

[11]An essential element in the Wicksell/Myrdal cumulative process is the supposition that certain behaviors must follow certain stimuli: "In the theory (of cumulative processes) is implied not only certain causal relations between them but also a
given order of sequence in their movements" (emphasis in the original) (Myrdal,
1939, p. 27).

272   *JOURNAL OF POST KEYNESIAN ECONOMICS*

Shackle's concentration on the theory of imagination, loosely connected with a theory of action, however, has led him to gradually
downplay these concerns for the evidence of uniformities. Even
similarities among individuals necessary for the existence of regularity
and order become only *ad hoc* assumptions. Shackle's economics, with
its attempt to clearly expose the fallacy of the neoclassical mechanical
time concept, correctly emphasizes expectational time. Unfortunately
evolutionary time (and its associated institutional developments),
which must interact with expectational time for a more complete description of the real world, has not been sufficiently emphasized.

It is necessary to consider "social" aspects that act as constraints on
decision-actions.[12] Decision choice analysis requires some information
about how the system operates to restrict agents' expectations *and*
feasible acts. Thus we must augment a theory of imagination with a
theory of action and interaction. One can then investigate the
"coherence" of social interaction in real History (e.g., the analysis of
financial instability by Minsky and the role of money by Davidson).[13]

A summing up of Shacklean economics

Shackle is interested primarily in the process of creation, of imagining
the future and taking decisions. The importance of constraints is clearly
underestimated and usually reduced to perception of "natural laws"
(Shackle, 1969, p. 12). "Social laws" are not dealt with although they
represent a constraint involving the *interaction* of decision-makers,
thereby reducing the "solitariness" of the decision process.

It is difficult to reconcile the complete freedom of the individual
with the existence of orderliness. In the absence of constraining social
laws, there are no connections between successive economic periods
and the carrying over of debt contracts and personal real property.
These can be discussed only within a theory of social actions and
relations in a historical (or institutional) frame.

Finally, an important part of the history of the system, its production
and reproduction, depends on the concept of orderliness. The impor-

---

[12]Vickers (1978), despite his adherence to the Shacklean approach, gives more importance to the influence of objective factors and the environment, through his concept of "inheritance" (p. 20).

[13]Although they share the same concept of uncertainty, different assumptions about
time lead Shackle and Davidson to stress the liquidity properties of money in very
diverse ways. While Shackle focuses on only the individual necessity of "safeness"
to answer the question "Why money?" Davidson refers to the Keynes's argument
about money's elasticities of production and substitution that are closely related to
the forms of social organization of capitalist economies.

tance of production and reproduction is absent in the works of Shackle. On the other hand, it is at the very core of Sraffa's 1960 work, *Production of Commodities by Means of Commodities* (1975).

Sraffian theory

Centers of gravity

The *Production of Commodities* is the result of Sraffa's lifelong concern with the theory of value. It is the culmination of a long struggle to escape the conventional theory of value as well as the problems connected with the Ricardian-Marxian alternative, either in terms of an invariant measure of value or in terms of the "transformation problem."

Sraffa's book deals with the determination of production prices: prices that allow a uniform rate of profit to exist (Roncaglia, 1978, p. xvii).These are equilibrium prices: if the rate of profit is the same everywhere, then capitalists have no reason to alter their activities.

Sraffa is concerned with the *logical* requirements for the determinations of production prices. He does not commit himself with any description of actual processes that would lead to equilibrium. Sraffa's analysis resembles those obtained in timeless models of general equilibrium. The method to obtain equilibrium prices is, in fact, the same, although the parameters are different.[14] Prices and the rate of profit (given wages) have to be defined simultaneously.

If prices of production are those prices that allow for a uniform rate of profit, they cannot be determined before that rate itself is determined. The profit rate, on the other hand, is a relationship between the "value" of the capital advanced and the "value" of the surplus generated in that economy. It cannot be known before the prices of production are determined.

In Sraffian economics, a time-dimension concept is introduced, not by Sraffa but by some of his followers.[15] The central question is, How

---

[14]". . . Sraffa's system is beyond doubt competitive and general equilibrium in nature" (Kregel, 1971, p. 39).

[15]It should be noted that the notion of dated labor does not really involve Time. Dated labor is only an alternative way of measuring the use of inputs to the production of each commodity (Sraffa, 1975, chap. 6). The means of production are continuously decomposed into their constituent labor and earlier means of production components up to a point in the "past" where there exists only labor and raw materials or objects in their natural states.

should production prices be interpreted? What is the relationship that price of production maintain to actual (or market) prices?

For some Sraffians, production prices are long-run equilibrium prices. For Garegnani [(1979) and Harcourt (1977)] production prices are a center of gravity around which the market prices fluctuate.[16] This gravitational conceptualization clearly involves the idea of a process and of a time span necessary for the production prices to emerge and assert themselves.

The process by which production prices emerge is a process similar to that imagined by the classical economists. Given technology implies that a given set of production prices would be sufficiently stable (in the long run) to permit them to serve as "lighthouses" to which the market prices would converge. Naturally, in order to be able to perform this role (and implicit in the idea of a gravitation center) it is necessary that these prices gradually become visible as "the solution" toward which the system converges (as a position consciously sought for or, more probably, as an "imposition" of the system operation).

The determinants of the equilibrium solution must be invariant to the equilibrating process. In Sraffian economics these determinants are (given) technical coefficients of production and (given) distribution of income. This means that the technical conditions of production are invariant to changes in the composition of output. At the same time, distribution of income must be invariant to changes in market prices. If fluctuations of market prices affect the general rate of profits no stable position could ever be determined.[17]

This decomposition process constitutes only an analogy with the actual "history" of each product. It does not refer to the historical record, only to the "past" that can be identified in an input/output table.

"The various labor quantities are not defined as the quantities actually expended in the historical past but as the quantities which would have been expended had technical conditions of production always been just as they are in the 'current' period. The 'resolution' into a backward time series of labor expenditures is thus purely conceptual" (Steedman, 1977, p. 70n). (See also Harcourt, 1974, pp. 185-186. Kregel, 1971, seems to take the opposite view—pp. 29-31.)

[16]For Marxians, production prices are a "potential state" which exists side by side with actual prices but is never attained because the gravitational process itself (if it could be defined) could contradict and jeopardize the determination of an equilibrium position itself.

[17]In a very general manner, this refers to the relationship between market prices and natural (or production) prices. C. Benetti, for instance, notes that "there is a contradiction between the idea that the deviations of market prices in relation to natural prices determine the future orientation of productive activities . . . and the absence of hypotheses about returns to scale in the definition of natural prices." For

"Reaching" equilibrium

There are two possible ways to "reach" the gravity center:

    (1) being "there" from the outset[18]; and

    (2) "groping" toward the position by adjustments in the structure of supply given the composition of demand.

The first possibility would mean that production prices are not only "long-run" prices but also "short-run" prices. None of the Sraffian economists, however, suggests that short-run prices are necessarily costs of production prices or that the rate of profit is uniform at each moment of time.

The "groping" approach implies a theory of investment. Capital flows from sectors with rate of profit smaller than the average to those sectors with rate of profit greater than the average. Agents, therefore, assume that *actual*, observed differences in rate of profits are due to a given structure of demand, and the latter is expected to remain the same whatever acts are decided (and performed) by firms. Expectations are entirely determined by current demand conditions no matter how wrong the early decisions have showed themselves to be. There is not any kind of "imagination," only a reflection of present conditions, that is, the current rates of profit.

A necessary feature of this process is the reversibility of action without losses. To keep the gravity center stable over time requires that agents can make mistakes, perceive them, and correct them without any destabilizing effects on the composition and level of demand and on income distribution.

In sum, in order to conceive of prices of production as a long-run gravity center we have to accept that the technique adopted and the income distribution profile and composition of demand are invariant to investment, realization, and price movements. Unexpected changes and uncertainty cannot be introduced in this scheme.

Short run versus long run

The Sraffian system displays a long-run equilibrium position when all mistakes have been corrected and all capitalists find the best employment of resources that allows them to earn the uniform rate of profit.

---

him this is a *"contradiction interne"* in the classical theory (see Maurisson et al., 1976, Introduction). Spaventa (1977, chap. 4) shows that the equilibrium solution in this system *and with constant returns* is invariant to the composition of output if transactions are always realized at equilibrium prices.

[18]Joan Robinson would say that, in fact, this is the only possibility!

Competition ensures that this result will obtain no matter what agents think or decide. A theory of production prices as a gravity center demonstrates that the indeterminacy associated with individual choices is just a temporary (and inoffensive) phenomenon.

The subjectivistic element contained, for instance, in Keynes's theory of investment is criticized by Garegnani. Keynes's weakness, in Garegnani's view (1979, p. 160; Garegnani et al, 1979, p. 182/3), is the importance given to the subjectivity of decision making. Garegnani believes that subjectivism in Keynes allows neoclassical economists to recover their dominance because it restricts Keynesian analysis to the short run, where it is impossible to achieve determinate results. The long run is therefore open to the introduction of neoclassical hypotheses. Garegnani considers the short run as a "minor" concern, because it lacks "determinateness": in the short run we can achieve only accidental positions, unexplainable by any "general" principle. Only in the long run can we obtain "determinate" results.

It should be noted that the "determinateness" of the long run in Sraffian economics is assured *by construction*. The long run *is defined* as the period in which the ultimate determinants predominate over supposedly *accidental* short-run circumstances.

Is it necessary to suppose the existence of a long-run position that is *independent* of short-run results and behaviors? After all, with investment decisions, inevitable "errors" are committed; are these errors neutral in relation to the given long-run position? If they are not neutral, the commitment of resources to a certain use would impose a whole new configuration of income distribution, capital, and technology on the system and create the necessity of looking for another set of "long-run" prices. The dilemma is, therefore, that a gravitation theory is meaningless in the short run but that, in order to be significant to the long run, it demands that the gravity center remain fixed over time no matter what actions are taken by the agents.[19]

In the "center of gravity" approach to Sraffian economics there is an overemphasis on "determinateness" in a world lacking this quality in expectational and evolutionary time. As far as investment "decisions" are involved it is difficult to see how to eliminate subjectivity without getting rid of the very problem to be resolved.[20] The supposition of a

[19]Besides, *ça va sans dire*, it is necessary to suppose that the actions will converge to equilibrium.

[20]That this is a result of methodological assumptions is perceptively but subtly noted by Harcourt: "The latter group, especially Garegnani, worry about concentration

determinate "subjectivity-free" long-run position is an answer that eliminates the question itself in the sense that it allows one to comfortably suppose that all steps are convergent as a function of time. It transforms that "long-run" position in a *deus ex machina* whose kingdom will be attained someday.

The notion of processes and of time in Sraffian economics is not an alternative to neoclassical economics in the sense that it cannot transcend the treatment of time we find in the traditional theory. The *method* is essentially the same in both schools: the search for gravity centers.[21] These Sraffian gravity centers are determined by the profile of income distribution and the given techniques. In neoclassical economics, the equilibrium centers of gravity are determined by utility functions, resources, and technical conditions of production. There is no theoretical time "duration" associated to these ultimate parameters in the sense that no change in them is explainable by either Sraffian or neoclassical schools. All that is possible to do is to determine what is the equilibrium position associated to each combination of them. There is no "traverse" but only comparisons between equilibrium positions. All "moments" (that is, all configurations of income distribution and technical coefficients) are co-valid. This means that time is reversible. Therefore, the theory of prices of production as gravity centers admits only mechanical time or no time at all.

Conclusion

Both Shackle and Sraffa are critics of conventional neoclassical economics, but their views are radically different. Shackle stresses individual behavior and the role of expectations in situations of fundamental uncertainty, in a theory of individual creative decision; Sraffa has as his main concern the conditions of reproduction of the system in a timeless world of parameter stability.

---

on the short-run because it gives over much emphasis to the importance of expectations so that definite results might not be possible (*this, of course, might be a strength*) . . ." (Harcourt, 1982, p. 14, my emphasis).

[21]"In Garegnani's view, a belief in long-period gravitation towards natural prices has been shared by all economists up until Hicks' *Value and Capital*. . . . Furthermore, it is *not* this methodological procedure which is at fault but rather, its use *in conjunction with the concepts of supply and demand* . . ." (Harcourt, 1977, p. 357, Harcourt's emphases). Harcourt quotes Garegnani as saying that "it is therefore apparent that this difficulty . . . (concerns) the theory, i.e., the way in which the centers of gravitation of the system are determined, and not the static method of analysis based on such 'centers' . . . " (p. 358).

278   JOURNAL OF POST KEYNESIAN ECONOMICS

The comparison between them, nevertheless, is important, if for no other reason than that what is being proposed as the "Post Keynesian" alternative to mainstream economics is, to some extent, based on the "visions" of these authors (Davidson, 1982, ch. 1). The Shacklean system and the Sraffian system are in their current states of development limited in their approach to the "real world"; neither deals extensively with the problem of historical, evolutionary time. In Shackle, time is the eternal present of the individual existential experience. From the point of view of the individual, moreover, all history is accidental. In Sraffian theory, on the other hand, there is no place given to historical time.

Nevertheless, both these brands of Post Keynesian thought point out important aspects to be considered in the formulation of a theoretical alternative to conventional economics. The stress on the uncertainty and fragility of the bases on which agents take decisions, characteristic of Shackle's approach, opens the way to the consideration of this decision-making theory for a broader theory of investment, money, and finance. Sraffian analysis, for its part, stresses fundamentally the necessity of taking into consideration the broader systemic framework, to approach (and solve) problems; a framework that is meaningless if we stick solely to the individual's point of view. Each approach, taken by itself, is incomplete; a viable alternative theory must approach interactions in historical time. A timeless or mechanical time approach can never suffice.[22]

Expectations and uncertainty are not only clouds hiding the sun. Agents do take decisions based in uninformed expectations. They know that their expectations are based on "flimsy" foundations. Their behavior can be "kaleidic." Decisions, once transformed into actions, however, are not necessarily easily reversed (certainly not instantaneously); they change the "face" of the world, and the value (or even the set) of determinants to be considered.

A theory of history is a theory of action *and* social interactions. This means that collective creations, habits, and customs or, more generally,

---

[22]The necessity of consideration of historical time is clear, for instance, in Minsky's theory of financial instability and the "incoherence" of capitalist economies. To define incoherence we need to be able to recognize the interdependence of agents, the unfolding of decisions, the verification of results, the influence on the reshaping of expectations, the settlement of debts, etc. (Minsky, 1980). On the other hand, historical time means taking in consideration that agents decide under uncertainty and that, as they know it, they try to insure themselves against unpredictable failures. As Kregel (in Maurisson et al., 1976) points out, this kind of problem "cannot be easily integrated . . . in the Sraffa system" (p. 158). For a contrary position, see Roncaglia (1978, chap. 2).

institutions have to be brought into light not only as "givens" but, to a great extent, as historical results as well. These institutions limit the individual's visions of things to come.

The problem of analyzing time is in fact the problem of adopting a philosophy of history. The idea of change (implicit in the concept of creative choice) must be combined with the notion of orderliness. Order requires a certain degree of permanence of features, of repetitiveness. This is obtained, on one side, through the creation of institutional constraints to what is permitted for agents to do. On the other side, the whole cultural ideological determination of modes of behavior considered as socially acceptable is a constraint. The very definition of goals and means to attain them that agents are socially permitted to adopt are culturally determined. It is essential to consider the limits to action imposed by the *social structure*; the set of social roles and institutions that frames that individual behavior.

This concern with history is not new. Both Marx and Schumpeter had history in the forefront of their economic theory. Change, not rest, is the characteristic "state" of capitalism.[23] The birth and evolution of structures themselves is a subject to Marx. History, in this sense, was also a concern to Keynes and it is an important part of his heritage left to Post Keynesian economists.[24]

All these approaches are certainly different in many respects. Some of them seem more appropriate to particular subjects. All of them have in common, however, in contrast to conventional economics, the assumption that substantive change and structural continuity (but not fixity!) are complementary rather than contradictory requirements of a method suitable to investigate economic reality.

[23]"The essential point to grasp is that in dealing with capitalism we are dealing with an evolutionary process. It may seem strange that anyone can fail to see so obvious a fact which more over was long ago emphasized by Karl Marx" (Schumpeter, 1976, p. 82. In the same work see chapter 3).

[24]E.g., "*Money can only be studied in an historical and institutional context*" (Davidson, 1982, p. 241, with emphasis in the original).

REFERENCES

Davidson, Paul. *Money and the Real World*. London: Macmillan, 1972.

—————. *International Money and the Real World*. New York: Halstead Press, 1982.

—————. "Rational Expectations: A Fallacious Foundation for Studying Crucial Decision-Making Processes." *Journal of Post Keynesian Economics*, Winter 1982-83, 5 (2), 182-198.

Dolan, Edwin G. *The Foundations of Modern Austrian Economics*. Kansas City: Sheed & Ward Inc., 1976.

280   *JOURNAL OF POST KEYNESIAN ECONOMICS*

Einstein, Albert, and Infeld, Leopold. *The Evolution of Physics*. New York: Simon and Schuster, 1966.

Foa, Bruno. "Marshall Revisited in the Age of DNA." *Journal of Post Keynesian Economics*. Fall 1982, *5* (1), 3-16.

Garegnani, Pierangelo, "Notes on Consumption, Investment and Effective Demand: A Reply to Joan Robinson." *Cambridge Journal of Economics*, 1979, *3*, 181-187.

Garegnani, Pierangelo, et al. *Debate sobre la Teoria Marxista del Valor*. Mexico: Siglo XXI Editores, 1979.

Georgescu-Roegen, Nicholas. *The Entropy Law and the Economic Process*. Cambridge, Mass.: Harvard University Press, 1971.

Harcourt, G. *Some Cambridge Controversies in the Theory of Capital*. Cambridge: Cambridge University Press, 1974.

_____. "The Theoretical and Social Significance of the Cambridge Controversy in the Theory of Capital: An Evaluation." *Revue d'Economie Politique*, 1977, *87*, 351-375.

_____. *Post-Keynesianism: Quite Wrong or/and Nothing New*. London: Thames Papers in Political Economy, 1982.

Kahn, Richard F. *Selected Essays on Employment and Growth*. Cambridge: Cambridge University Press, 1972.

Kregel, Jan A. *Rate of Profit, Distribution and Growth: Two Views*. London: Macmillan, 1971.

Maurisson, Patrick, et al. *Actes du Colloque Sraffa*. Amiens: Cahiers d'Economie Politique, Presses Universitaires de France, 1976.

Minsky, Hyman P. "Money, Financial Markets, and the Coherence of a Market Economy." *Journal of Post Keynesian Economics*, Fall 1980, *3* (1), 21-31.

Myrdal, Gunnar. *Monetary Equilibrium*. London: William Hodge & Co., 1939.

Nordmann, Charles. *Einstein et l'Univers*. Paris: Librairie Hachette, 1921.

Robinson, Joan V. "Keynes and Ricardo." *Journal of Post Keynesian Economics*, Fall 1978, *1* (1), 12-18.

Roncaglia, Alessandro. *Sraffa and the Theory of Prices*. Chichester: John Wiley and Sons, 1978.

Schumpeter, Joseph A. *Capitalism, Socialism and Democracy*. London: George Allen and Unwin, 1976.

Shackle, G. L. S. *A Scheme of Economic Theory*. Cambridge: Cambridge University Press, 1968.

_____. *Decision, Order and Time*. Cambridge: Cambridge University Press, 1969.

_____. *An Economic Querist*. Cambridge: Cambridge University Press, 1973.

_____. *Epistemica y Economia*. Mexico City: Fondo de Cultura Economica, 1976.

_____. "Comment." *Journal of Post Keynesian Economics*, Winter 1982-83, *5* (2), 180-181.

Sraffa, Piero. *Production of Commodities by Means of Commodities*. Cambridge: Cambridge University Press, 1975.

Spaventa, Luigi. *Apontamentos de Economia Politica*, mimeo. Rio de Janeiro; 1977.

Steedman, Ian. *Marx After Sraffa*. London: New Left Books, 1977.

Vickers, Douglas. *Financial Markets in the Capitalist Process*. Philadelphia: University of Pennsylvania Press, 1978.

[5]

G. L. S. Shackle:
A Brief Bio-Bibliographical Portrait

by J. L. Ford
University of Birmingham

George Lennox Sharman Shackle is now in his 82nd year having been born on 14 July 1903. Yet during the 25 years that I have known him (beginning when I was an undergraduate at the University of Liverpool in 1957) he has hardly seemed to change at all, in physical appearance, in temperament, and in his attitude to his work: retirement is a word that does not enter his vocabulary. In appearance, Professor Shackle lives up to the popular image: out of any crowd, "the man in the street" would have no hesitation in identifying him as a professor. He looks the true scholar (rounded glasses and all), benign, self-contained, appearing absent-minded, preoccupied with higher thoughts. Since, indeed, he has altered so little over the years it is difficult to think of him as having had to pass through the "ages of man". As he has done so, however, his temperament has also hardly changed. He is a most modest and kind person, ever willing to assist those, young and old, who seek his help with the unravelling of economic theory. As with all true scholars and researchers of distinction, Professor Shackle's byword is humility.

Throughout his life Professor Shackle has been, to use the vogue word, a "workaholic"; this will be apparent to all since the time he became a university academic, fifty years ago, from his continuing stream of research papers and books. Even in that regard probably very few are aware of the extent to which Professor Shackle has devoted himself to the pursuit of his academic writings. He has always begun work in the early hours of the day and he seems to continue for most of every day; his relentless schedule is rarely interrupted for high days and holidays (one factual example, for instance, is given in his *Years of High Theory*, where he indicates that he spent a Christmas Day re-reading Sir John Hicks's 1935 *Economica* paper on money, for the chapter on Keynes's Liquidity Preference Theory). But Shackle loves the country, having a passion for the quiet, the peace and the isolation often associated with it, and he used to take vacations each year in Oban and Aldeburgh, with their contrasting hinterlands. It was whilst visiting Aldeburgh that he found the bungalow in which, since 1969, he has spent the whole of his retirement.

George Shackle seems, however, to have been a hard worker and a scholar with a thirst for knowledge ever since his very earliest days. His father, Robert Shackle, was a master at the Perse School, Cambridge; his specialism was mathematics and it was he who coached John Maynard Keynes for the scholarship which took him

4   Journal of Economic Studies 12,1/2

to Eton College. George Shackle attended his father's school, but left at the age of 17 to assume employment as a bank clerk. But he did not, in fact, choose banking as a possible career. He has intimated (Shackle, 1983(c) and in private conversation) that it was the family's financial circumstances which prevented his going on to obtain a university education at the usual age. Yet the work in the bank opened the academic door. George Shackle decided that he would improve his knowledge of the banking world by reading economics; he became spellbound immediately by the subject and devoted all his spare hours to devouring its literature. He had obviously benefited from discussing mathematics and logical analysis with his father, and this gave him the appetite for, and a comparative advantage in, economic theory[1]. His chance acquaintance with economics was fortunate for the profession.

It is hard for those who know him to think of George Shackle as a bank clerk; in his terminology they would attach an infinite degree of potential surprise to such a notion. He is a man who deals with ideas and thought-constructs, in a most imaginative and original way. The filling of ledgers and the balancing of the resulting accounts must, indeed, have seemed as mundane to him as his handling them appears incongruous to us. Nevertheless, it is easy to imagine why he would have been viewed as a potential first-class clerk. The assiduity and thoroughness which he applies to every task and his impeccable hand-writing (which to my knowledge has not wavered over the last 25 years) must have been a boon to his bank manager; for in those far off days the benefits of computer technology were barely fantastic imaginings, and all a bank's dealings had to be recorded painstakingly by hand, copies also being made in the same way.

It seems that George Shackle remained at the bank for another four years. He then also joined the staff of the Perse School, Cambridge, where he was a master for ten years. During that time he continued the studies he had begun at the bank, eventually entering for a BA degree of the University of London, which he was duly awarded in 1931. He seems to have taken the decision in that year to become an academic economist. He has written:

> Then, in 1931, I received the "sealed orders" for my career, in two momentous books: *A Treatise on Money* by John Maynard Keynes, and *Prices and Production* by Friedrich A. von Hayek. In these books I embarked on a thrilling voyage. The genial, brilliant and at times paradoxical *Treatise* gave me the feel and vision of a world of scholarly discourse and debate, relaxed, Olympian, intoxicating. *Prices and Production* which I read next, brought an extra, astonishing excitement. A diagram which I had invented for myself, to illustrate Keynes's rudimentary account of the Austrian theory of capital (in the *Treatise*, volume two) suddenly appeared before my eyes in print, in Hayek's book, the rising columnar representation of the time-structure of production. At this moment there began, in various journals, the debate between the two writers, with Frank Knight as a third contender. The torrent of ideas swirled and swept around me. My voyage had begun. (Shackle, 1983(c), p. 108).

In 1934 the opportunity eventually presented itself which enabled George Shackle's dream to come true. He was awarded a Leverhulme Research Scholarship, which he held at the London School of Economics writing a Ph.D thesis, which initially was indeed concerned with the Austrian theory of capital. His thesis was completed in 1936 and his degree awarded in 1937.

During 1937 he moved to the Oxford Institute of Statistics (now the Institute of Economics and Statistics) and to New College, where he rewrote his thesis. That task was completed in July 1937, by virtue (again) of much hard labour in the early and late hours of each day before and after work at the Institute as Research Assistant to Professor Henry Phelps Brown, who was then a Fellow of New College. The revised thesis appeared as a book in May 1938 under the imprint of Oxford University Press, and with the title *Expectations, Investment and Income*. The book was re-issued in 1968 by the Clarendon Press.

The theme of the book is the construction and analysis of a Keynesesque theory of the business cycle, the key feature in Shackle's story being the role played by expectation and uncertainty; and the related concepts of *ex ante* and *ex post*. These latter notions Shackle came across whilst taking a course at the LSE given by Brinley Thomas on the Swedish school of macroeconomists; especially the ideas of Myrdal (derived from Wicksell) on expectations, dynamic (period) analysis, and the distinction between *ex ante* and *ex post* magnitudes. Shackle calls his book " a study of the new Keynesianism in the light of the new Wicksellianism".

In the second edition, Shackle provides a most illuminating and lucid account of the intellectual background to the circumstances surrounding the writing of the original thesis. *Inter alia* he tells how he did intend originally to tackle aspects of the Austrian theory of capital, but abandoned the idea after a year's research. What was responsible for this was a visit to Cambridge made in October 1935 during which he heard Joan Robinson and Richard Kahn give a summary of the main threads of Keynes's forthcoming *General Theory*. What especially it was that he heard that provoked him to tear up his particular thesis Shackle does not make clear. But the clue lies in the theory of the rate of interest as Shackle himself confirmed (Shackle, 1983(c)). The Austrian theory of capital supposes that "lapse of time" is a factor of production and earns as its reward a rate of interest. The Austrian theory postulates that the level of the rate of interest is then determined by the equality of desired (*ex ante*) saving and of desired investment. Keynes's theory of liquidity preference challenged that notion and provided a new theory of interest rate determination. It was acceptance of that fact which persuaded Shackle to switch the theme of his thesis. Ever since that time Shackle has maintained in all of his writings on Keynes that he holds to the opinion that Keynes's *tour de force* was the theory of liquidity preference.

George Shackle remained at Oxford until 1939, being involved on various projects for Phelps Brown, most of which were concerned with the construction of money supply data and with the behaviour of velocities of circulation. He maintained his own interests in expectation and employment whilst at Oxford and published papers on this theme. In 1940 he was awarded an Oxford D.Phil. (for the discerning, this is why, when the second edition of *Expectations, Investment and Income* appeared, OUP had become the Clarendon Press: Shackle had become an Oxford graduate).

His move from Oxford took him to his beloved Scotland in the form of a lectureship at St. Andrews. However, he was to spend little time there because, at the outbreak of the Second World War, he was called into government service in which he remained for eleven years. During the hostilities he was a member of Sir Winston Churchill's Statistical Branch in the Admiralty and Cabinet Office. The period 1945-1950 was spent in the Economics Section of the Cabinet Secretariat. He became Reader in Economic Theory at the University of Leeds in 1950, but within a year or so he had been appointed to the Brunner Chair of Economic Science at the University of

Liverpool. No further moves took place and George Shackle did not leave that post until his retirement in September 1969, whereupon he was awarded the title of Emeritus Professor. If you were to ask him whether over that period he had not thought of moving to one of what we might consider the major Chairs of Economics in the UK, he would look at you with surprise. The fact that he had a Chair was sufficient for his purposes: it allowed him the freedom to pursue his researches with rigour and to concentrate his efforts, almost, but not quite, exclusively on the theme of expectations and uncertainty in economics and on his own special theory of decision making under uncertainty.

Professor Shackle had many honours bestowed upon him and he held several offices during his tenure of the Chair at Liverpool. Thus, for example: in 1957 he delivered the F. de Vries Lectures in Economic Theory in Amsterdam, which appeared as *Time in Economics,* this being a most distinguished series, having opened with James Meade's celebrated *Theory of Customs Unions;* in 1957-1958 he was Visiting Professor of Economics at Columbia University; Visiting Professor of Economics and Philosophy, University of Pittsburgh, 1967; Keynes Lecturer, British Academy, 1976; President, Section F, BAAS, 1966; Member, Council of Royal Economic Society, 1955-1969; made a Fellow of the Economic Society, 1960; made a Fellow of the British Academy, 1967; and awarded Honorary Doctorates from the New University of Ulster (D.Sc), 1974; and the University of Birmingham (D.Soc.Sc), 1978.

Apart from the period 1934-1939 Professor Shackle had then less than 20 years of full-time academic life before his retirement, all but one of which were spent at Liverpool. His output whilst there has been phenomenal, including many papers, review articles, contributions to books: but his output of books has been especially prolific. Over the period 1951-1969 these include: *Uncertainty in Economics and Other Reflections* (1955), a collection of his previously published articles; *Time in Economics* (1958), which we have already noted; *Economics for Pleasure* (1959); *Decision, Order and Time in Human Affairs* (1961, second expanded edition 1969); *A Scheme of Economic Theory* (1965); *The Nature of Economic Thought: Selected Papers 1955-1964* (1966); *The Years of High Theory: Invention and Tradition in Economic Thought, 1926-1939* (1967); second, extended, edition of *Expectations, Investment and Income* (1968).

Just by virtue of sheer arithmetic this is an amazing list. Then we have to add to it the articles that Professor Shackle was writing at the time (all catalogued in the Shackle Bibliography at the end of this volume) and bear in mind the fact that his writings were not just on expectation and uncertainty, some were textbooks; others, such as the *Years of High Theory,* demanded a wide knowledge of economics and the talents of an historian and a detective. To us lesser mortals, such production in quantity or quality is beyond our wildest dreams.

As I have said previously, Professor Shackle has always been something of a human dynamo, and he has always devoted himself passionately (if that is not too strange a way of describing it) to the pursuit and unravelling of ideas. He drives himself on inexorably[2]. We have seen this in his formative years where he was in full-time employment, yet beavering away at his studies at every conceivable opportunity. He continued in the same vein whilst at the Oxford Institute. It is also clear that the 11 years spent in the Civil Service hardly represented an interlude from academic life; they certainly did not in "the spirit" and barely did so in "the letter" since Shackle's output of academic publications matched that of the best of those in full-time academic life[3]. There were papers in *The Economic Journal, Oxford Economic Papers, Economica* and the *Review of Economic Studies,* and his most original book *Expectation in Economics.*

Since his so-called retirement, George Shackle seems to have done the impossible and increased the pace of his activity. From 1970 to date he has published five books and numerous papers. The papers, indeed, demonstrate a new dimension to his interests; and the books include a work that is Gargantuan both in its size and in the range of its scholarship and ideas, namely *Epistemics and Economics,* a critique of economic thought and doctrines.

Most of Shackle's academic writings have been devoted to an investigation of expectations and uncertainty in the analysis of economic behaviour; a related theme has been the question of time in economics. One thread was that started with his doctoral thesis: the role played by expectations of (largely) entrepreneurs and consumers in generating the business cycle, and hence in causing employment at certain times to be less than full. That thread was carried through a series of papers on expectations and unemployment but it enjoyed its fullest expression in two books, the major one being *Epistemics and Economics,* the other, much less ambitious, book, being *Keynesian Kaleidics* (1974). These volumes reiterate and amplify the main ideas contained in *Expectations, Investment and Income.* In the 1968 Introductory Chapter to the latter, after describing how he tore up his originally-conceived thesis on the Austrian theory of capital, upon learning of the momentous ideas contained in the *General Theory,* Shackle continues:

> When the *General Theory* itself appeared, in the evening of 3 February 1936, the *Treatise* was discarded from one's thoughts. It seemed to have been superseded by something radically different, brilliantly new, subversive of old ideas yet assured in its air of science and respectable by its origin. Only gradually, for me, its curious puzzles came to light. How was the equality of investment and saving brought about at that time when they were still mere thoughts and intentions in the minds of people acting independently of each other, if, after all, the interest-rate did *not* provide an equilibrating price? Keynes said that they were *necessarily* equal. But this was surely only true *ex post,* when disparate thoughts had been forced to lie in the one Procrustean bed of fact? And how was that income *already known as fact,* out of which people were *still free* to decide how much to spend on consumption? Had they a Wellsian time-machine, to explore the arcana of future time and return again to the present to make use of their knowledge? The *General Theory* performed the conjuring tricks, but not all of them were convincing. I started to try and explain the *General Theory* to myself. To make it understandable to my new frame of mind, I had to couch it in terms of *ex ante* and *ex post.* The result was *Expectations, Investment and Income* (Shackle, 1968(b), p. xviii: italics in original).

That study of expectations in a macroeconomic setting led to two new possible explanations of the business cycle, one of which highlighted the role played by the changing nature of business men's expectations in imparting the dynamic impulses into the economic system that were necessary to generate the cycle. The latter was centred around the distinction between *ex ante* and the *ex post* multipliers; a distinction that is central to a Keynesesque theory of output and employment over the cycle, and yet which is almost totally ignored in the literature. Professor Shackle stressed its importance in a major, sadly much neglected, paper, on both open and closed economy multipliers (Shackle, 1939(a)), but especially in *Epistemics and Economics.* In summary of his theory Shackle writes as follows:

8 Journal of Economic Studies 12,1/2

> The Multiplier effect of a first increase in the aggregate flow of business men's net investment in facilities will be unexpected by them, and will improve the profit outlook and lead to a further acceleration of investment, with a further Multiplier effect, and so on. Such Multiplier effects will, however, finally come to be *expected,* and at that stage net investment flow will have attained a maximum, there being no more unexpected increases in aggregate income to stimulate it further. But the failure of net investment to accelerate further will deprive the business men of the Multiplier effect which they have now come to expect. The expected "growth" will have let them down, merely by having come to be expected. With growth reduced or stopped, their pace of investment is now too high, and they will reduce it. The downswing, and its reversal, can be explained as a mirror image of the upswing. The whole cycle is thus explained by changes of expectation which are generated continuously by the effects of former changes. (Shackle, 1972, p. xxvi.)

A recurring theme in Shackle's "macroeconomic" writings, and one which, again, is considered at great length in *Epistemics and Economics,* is that traditional economic analysis for dealing with choice and the interrelationships between economic agents' choices in markets, as personified in the ultimate by GE theory, is *otiose:*

> Analysis of conduct by the economist's methods is only possible where that conduct is a reasoned response to known circumstances. Where the knowledge of circumstances is a mere heap of items instead of a structure seen to be relevantly complete, how can there be reasoned conduct based on sufficient knowledge? (Shackle, 1972, p. xxix.)

and

> General equilibrium is the natural and even the logical arrival point of that procedure of theorising which assumes that men pursue their interests by applying reason to their circumstances. . . reason can only be applied to circumstances in so far as those circumstances are taken as known. But the circumstances relevant to the choice of actions include other men's chosen actions. If the solution is to be *general* or *symmetrical,* if it is to accord to any and every person, no matter whom, a freedom and knowledge formally identical with those of every other person, if the rules of the games are to be precisely the same for all, the various actions of all these persons must be pre-reconciled. But choices which are pre-reconciled are effectively simultaneous. . . *Sequential* actions, transformations of one situation into a subsequent and different one, occurring successively, are excluded in the nature of things from being studied as the consequences of pure reason, unless these successive transformations all belong to simultaneously pre-reconciled plans. (Shackle, 1972, pp. 90-91.)

Some would probably not share Shackle's view that rationality requires full information, perhaps instead favouring the notion of "bounded rationality" suggested by Henry Simon, whereby we can hypothesise that economic agents can take that course of action which is the best that presents itself to them in the light of their available set of information, even if some of the items in that set have, of necessity, to be expectations which are also accompanied by a degree of uncertainty. It is difficult, however, not to accept Shackle's strictures against GE *per se.*

Those strictures (repeated in most of his publications) include one that Shackle has levelled against economic doctrines in general. This relates to the use of mathematical formulations in economic theory and to the concomitant desire of economists for an exactitude in their conclusions, which is almost impossible given the nature of our subject. That opinion might seem rather paradoxical, *prima facie,* in view of Shackle's training and interest in mathematics. But, on closer inspection, given his overriding concern with the role and nature of expectations in economics, the paradox vanishes. As Shackle has once described his feelings:

There is nowadays a movement of thought which would like to persuade itself that mathematics, the apotheosis of reason and certainty, can discover a new language or notation for describing the process of original thought, the business of exploiting the unknown by untrammelled invention. I cannot doubt that a peculiarly felicitous notation has sometimes exhibited suggestive powers amounting almost to being able to "think for itself". Who shall say what paradoxical powers mathematics may bring forth? Yet it is difficult to banish the suspicion that systems and freedom have an ultimate mutual intolerance. . . The nature of history is the nature of humanity. And economics, like every other scholarly involvement, is an art-form. "Polymath" is not always a polite appellation. But the economist needs to be a great enjoyer of ideas and a connoisseur of their means of expression, a daring sculptor of argument, an eclectic and sometimes an heresiarch. (Shackle, 1983, pp. 108-109.)

Shackle has certainly lived up to his notion of the ideal economist. He has been, as they say, a man of ideas. The majority of his writings have exhibited much originality and profundity of thought. He has been one of the very few economists who have developed their own theory encompassing a major (if not *the* major) area of the discipline: the theory of individual decision-making under uncertainty. His *Expectation in Economics* is a most stimulating, seminal and provocative monograph.

Naturally, it has been the ideas portrayed there that have been the focal point for most of his research writings for the last 40 years. It is that theory which Professor Shackle himself views as his greatest work and hence for which he would most like to see acceptance. That is the message implied by the overview of the development of his ideas that he has provided in "A Student's Pilgrimage" (Shackle, 1983(c)). The predominant theme is the need to view uncertainty as uncertainty, and not risk; and so for the need to replace probability descriptions of the likely, uncertain, outcomes arising from competing, alternative strategies or choices. Shackle's argument is that the use of the probability calculus is inappropriate simply because the conditions appertaining to its application just do not exist in respect of decisions taken in an economic context (and Shackle would extend this to any human context). A statement as proof of that proposition can be found in several of Shackle's publications. All are similar but perhaps the most vivid and succinct is the latest made available in "A Student's Pilgrimage":

Agatha Christie has told us that she made up her plots while standing at a kitchen sink. I am in good company, for it was amongst the vapours which there envelop one that I came to the decisive conviction that probability cannot serve the ultimate business of choice. Uncertainty, I thought, is surely not a pyramid of clustering hypotheses each "partly" believed in, but a wide-spreading plain where things widely unlike each other all claim to be *possible*. What gives an hypothesis the entrée to the counsels of the mind is not the being believed in, but the *not being disbelieved in*. A "mathematical expectation", it seems to me, is an adding together of mutual exclusives. Does that make sense? Only if every one of those mutual exclusives is going to make its appearance, more or less *often*, in a far-stretching series of trials of some system capable of only restricted variation. When such a series of trials is in contemplation, and when an extensive series has already been performed with that same system, the recorded frequencies of that past series may legitimately be looked upon as *knowledge*, in some practical sense, about the outcome of the contemplated series *as a whole*. But where there is knowledge there is not uncertainty. Uncertainty, *unknowledge*, is what confronts the chooser of action — when his act of choice is going to be *once-for-all*, when it is going to be crucial, when it is going to be an experiment the making of which will *destroy the possibility* of ever making that experiment again. In such a case we cannot say what *will* happen, even if we only claim to say it half-heartedly, as a "probability". We can only attain some notion of the kind of thing that *can* happen. (Shackle, 1983(c), p. 109.)

The notions of relative frequencies (probabilities) and of "mathematical expectation" are replaced (we might say in a loose manner) by those of potential surprise and focus-

10   Journal of Economic Studies 12,1/2

gains/focus-losses in Shackle's new theory. The edifice that he has constructed on the foundations provided by the concept of potential surprise is the focus of discussion in the ensuing essay in this volume.

It has obviously been a source of disappointment to George Shackle that his own theory has had virtually no impact on the profession. It is only now that his work is being acknowledged, but it is not his own theory as such which receives the recognition, but his general views on the disequilibrium brought about in markets and, hence, in the macroeconomy, by divergent forces themselves generated by the disparate expectations of economic agents, which can only dovetail fortuitously, so that equilibrium can be attained only in likewise fashion. Such general views have been seized on avidly by those seeking to find a pedigree for the Austrian School's views about the behaviour of markets, which are so much in the vanguard these days. The hope must be that once economists do become more familiar with Shackle's writings they will be given the stimulus to look into his own theory of expectation.

There are, perhaps, a number of reasons why Shackle's theory has not had more acknowledgement and gained the recognition it deserves. For example, the theory appeared during a period when the profession was largely preoccupied with macroeconomic theory and policy. But where it was concerned with microeconomics it was with the orthodox certainty-based paradigms, or with individual decision-making under uncertainty, founded on the (it must be conceded, elegant) *Expected Utility Theory* developed by Von Neumann and Morgenstern. That theory embraced formal statistical and mathematical analysis and appeared to provide empirically appealing hypotheses.

The psychological, subjective, foundation of Shackle's theory did offer a sharp contrast to the seemingly scientific approach embedded in the expected utility theory. It was probably viewed (and, of course, one can only hazard a guess about this) as a rather imprecise, "descriptive", theory. Apart from a comparative few, the technicians, as it were, won the day.

Another reason, perhaps, why Shackle's theory did not have appeal was that it purported to be a *general* theory to explain *human behaviour* under uncertainty. The context in which the relevant decisions were to be taken need not be confined, so Shackle has argued (Shackle, 1961(a)), to an economic one. The alleged generality of his theoretical model (supported, so Shackle has claimed, by psychological enquiries, such as those undertaken by Professor Sir Cyril Burt in the 1930s and 1940s) probably meant that Shackle did pay too little attention to providing purely economic examples wherein his theory could be used to understand behaviour. It might have been better for the propagation of his approach for him to have provided those illustrative examples. Maybe another concomitant reason has been the view that an empirical test of Shackle's theory is not feasible. Yet another could lie with the insurmountable obstacles it seems to place on the development of an explanation of the *aggregate* behaviour of a group of economic agents in regard to the choice of strategy in an uncertain situation, for example, the choice of type of machinery to instal.

Yet, to reiterate the point, that theory still retains pride of place in Shackle's own (implied) assessment of his own endeavours. For my part, I think that it is indeed a veritable *tour de force* despite its comparative neglect, and the conundrums that I think it contains. It does offer insights into economic behaviour under uncertainty and provides scope for the development of more internally consistent theories of such behaviour; and it *will* also admit of empirical evaluation. Its basic approach, concerned as it is with the notion that economic agents can only map out the outcomes for a range of possible actions, where they do not have perfect information on their outcomes, in a loose fashion (compared with the probability approach) and with the notion that agents ultimately have to edit the expectational set they do possess in order to simplify it, offers a starting-point also for the derivation (by questionnaire, say) of axioms of economic behaviour that could produce a more satisfactory theory than Shackle's own, my own development of it, or the exciting paradigms (Expected Utility, Prospect Theory, Regret Theory) based on the probability calculus.

So I would select *Expectation in Economics*, and its re-statement (with commentary on the critical literature on it) *Decision, Order and Time*, as two of Shackle's greatest works. But one other ranks perhaps as high as these even if it is less seminal: that is, *The Years of High Theory* mentioned earlier on. This is a splendid book exhibiting the highest quality of scholarship; and it must be one of the very best books ever written on the history of economic *theory* (rather than *thought*). *Expectations, Investment and Income* I would myself place on a par with that book. As scholarly a book as it is, *Epistemics and Economics* I feel falls short of providing the lasting quality contained in the previously mentioned books. It is very much a nihilist book as far as economics *per se* is concerned; it tends to gather together many of the critical and rather negative ideas mentioned in his preceding writings.

Throughout all his works the special hallmarks of George Shackle's writing can be discerned. Above all, he has demonstrated a felicity of style, a command of the English language, an eye for the precise phrasing and for definitive exactitude that is reminiscent of the master of economic exposition, the late Sir Denis Robertson. Shackle's writings, like Robertson's, even though they are centred largely on theoretical ideas, have a remarkable facility for drawing on empirical observations, to give the esoteric arguments a readily understandable factual base. Furthermore, Shackle's writings are erudite, peppered as they are with illustrative examples, drawn from a wide field of literature, also from science and even sometimes from sport[4].

George Shackle's works could live on solely as masterpieces of economics literature. But the four books that we have selected deserve more than that. They merit longevity of life because of their major contributions to the development and synthesis of economic theory. They will testify to the imaginative and scholarly gifts of a man who was indeed, a "polymath" in the best possible sense[5]. A man, indeed, who is both a gentle man and a gentleman; whom it has been a privilege to know and to have as one's mentor in economic theory[6].

Notes
1. One gains the impression that these discussions started at a young age, and that they gave Shackle the idea for his book, *Mathematics at the Fireside* (1952). This is a delightful book based on a question and answer style between a father and his two children, George and Lucy. I read this book as a student at Liverpool but have been unable to check that hypothesis for this article.
2. It has been known for him to become so immersed in his research that he has forgotten that he is, indeed, only human, so going for long stretches without food and sleep, with inevitable consequences. One occasion when this happened was shortly after he moved from Leeds to Liverpool when, at the start of the day, he was found in the Department in a collapsed and exhausted state.

His wife and family were still in Yorkshire waiting for the sale of their house to be completed and so there were no reminders of the schedule of daily life.

3. One can imagine, therefore, how difficult it might have been to gain access to him. Richard Sayers, Shackle's boss 1945-47, has related, for example, how he once needed to consult him one day about a report he was preparing on food supplies. There was continually no reply from Shackle's office. Eventually the report on food supplies duly appeared and on time, but Sayers was sure that Shackle was making a determined effort to complete the first draft of *Expectation in Economics!*

4. These comments echo those offered by Sir Charles Carter and myself, on another occasion (*Uncertainty and Expectations in Economics: Essays in Honour of G. L. S. Shackle,* Oxford, Basil Blackwell, 1972) except that having had the further opportunity to consider *The Years of High Theory* and *Expectations, Investment and Income,* I believe that our earlier "rankings" should be widened.

5. In his Inaugural Lecture (1953), entitled "What Makes an Economist?", Shackle has summarised his answer in the following passage: "To be a complete economist, a man need only be a mathematician, a philosopher, a psychologist, an anthropologist, a historian, a geographer and a student of politics; a master of prose exposition; and a man of the world with experience of practical business and finance; an understanding of the problems of administration, and a good knowledge of four or five foreign languages. All this, in addition, of course, to familiarity with the economics literature itself. This list should, I think, dispose at once of the idea that there are, or ever have been, any complete economists, and we can proceed to the practical questions of what arrangements are likely to provide us with men who will feel not wholly confounded when an important economic decision confronts them." (*Uncertainty in Economics and Other Reflections,* p. 24). These are very demanding qualifications. But we can see that Shackle himself goes a long way towards fulfilling them.

6. Shackle's main teaching duties in my day were to run a second and third year seminar in economic theory and to supervise any relevant graduate theses (there were no taught postgraduate courses at that time). The ten or so of us specialising in economics had to present a theory paper to be discussed by our fellow students and George Shackle. This was a rewarding experience, for no matter how bad our offerings were he always considered them seriously and with the utmost care. Suggestions for improvement were made, ideas and reading to be pursued were given; but there was no disparagement, only encouragement. One other way in which he made us feel that our efforts were at least of some value and which also showed his humility, was that he would always take copious notes from our papers. Whether he did ever find that we had, by accident, cast out a pearl or two I never discovered! My own two papers, I recall, were on Interest Rates and Investment and the Swedish School of the 1930s and Keynes. I am sure that they were pedestrian enough but they did introduce me, *inter alia,* to Shackle's own work, and the role of expectation in economics, especially in macroeconomics. But more than that Shackle's third year seminar, especially, was instrumental in sealing my interest in economic theory.

[6]

Smith and Shackle:
History and Epistemics

by Andrew S. Skinner
University of Glasgow

This article|1| does not constitute a commentary on George Shackle either as an economist or as an historian. Rather it sets out to explain the reference to Smith which was introduced to the foreword of the 1983 edition of *The Years of High Theory*, and further to elaborate some striking similarities between two philosophers whose writings on the origin of theory are separated by more than 200 years.

Adam Smith

Smith's interest in the principles of human nature is well known, especially to students of the *Theory of Moral Sentiments* (1759). Less familiar, perhaps, is the knowledge that Smith found his evidence in a number of areas, which included the study of language and of all forms of literary composition. John Millar, perhaps Smith's most distinguished pupil, described his teaching from the Chair of Logic in these terms:

> The best method of explaining and illustrating the various powers of the human mind, the most useful part of metaphysics, arises from an examination of the several ways of communicating our thoughts by speech, and from an attention to the principles of those literary compositions which contribute to persuasion or entertainment. By these arts, everything that we perceive or feel, every operation of our minds, is expressed and delineated in such a manner, that it may be clearly distinguished and remembered (Stewart, 1, 16).

Smith addressed himself to three major types of discourse, the oratorical, narrative and didactic (by which he meant scientific) arguing in each case that the writer should organise his material in a manner which reflected the purpose in hand (for example, persuasion or instruction) and the psychological characteristics of the audience to be addressed|2|.

In the case of scientific writing, Smith argued that this type of discourse may have one of two aims: either to "lay down a proposition and to prove this, by the different arguments that lead to that conclusion" or to deliver a system in any science. In the first case the writer may seek to present a complex proposition which requires the proof of several subordinate ones, and here Smith recommends that these "should not be above five in number" (*LRBL*, ii, 126) if mental confusion and stress is to be avoided. In the second case Smith advises use of the Newtonian method of *exposition* whereby we "lay down certain principles, known or proved in the beginning...whence we account for the several Phenomena, connecting all together by the

14   Journal of Economic Studies 12,1/2

same Chain" (*LRBL,* ii, 133). He added that this method was the most "philosophical" one and noted further that: "It gives us a pleasure to see the phenomena which we reckoned the most unaccountable, all deduced from some principle (commonly a well known one) and all united in one chain" (*LRBL,* ii, 134).

Smith was to continue this broad theme in an essay which he allowed to be published after his death, the still relatively neglected piece on Astronomy, where he set out to consider not so much the question of the *mode* of delivery as that of the *origins* and characteristics of theory[3].

The assumptions employed in the essay on Astronomy are fundamentally simple: Smith assumes that *all* men are endowed with certain faculties and propensities such as reason, reflection and imagination, and that they are motivated by a desire to acquire the sources of pleasure and avoid those of pain. In this context pleasure relates to a state of the imagination: the "state of. . .tranquility, and composure" (*Imitative Arts,* II, 20). Such a state, Smith suggested, may be attained even where the objects contemplated are unlike or the processes involved are complex, provided only that the connection is a customary one.

Smith argues that when certain objects or events are seen to follow in a particular order, "they come to be so connected together in the fancy, that the idea of the one seems, of its own accord, to call up and introduce that of the other". Under such circumstances, he continued:

> There is no break, no stop, no gap, no interval. The ideas excited by so coherent a chain of things seem, as it were, to float through the mind of their own accord, without obliging it to exert itself, or to make any effort in order to pass from one of them to another (*Astronomy,* II, 7).

While the imagination finds no stimulus to thought under such conditions, Smith went on to argue that this would not be the case where the "appearances" studied were in any way *unexpected.* We feel *surprise* when some object (or number of objects) is drawn to our attention which does not fall into a recognised pattern; a sentiment which is quickly followed by that of *wonder,* where the latter is defined in these terms:

> The stop which is thereby given to the career of the imagination, the difficulty which it finds in passing along such disjointed objects, and the feeling of something like a gap or interval betwixt them, constitute the whole essence of this emotion (*Astronomy,* II, 9).

Wonder, in short, involves a source of pain (a disutility); a feeling of discomfort which gives rise to uncertainty and "anxious curiosity" and even to "giddiness and confusion". The *response* to this situation involves the pursuit of some explanation, with a view to relieving the mind from a state of disequilibrium (i.e., lack of "composure"); a natural reaction, given Smith's assumptions, designed to eliminate the sense of wonder by providing some appropriate ordering of the phenomena in question, or some plausible account of the links between different objects. Finally, Smith suggested that once we have succeeded in providing an acceptable and coherent account of a particular problem, the very existence of that explanation may "heighten" our appreciation of the "appearances" in question. In this way, for example, we learn to *admire* a complex social and economic structure once its "hidden springs" have been exposed, while in the same way a theory of astronomy may help us to admire the heavens through presenting the "theatre of nature" as a coherent "and therefore a more magnificent spectacle" (*Astronomy,* II, 12).

Surprise, wonder, and admiration are, therefore, the three *sequential* sentiments on which Smith's account of mental stimulus depends, thus helping to explain the emergence of *theory* as a characteristic output of the mind.

Most of these points find further illustration in the "History of Astronomy" itself, where Smith reviewed four main systems of thought, not with a view to judging their "absurdity or probability, their agreement or inconsistency with truth and reality", but rather with a view to considering how far each of them was fitted to "soothe the imagination" — "that particular point of view which belongs to our subject" (*Astronomy*, II, 12). Looked at in this way, the analysis has a "static" aspect, at least in so far as it is designed to show the extent to which each of the four main astronomical systems reviewed did, in fact, "soothe" the imagination, isolating by this means the characteristics which they have in common. But Smith goes further than his stated object in noting that the systems of astronomy reviewed followed each other in a certain historical sequence, and in exposing the causal links which, he felt, might explain that sequence. The essence of Smith's argument would seem to be that each system at the time of its original appearance did satisfy the needs of the imagination, but that each was subject to a process of modification as new problems came to light; a process of modification which resulted in a growing degree of complexity which ultimately became unacceptable to the imagination, i.e., to the mind. This in turn paves the way for a new kind of response — the production not just of an account but of an *alternative* account (in this case of the heavens); a new thought-system designed to explain the same problems as the first, at least in its most complex form, but cast in a more acceptable style, i.e., in a form which relied upon a smaller number of familiar or plausible principles, and which was for this reason more acceptable to the mind.

While theory and the theoretical system emerge as the means of escaping the disutility associated with the sentiment of wonder, Smith also described the activity involved as "an original pleasure or good in itself" (*Astronomy*, III, 3). Theoretical work is a source of positive enjoyment as well as of relief; a point already made in the discussion of the Newtonian method and confirmed by Smith's likening of the intellectual system to the "delights of a well composed concerto. . .of instrumental music" (*Imitative Arts*, II, 29). In the *Wealth of Nations* reference is made to the "beauty of a systematical arrangement of different observations connected by a few common principles" (*WN*, V, i, f, 25); elsewhere attention is drawn to a propensity, natural to all men, to "account for all appearances from as few principles as possible" (*TMS*, VII, ii, 2, 14).

Smith added a further dimension to the discussion in considering the attachments men form for particular systems and in referring to the problems of communication which can arise when currently accepted systems are threatened by some alternative — a necessary feature of the historical process as Smith outlines it. It was in this connection that he commented on the ease with which the "learned give up the evidence of their senses to preserve the coherence of the ideas of their imagination" (*Astronomy*, IV, 13) and on their unwillingness to give up any part of a system or theory once completely formed (IV, 19). He also noted the desire which some philosophers had shown to "slur over" difficulties rather than qualify in any respect the pleasure to be derived from a given thought-system, and later drew attention to the importance not just of the "prejudices of the imagination" (IV, 52) but also to those of education in regard to the reception of new ideas. In this Smith was at one with Hume|4|:

16   Journal of Economic Studies 12,1/2

> But though education is disclaimed by philosophy, as a fallacious ground for assent to any opinion, it prevails nevertheless in the world, and is the cause why all systems are apt to be rejected at first as new and unusual (*Treatise of Human Nature*, I, iii, x, 1).

G. L. S. Shackle

Shackle's purpose differs from that of Smith in one very important respect: Smith had not set out to write a history of astronomy as such, but rather to use historical materials drawn from that field to illustrate the principles which lead and direct scientific enquiry[5]. Shackle, in contrast, set out to provide a record of developments primarily in the 1930s and may, therefore, be appraised as an historian of economic thought. Brian Loasby's recent essay is very much in this genre[6]. As Loasby (1983) has reminded us, Shackle passes in review a number of important historical developments such as the re-emergence of indifference curve analysis at the hands of Hicks and Allen, the re-definition of marginal revenue and its deployment as a curve which can be given geometric representation, and Leontief's input-output table, to name but a few. These themes allowed Shackle to illustrate a number of interesting features of the historical process and in particular to demonstrate that the materials necessary to each of the developments just mentioned were to hand long before they were successfully elaborated. But, of course, the book is dominated, as to the historical record, by the emergence of the theories of imperfect and monopolistic competition on the one hand, and by the macroeconomic revolution, with Myrdal and Keynes as the chief actors, on the other.

The *organisation* of the material brings to light a closer parallel with Smith in the sense that Shackle begins his study by describing a single intellectual system before going on to consider the work of those who attacked it. As Shackle noted:

> The forty years from 1870 saw the creation of a Great Theory or Grand System of Economics, in one sense complete and self-suficient, able, on its own terms, to answer all questions which those terms allowed. The briefest statement of those terms may be that they took as the sole purpose of economic theory the demonstration of the logical implications of given tastes or needs combined with perfect knowledge and confronted with a scarcity and versatility of resources... This Great Theory was thus the theory of general, perfectly competitive, full employment, stationary (or better, timeless) equilibrium. (Shackle, 1967(a), pp. 4-5.)

He added:

> In its arresting beauty and completeness this theory seemed to need no corroborative evidence from observation. It seemed to derive from these aesthetic qualities its own stamp of authentication and an independent ascendancy over men's minds. (*Ibid.*, p. 5.)

The whole of the subsequent record is represented by Shackle as a response to the inadequacy and irrelevance of the theoretical perspective just described as exposed by the social, political, and economic conditions of the inter-war period. The "value-theory revolution of the early 1930s" was described as a "a struggle, not of man against man, but of the whole body of trained economists against the tremendous grip of received doctrine, the established image of the economic world" (*ibid.*, p. 43). The generalisation of the model of monopoly by Joan Robinson, (and the development of oligopoly by E. H. Chamberlin) conspired "to risk the dissolution of value theory and even the whole fabric of economics as a deductive system" (*ibid.*, p. 26). In the sphere of macroeconomics, Shackle gave particular credit to Myrdal (rather than

Keynes) for releasing economic theory from "the tacit, imprisoning assumption that the economy moves like the planets" (*ibid.,* p. 116). Uncertainty was the "new strand placed gleamingly in the skein of economic ideas in the 1930s" (*ibid.,* p. 6); uncertain expectation was seen to lie at the root of the new economics of the *General Theory.* The implications were grave; as Shackle put it, by way of summary:

> When economic theory elects to bring in imperfect competition and to recognise uncertainty, there is an end to the meaning of general equilibrium. Economics, thereafter, is the description, piece by piece, of a collection of fragments. These fragments may fit together into a brilliant, arrestingly suggestive mosaic, but they do not compose a pattern of unique, inevitable order. (*Ibid.,* p. 295.)

Smith would no doubt have been quick to appreciate an argument cast in the form of an attack on a prevailing orthodoxy which had been shown to be of questionable relevance.

The parallels become even closer when we go beyond the issues of historical content and organisation to recall that Shackle's interest was in economics as a "department of thought" (*ibid.,* p. 2) and that he was also searching for an episode which could be used "to cut a few sods in aid of an eventual theory of the origins of theories" (*ibid.,* p. 3). Here the generalisations which Shackle was able to offer on the basis of his historical study seem to follow even more closely in the footsteps of Adam Smith.

In the Foreword to the edition of 1983 Shackle recalled Smith's claim that the chief purpose of theory "is to set men's minds at rest", thus echoing his own earlier statement:

> The chief service rendered by a theory is the setting of men's minds at rest. So long as we have a satisfying conceptual structure, a model or a taxonomy which provides for the filing of all facts in a scheme of order, we are absolved from the tiresome labour of thought and the uneasy consciousness of mystery and a threatening unknown... Theory serves deep needs of the human spirit; it subordinates nature to man, imposes a beautiful simplicity on the unbearable multiplicity of fact, gives comfort in the face of the unknown and unexperienced. (*Ibid.,* p. 288.)

In this connection we find exactly the same emphasis on the importance of coherence, consistency and order, as recorded in the following passage:

> The question for the scientist is what thought scheme will best provide him with a sense of that order and coherence, a sense of some permanence, repetitiveness and universality in the structure or texture of the scheme of things. (*Ibid.,* p. 286.)

Moreover, it is suggested, much in the manner of Smith's description of the "Newtonian method", that the "scientist's ultimate aim is to see everything as an illustration of a very few basic principles incapable of further unification" (*ibid.,* p. 287). A theoretical structure, thus constituted, can also be appreciated as a thing of "arresting beauty and completeness" (*ibid.,* p. 5) so that it comes as no surprise to find the model described as:

> A work of art, freely composed within the constraints of a particular art form, namely the logical binding together of propositions. In this bounded freedom it resembles any other art form, the sonnet, the symphony, the cabinetmaker's or architect's conception. (*Ibid.,* p. 47.)

Elsewhere Shackle made a related point, also to be found in Smith, when noting that:

> Theories by their nature and purpose, their role of administering to a "good state of mind", are things to be held and cherished. Theories are altered or discarded only when they fail us. (*Ibid.,* p. 289.)

18   Journal of Economic Studies 12,1/2

In the same way, Shackle took note of the problems associated with change from one major system to another in a passage which recalled Smith's own preoccupation with the prejudices of education:

> The innovating theoretician needs a ruthless self-belief. He must overturn the intellectual dwelling-places of hundreds of people, whose first instinct will be resistance and revenge. Yet reconstruction must inevitably use much of the old material. Piety is not only honourable, it is indispensable. Invention is helpless without tradition. (*Ibid.,* p. 295.)

A further implication of the argument is that change is both inevitable and continuous, thus echoing Smith's bold assessment of the Newtonian system:

> . . .even we, while we have been endeavouring to represent all philosophical systems as mere inventions of the imagination, to connect together the otherwise disjointed and discordant phenomena of nature, have insensibly been drawn in, to make use of the language expressing the connecting principles of this one, as if they were the real chains which Nature makes use of to bind together her several operations. (*Astronomy,* IV, 76.)

Such parallels are surely interesting and, indeed, remarkable when one stops to consider that Smith and Shackle based their observations on two very different branches of science and to recall that Shackle was at the time of writing quite unaware of the work done by his distinguished predecessor in this field.

Of no less interest is the fact that Shackle offered the generalisations just considered as applicable not merely to the Grand (and beautiful) System of *classical* economics, but also to the theoretical constructions of the 1930s; the years of *"high theory"* dominated as they were by the preoccupation with uncertainty rather than by the assumption of perfect knowledge.

Chamberlin, for example, may be seen to have provided a "progression of ideas" in the form of an argument which gradually increases the number of variables and which culminates in an account of competition where numbers are small. Keynes produced a *General Theory* which featured a number of interdependent functions capable, as Hicks demonstrated, of exposition in the form of an IS/LM system. Both theories are, from this point of view, coherent, systematic and attractive.

At the same time, both theoretical structures are formulated in a way which is designed to convey something of the underlying economic reality which their authors sought to understand. Chamberlin provides us with a means of comprehending the phenomenon of oligopoly and of appreciating the problems of prediction which arise in the context of small numbers and interdependent functions.

At the same time Chamberlin showed himself willing to confront the implications of these findings. In this framework:

> The only defensible scientific attitude seems to be to "let the chips fall where they may", to give full importance to the indeterminate as well as to the determinate and carefully to avoid the temptation of formulating problems with the *objective* of securing a determinate answer. (Chamberlin, 1957, p. 62.)

In the case of Keynes, Shackle noted the quality of coherence provided by the new system, while observing that:

> A theory of unemployment is, necessarily, inescapably, a theory of disorder. The disorder in question is the basic disorder of uncertain expectation, the essential disorder of the real, as contrasted with the conventionally pretended, human condition. (Shackle, 1967(a), p. 133.)

He added:

> It is not surprising that an *Economics of Disorder* was not intellectually acceptable to those trained in the Economics of Order, *viz.* in Value Theory, the theory of how to cope, by the best use of *all available* resources, with ineluctable scarcity, that gravitational principle of economics. (*Ibid.,* p. 134.)

To what extent has this kind of perspective proved to be acceptable to a later generation? In 1967 Shackle wrote that *after* the 1930s economics provided an "account of how men cope with scarcity and uncertainty. This was far the greatest of the achievements of the 1930s in economic theory" (*ibid.,* p. 7). But in another interesting passage, added to the Foreword of the 1983 edition, he drew attention to the resurgence of neoclassical thought in the years after 1945:

> Economics re-asserted its claim to be the science of rational conduct, able to inform itself adequately about the determining conditions in which its actions would work out their consequences. The 1970s have opened afresh the gulf between what we see around us and what the theory of business as a rational self-co-ordinating and foreknowing action can explain. (Shackle, 1983(f), p. vi.)

The Importance of Commentary
After the 1930s, the period of Shackle's study, the work of Chamberlin was reduced to a series of tangency solutions and the wreckage of value theory obscured to such an extent that modern texts frequently *conclude* with a theory of general equilibrium in a manner which conceals the underlying theoretical tensions. The exposition of the *General Theory* was conducted almost exclusively in terms of an apparatus which may obscure Keynes' preoccupation with a world of volatile functions. Far from exploring the implications of monopolistic competition for the macroeconomic model, supply functions have been added in a way which suggests that perfect competition and the assumption of perfect knowledge have not been entirely abandoned.

The reason for this kind of development, which Shackle does not explore, may very well be rooted in those psychological judgements which he was able to offer; notably in our desire for coherence, simplicity, order and continuity.

Shackle concentrated on the *innovator* confronting a body of received doctrine and on the struggle which this involved. But while Smith concentrated most of his attention on the development of new theoretical structures, he did not neglect the role of the *commentator* whose task it was to *deliver* a system in any science. Scientific literature was seen by Smith to be a form of discourse, to be expounded in a way which the writer found attractive and which would appeal to his audience. This view of science as literature was part of Smith's original contribution to eighteenth-century rhetorical theory and still remains a result of some importance[7]. While the innovator and the commentator may share the same psychological characteristics, it is the latter who may unwittingly compound the "prejudices of education", and at the same time exercise real authority in the development of ideas.

Perhaps the textbook deserves almost as much attention as the original materials on which it is based, from those seeking an understanding of the "principles which lead and direct" philosophical enquiry.

The record would at least seem to suggest that order and coherence in a theoretical structure ("the brilliantly suggestive mosaic") may be insufficient if the conclusion which it prompts is disequilibrium.

20   Journal of Economic Studies 12,1/2

Notes

1. This article is a development of ideas stated in Skinner (1979(a)) and designed to concentrate only on some parallels (and differences) in the work of Adam Smith and George Shackle. I am indebted to the editors of the *Scottish Journal of Political Economy* for permission to reproduce the short account of Smith's *Astronomy* which appeared in the 1979 article above cited. The present writer accidentally introduced Shackle to a neglected aspect of Smith's work, and although the point is hardly as important as other themes in this volume, it was a great source of pleasure at the time.
2. For comment see Howell (1975). The present writer's views on Smith's lectures on rhetoric are set out in Skinner (1983).
3. The present writer has commented on the essay on Astronomy as a subject in its own right in Skinner (1979(b)), and in sections I-IV of the General Introduction to *EPS*, to which reference may be made for a summary of the critical literature. Joseph Schumpeter was among the early writers to appreciate Smith's work in this field, even if he did feel moved to express surprise that the *Astronomy* could have been written by "A. Smith" (Schumpeter, 1954, p. 182)!
4. The link with Hume has been particularly emphasised by D. D. Raphael (1979) and in section V of the General Introduction to *EPS*.
5. W. P. D. Wightman has developed this point in *Essays* and again in the editor's Introduction to the *EPS*.
6. Loasby also further developed the parallels between Smith and Shackle from the point of view of the "origins of theory".
7. This point is owed to Howell, *Essays*.

References

Adam Smith
References to Smith's works follow the usages of the Glasgow edition of the *Works and Correspondence* (Oxford), and normally cite Part, Book, or Volume; section, chapter, sub-section and paragraph. Abbreviations used are as follows:

TMS = *Theory of Moral Sentiments* (1759), ed. D. D. Raphael and A. L. Macfie (1976).
WN = *The Wealth of Nations* (1776), ed. R. H. Campbell, A. S. Skinner and W. B. Todd (1976).
EPS = *Essays on Philosophical Subjects* (1795), ed. W. P. D. Wightman (1980). This volume includes:
       Astronomy = The Principles which Lead and Direct Philosophical Enquiries: Illustrated by the History of Astronomy
       Imitative Arts − Of the Nature of that Imitation which takes place in what are called the Imitative Arts
LRBL   *Lectures on Rhetoric and Belles Lettres*, ed. J. C. Bryce (1983).
Stewart = *Account of the Life and Writings of Adam Smith, LL.D.* ed. I. S. Ross, in *EPS* (1980).
Essays = *Essays on Adam Smith*, ed. A. S. Skinner and T. Wilson (1975).

Additional References

Chamberlin, E. C., *Towards a More General Theory of Value*, Oxford, Oxford University Press, 1957.
Howell, W. S., "Adam Smith's Lectures on Rhetoric: An Historical Assessment", *Essays*, 1975, pp. 11-43.
Loasby, B., "G. L. S. Shackle as an Historian of Economic Thought", in *Research in the History of Economic Thought and Methodology*, Vol. 1, 1983, pp. 209-221.
Raphael, D. D., "Adam Smith: Philosophy, Science, and Social Science", in S. C. Brown (Ed.), *Philosophers of the Enlightenment*, Brighton, Harvester Press, 1979.
Schumpeter, J. A., *History of Economic Analysis*, London, George Allen and Unwin, 1954.
Skinner, A. S., "Adam Smith: An Aspect of Modern Economics?", *Scottish Journal of Political Economy*, Vol. 26, 1979(a), pp. 109-125.
Skinner, A. S., "Science and the Role of the Imagination" in *A System of Social Science*, Oxford, Oxford University Press, 1979(b), pp. 14-41.
Skinner, A. S., "Adam Smith: Rhetoric and the Communication of Ideas" in A. W. Coats (Ed.), *Political Economy and Public Policy*, London JAI Press Inc., 1983, pp. 71-88.
Wightman, W. P. D., "Adam Smith and the History of Ideas", in *Essays*, 1975, pp. 44-67.

[7]

Profit, Expectations and Coherence in Economic Systems

by Brian J. Loasby

Stirling University

Introduction

Professor Shackle is the most courteous, the most erudite, and the most radical critic of orthodox economics. The concept of profit, which apparently serves as such a convenient instrument of equilibrium, on closer enquiry is revealed to be necessarily subversive of such schemes of order; for profit can arise only where knowledge is not adequate to support any agreed — even probabilistically agreed — assessment of a situation. Thus any consideration of Professor Shackle's (1972, Chapter 35) discussion of profit focuses our attention on the insufficiency of knowledge which is the core of his criticism of orthodoxy. It should be no surprise, therefore, to find that the problem of coherence within economic systems resembles the problem of coherence in the growth of knowledge. Both appear to depend upon a productive but precarious tension between imaginative conjectures and a framework of serviceable conventions within which they may be tested.

Profit is the difference between two valuations, for example between the price that a merchant pays for his goods and the price, net of expenses, at which he sells them, or between the price of a manufacturer's output and the total costs of all the inputs used in its production. Now it is a commonplace of conventional economics that if all inputs, including the labour and capital contributed by the merchant or manufacturer himself, are properly accounted for, no such difference can exist in a competitive equilibrium. In Schumpeter's words (1934, p. 29): "Production realises only the values foreseen in the economic plan, which previously exist potentially in the values of means of production." Normal profits are no more than wages or interest, misleadingly classified. Indeed, even in a monopolistic equilibrium no such difference of value can arise, since what are usually called monopoly profits are imputed to the monopolised input: the value of that input is the net present value of its future income stream, and on that value no more than a normal return can, therefore, be earned. If we are to discuss profit, we cannot be discussing equilibrium prices and quantities. Whether we can be discussing tendencies towards equilibrium is a major question for this article.

The definition of profit given above was deliberately couched in the present tense; in equilibrium models all dates are simultaneously available for analysis and so the tense is appropriate. But if profit is to be analysed, then it must be within an analytical framework which allows for the passage of time — in Professor Shackle's terms, a diachronic model. Profit may now be defined, in accounting terms, as the change in net worth between two dates. A period of time may be considered from either end, and so may the profit attributed to it, as forecast or as record. In view of the supreme importance which Professor Shackle (1967(a), Chapter 10) has assigned to Myrdal's distinction between *ex ante* and *ex post* appraisals it is not surprising that he distinguishes these two perceptions of profit, which he labels expectational and resolutional. These two perceptions have different but complementary roles to play in Professor Shackle's human drama: expectational profit is the incentive to action, resolutional profit the stimulus to thought. In the language of a very different kind of economist (Hahn, 1973), expectations trigger policy, outcomes modify theory.

Perception or Imagination?
Let us begin with expectational profit.

> Cantillon regards his merchant as able to buy goods at a known price with a view to sell them later at a price which, when he buys them, he cannot know. We can equally regard a producer as able to buy the means of production at contractual prices, in order to combine them into a product which will be available only after a lapse of time, and saleable then at a price which cannot at the outset be known. (Shackle, 1972, p. 415)

It is clear that we are here concerned with future prices which are not describable by any objective probability distribution, and certainly not with prices for future goods which are settled in markets for contingent commodities before present purchases are agreed. We are dealing with a world of uncertainty. Moreover, this uncertainty is interpreted in different fashion by agents within a single market: for if suppliers of inputs and the prospective purchasers of those inputs all took the same view of the prospects for output prices and quantities, then this common presumed value of outputs would be imputed to the inputs, and there would be no profit. What matters is that there should be differences of view. How may these differences emerge?

One answer has been provided by Professor Kirzner (1973). He invites us to take as our starting-point an equilibrium configuration of prices and quantities, without profit but with an established self-sustaining pattern of production and exchange. What now happens if there is a change in preferences, the discovery of a new source of inputs, or the invention of a superior method of production? To an omniscient analyst, any of these entails a new equilibrium price vector — and the analyst is likely to concern himself with its configuration, to the exclusion of any interest in the process by which it might be established. Now it is precisely this process of adjustment to equilibrium to which Professor Kirzner directs our attention. The change, he asserts, may not be widely known, and its implications not necessarily obvious even to those who do know. But for those who recognise the change, and perceive its implications, the disparity between currently established prices and those which they deem to correspond to the new data offers the prospect of profit.

> Profit opportunities arise when the prices of products on the product markets are not adjusted to the prices of the resource services on the factor markets. In other words, "something" is being sold at different prices in two markets, as a result of imperfect communication between the markets. (Kirzner, 1973, p. 85.)

Recognition of the profit opportunities, even by a single individual, leads to decisions

Profit, Expectations and Coherence **23**

which reallocate resources in the direction of a new equilibrium. The success of the pioneer or pioneers encourages others to follow, since it is less difficult to perceive and interpret the profits achieved by others than the profit potential inherent in a situation; and the reallocation continues until the new equilibrium configuration is attained and the profit opportunity thereby extinguished. Professor Kirzner's ideas have recently been developed and extended by Professor Casson (1982).

Now there are some difficulties with this story of the adjustment process, which arise from the view of knowledge which it embodies. There is an unambiguous change in the data, as a result of which some business decisions, hitherto correct, are now in error. The problem, therefore, is to correct these errors by amending the decisions to conform with new knowledge; and this problem is solved through the recognition by one or more alert entrepreneurs of the profit which can be secured — without cost, in Kirzner's (1973, p. 48) view, and the incentive which this costless profit provides. The magnitude of the profit opportunity reflects the value of the new information; as the information is applied, the profit opportunity shrinks; when it is fully used, profits are extinguished, and we are in equilibrium.

This appears to be a very neat self-regulating system. But its self-regulating properties are derived from the assumption that entrepreneurial expectations are correct. Like the rest of us, the entrepreneur does not know the whole truth; but what he does know is nothing but the truth. Professor Kirzner has defended this assumption with the argument that the profit opportunity will only yield profits *ex post* if it is a genuine opportunity, and that the entrepreneur has a very powerful incentive to ensure, before committing himself to action, that it is indeed genuine (Kirzner, 1982, p. 149). Casson (1982, p. 14) similarly emphasises that the entrepreneur is in the business of being "right, while everyone else is wrong". The argument that the truth can be found by those motivated to look for it rests on the proposition that objective truth lies around us, awaiting discovery, and that those who are sufficiently alert will perceive more and more of it. In Popper's (1972(b) p. 341) metaphor, "according to this view. . .our mind resembles a container — a kind of bucket — in which perceptions and knowledge accumulate". Kirzner's and Casson's entrepreneurs profit from the contents of their buckets.

In contrast to the "bucket theory of knowledge", Popper advocates a "searchlight theory":

> . . .the aim of the scientists is not to discover absolute certainty, but to discover better and better theories (or to invent more and more powerful searchlights) capable of being put to more and more severe tests (and thereby leading us to, and illuminating for us, ever new experiences) (Popper, 1972(b), p. 361).

His metaphor is unconsciously adopted by Professor Shackle (1972, p. 118).

> The rôle of theory is to be an illuminant. It throws features of the scene into relief, gives them substance by eliciting a shadow, defines profiles and lends colour. The illuminating beam is not itself the object of study, and it will not do to mistake theories for realities. But without the illumination there is nothing to be seen.

A Popperian entrepreneur does not have the luxury of exploiting a profit opportunity solidly based upon a newly-discovered truth; his profit opportunity is founded upon a novel conjecture, which must be tested in the market place, where it may prove a mirage — more successful, perhaps, as a stimulus to thought than as an incentive to beneficial adjustment towards a newly-defined equilibrium. And indeed, most entrepreneurial conjectures are refuted by the market test — after a good many more have been refuted by a great variety of pre-market tests.

For Shackle, as for Popper, the inadequacy of knowledge is liberating.

> If he is aware that his basis of supposed fact is incomplete, and thus insufficient to support any valuation at all until supplemented by suppositions originated by himself *ad hoc,* plainly he has freedom in choosing these supplemental ideas, to reach many rival and mutually contradictory valuations. (Shackle, 1972, p. 410.)

The encouragement of bold conjectures by practising scientists has been, perhaps, the most obvious impact of Popper's philosophy of science upon scientific practice: such conjectures provide the hazardous opportunities for the kind of profits which scientists value.

Shackle's assertion (1972, p. 411) that "profit. . .involves conjecture and arises from it" is also consilient with Schumpeter's explanation of economic development. The mere recognition of changes which have taken place outside the economic system is not, for Schumpeter, a source of economic development; such development springs from entrepreneurial conjectures of what might be, described, in terms which we have come to associate with Professor Shackle, as "a figment of the imagination" (Schumpeter, 1934, p. 85). G. B. Richardson, too, after considering in some detail the problems of equilibration in response to exogenous change, observes, like Schumpeter, that this conception of the economic problem of change is unacceptably restrictive, and that "it is necessary to adopt a conception of entrepreneurial activity different from that appropriate to the hypothetical world of perfect competition" (Richardson, 1960, p. 104). His proposals invoke the same central idea of imaginative conjectures which go beyond the evidence.

> Imagination, rather than information in any ordinary sense, is what entrepreneurs require in order to discover new ways of combining resources so as to meet consumers' desires; production functions exist unknown to entrepreneurs only in the sense that musical tunes await discovery; in either case originality, rather than the possession of "information", as considered exclusively hitherto, is what is required for successful new combinations to be produced. (Richardson, 1960, p. 105.)

Conjecture and Calculation

That an economic system might achieve coherence through the gradual discovery of "correct information" may seem a tolerably plausible proposition, and it is, indeed, currently the focus of some of the most advanced theoretical work in economics; but that coherence might be achieved on the basis of figments of entrepreneurial imagination appears distinctly dubious. Faced with such a proposition, a well-trained economist looks for some way of constraining the imagination.

Let us start with the apparently simplest question. Since expectational profit is a difference between two valuations, can we ensure that only one of them is the product of imaginative conjecture? May not input prices, at least, be grounded in established knowledge? At one point Professor Shackle seems to assume that they may: he writes, in the passage quoted earlier (1972, p. 415) of a producer "able to buy the means of production at contractual prices", and, immediately after, of "known cost". However, as he has himself insisted, action always relates to the future, and what matters is not what inputs have cost but what they will cost when the entrepreneur comes

Profit, Expectations and Coherence   **25**

to buy them. It is possible (though it cannot be guaranteed) that merchants will be able to buy tomorrow at prices little different from those of today; but many entrepreneurial plans offer the prospect of profit only if projected over a considerable interval, whether or not they require the acquisition or construction of physical capital. For such projects, as Professor Shackle observes (1972, p. 417), expectational profit,

> . . .will be reckoned by taking for each future year of the proposed plant's operating life, some supposition of the sale-proceeds of the product to be produced with its aid in that year, and some supposition concerning the corresponding outlay for the necessary materials, power, labour and other things necessary for operating the plant in that year, and subtracting the latter from the former to obtain one hypothesis of trading revenue for that year.

Are both kinds of supposition open to unrestricted conjecture, or can we find some anchor for expectation?

Schumpeter argued that we can, and indeed that we must, if entrepreneurs are to flourish. Entrepreneurship, he claimed, requires a combination of imagination and calculation — imagination to conceive of a novel use of resources, the profit from which can be calculated on the basis of prices which are not likely to change before the profit has been attained. He begins with an analysis of the circular flow of economic activity, from which innovation is absent. Here prices are stable, and economic activity follows established routines, which have been adjusted to experience. Within the circular flow, the value of current output is fully imputed to inputs, and there is no profit. It is this situation which gives the entrepreneur his calculable opportunity. He conceives of a "new combination" which either permits increased revenue to be generated from a given quantity of inputs, or reduces the quantity of inputs necessary to obtain a given revenue. He then evaluates this new combination:

> . . .the value of the new products must be compared with the value of those products which the same means of production have been producing so far in the normal circular flow. Clearly this valuation is necessary in order to make any estimate of the advantage of the new combination, and without it no action would be possible. . .(Schumpeter, 1934, p. 141).

Schumpeter insists that it is the value generated by the means of production in their present uses which must be imputed to them in order to calculate the potential profit: for this is their opportunity cost (though he does not use the phrase) within the existing circular flow; and that circular flow will continue unchanged unless a new combination is introduced.

Thus the circular flow provides a general equilibrium framework within which the prospective entrepreneur can make his partial disequilibrium calculations, with no apparent need to consider the impact of his own decisions on the remainder of the system. It thus serves an analogous purpose to the problem-situation which, in Popper's view, normally faces the scientist: the area for conjecture is reasonably well defined against a background of what may be regarded as reliable knowledge. This is a theme to which we shall return; but it is appropriate here to point a contrast with the views of Schumpeter's fellow Austrian, Machlup, who relies on the system constraint of the competitive market to secure uniformity of action, thus permitting the construction of general theories which require no particular specification of individual behaviour, and so apparently preserving both free-will and the ability (in appropriate circumstances) to predict the results of its operation. Now Schumpeter shares this approach to the point of inferring the regularity of activities within the circular flow; but it is precisely this regularity which in his model provides the opportunity for the most striking exercise of free will.

Professor Shackle (1972, p. 227) also draws attention to the advantages of stable prices, in commenting on Townshend's suggestion that established prices might reflect established routines which it is not worth anyone's while to disrupt. Neither Townshend nor Professor Shackle, however, suggests that these routines are more than serviceable conventions, whereas Schumpeter claims that the circular flow is not merely a coherent but a rationally adapted system. But though pointing to the inadequate basis for the apparent implication of conventional value theory that prices should be fluid, in order to secure that allocation of resources which best reflects the current state of technology and preferences, Professor Shackle does not explicitly consider whether stable prices might assist or impede the exercise of economic imagination. Professor Casson, by contrast, leaves us in no doubt about the advantages, and incidental disadvantages, of price stability to the entrepreneur's operations.

Stability and Adjustment
To be fully effective, as has been pointed out, this price stability must be expected by the entrepreneur to extend into the future long enough to allow him to reap at least sufficient of the profit which he calculates will result from his conjecture to cause him to take the risk that this conjecture is ill-founded. This condition embodies in another form the requirement emphasised by G. B. Richardson, that the prospective entrepreneur should not be dissuaded from action by the fear that others may duplicate his action and frustrate his potential gains; for

> ...a general profit opportunity, which is both known to everyone and equally capable of being exploited by everyone, is, in an important sense, a profit opportunity for no-one in particular (Richardson, 1960, p. 57).

Professor Shackle, Schumpeter, and Richardson himself all provide some protection from this danger by attributing the perception of apparent opportunities to the exercise of imagination rather than alertness to new data: entrepreneurs' imaginations may be more fertile than those of other people (at least in the particular field of enterprise which each is cultivating — and that is all that matters), and there is no particular reason to believe that equally imaginative entrepreneurs will have very similar ideas — though there is no reason to rule out the possibility either.

Schumpeter (1934, p. 239) insists on the "mere businessman's" dependence on routine, which serves to ensure — in his model — the perpetuation of the practices of the circular flow, and their concomitant prices, for long enough to allow the entrepreneur to secure his reward from successful innovation — a reward which depends, in Professor Shackle's words (1972, p. 423), on "the exploitation of the opponent's lack of knowledge, or of his reliance on what he wrongly believes to be knowledge". Similarly, Kirzner's entrepreneur can profit from the error which he perceives only while that error is perpetuated by others. Even when the "mere businessman's" well-corroborated belief in the efficacy of established routines suffers a Popperian refutation, the routines may continue for some time.

This persistence in once-effective methods despite evidence that they are no longer adequate is not simply a matter of inertia or limited mental capacity. The evidence is often debatable, the possibly-refuted theory may still be serviceable in other contexts, and there may be no obvious replacement. Moreover, as Nelson and Winter (1982) have emphasised, every organisation depends on an interlocking set of routines which are imperfectly specified and perhaps impossible fully to articulate — and for those reasons not easy to amend, even when the need for amendment is agreed; since these routines are also likely to embody an implicit truce which preserves the organisational coalition, the need to reconstruct the coalition, and the practices and procedures which maintain it, is a second major obstacle to quick adjustment.

The competitive threat to entrepreneurial activity is extensively discussed both by Richardson and by Casson. But Richardson also draws attention to another, and opposite, threat in the failure to act of others whose activities are complementary to those of the entrepreneur. In conventional theory, the firm is a construct which acquires primary inputs (usually thought of as homogeneous) and supplies outputs directly to final users. In practice, of course, most firms rely very heavily on purchases of intermediate goods and services, some of which are precisely tailored to their particular requirements, and few manufacturing organisations are in direct contact with consumers. Effective innovation often requires the active co-operation of many outside the organisation within which that innovation originates, and at least the acquiescence of others.

Neither co-operation nor acquiescence is always to be secured by the anonymous transactions of the textbook price mechanism. As Richardson (1972) has pointed out, the organisation of industry is heavily dependent on specific relationships for the co-ordination of closely complementary activities; these relationships, though not — usually — incompatible with the operations of the market, are not adequately represented by it. The need to organise the activities of a network of organisations in order to secure innovation is not a theme which either Schumpeter or Shackle makes much of; but the greater ease with which new networks can apparently be created, or existing networks adapted, in America and in Japan than in Britain does seem to be a partial explanation of the failure to turn entrepreneurial imagination into an expectational profit which is sufficient to produce innovation. Of course, existing networks, in support of established routines, extend the problems of changing organisational routines beyond the bounds of a single organisation; and the power and rigidity of existing networks in Britain seems also to contribute to the difficulties often experienced in responding to new challenges from outside.

The Problem of Convergence
Let us suppose that an innovative process is somehow started. Is there any reason to expect that it might converge on some new stable set of routines, whether these represent some new circular flow, or some self-sustaining pattern of conventions? If we have abandoned the "bucket theory of knowledge" in favour of the concept of knowledge as a set of corroborated but still potentially refutable conjectures, we cannot simply argue that entrepreneurial expectations are based upon some superior ability to perceive what, though concealed from others, is undoubted truth, or even that they rest upon "intuition, the capacity of seeing things in a way which afterwards proves

to be true" (Schumpeter, 1934, p. 85). We must accept that entrepreneurial expectations are likely to prove mistaken. Why, indeed, should entrepreneurs be more successful than scientists in their attempts to invent new knowledge? The commonest experience of both is to see their conjectures refuted, in the laboratory or the experimental arena of the market.

Then the valuation made at the end of the trading period is not what was expected at its beginning; and this contrast between outcome and expectation defines what Professor Shackle terms a resolutional profit. Note that a resolutional profit is defined not as an increase in net worth, but as a departure from an increase written into the budget. Such an outcome, being contrary to expectations, is, in Shackle's terms, surprising. "It would constitute the actual occurrence of something which had been disbelieved in" (Shackle, 1972, p. 419). It thus refutes the hypothesis on which decisions had been based, and calls, not for different action merely, but for a revision of theory. It defines an error, but does not show how to correct it. That, in Professor Shackle's view of human affairs, calls for an activity much less welcome than a fresh decision; for the apparent failure of a theory to accommodate the emerging data exposes us to "the tiresome labour of thought, and the uneasy consciousness of mystery and a threatening unknown" (Shackle, 1967(a), p. 288).

Professor Shackle's psychological argument, as has been observed (Skinner, 1979 and the preceding paper of the present collection), is an unconscious paraphrase of Adam Smith's: successful theories soothe the indolent imagination, and their breakdown occasions an unpleasant surprise, followed by a search, first for some plausible supposition to patch up the defect, and, if that fails, for a new scheme of order which will restore tranquillity. However, he does not develop his theory of theory creation in the context of business decisions; a resolutional profit simply induces a quantitative change within a continuing scheme of action, a change in the expected value of that plan and possibly in the scale of activity and investment. The relationship between the magnitude of such revisions and of the resolutional profit which precipitates them produces a set of elasticity measures, and demonstrates the potential leverage (or "multiplier effect") on the economy of unanticipated outcomes (Shackle, 1972, pp. 419-20).

Such simple reactions, however, imply that the conjectural basis of the refuted expectations requires no more than numerical revision: a simple adjustment to the coefficients of an otherwise unchanged model, which is tolerant of such adjustments (as are so many econometric models). Such revisions may sometimes seem adequate; often they do not — and even if the results can be accommodated in this way, such accommodation may not inspire confidence as a basis for new action. Resolutional profit always calls for some revision of theory, which may be small or large; and a revision of theory entails a novel conjecture. Have we any reason to expect that such a novel conjecture will be forthcoming, and have we any reason to believe that a sequence of such conjectures, in response to a series of refutations, will tend to converge upon the conjectures simultaneously being made by others? If not, then unless somehow the entrepreneurs all guess right first time, it is not easy to see how the economy can work. In conventional equilibrium theory, the trick is to assume that the whole of the experimental process can be carried on in the auctioneer's laboratory (or some other place not always specified) so that the economy does get it right first time; more cautious theorists confine themselves to the question of what an economy would look like if it did get everything right first time. But this trick is an evasion of the central question about a decentralised economy. Can it learn from its mistakes?

Research Programmes

This central question of economics is a central question of the theory of knowledge. Popper's answer is that learning from our mistakes is the only proper basis of scientific knowledge — to which he adds that the process of identifying mistakes and generating fresh conjectures will be carried on most effectively in the critical atmosphere of an open society. A competitive economy, like the competition among scientists, may well prove an effective instrument for exposing mistakes; but the generation of new conjectures presents more of a problem. Since they are products of the imagination, not intuitively perceived fragments of the truth, there appears to be no constraint on their content; and a random search for knowledge is not appealing. (That is not to say that it may not sometimes be as effective as any other kind: different, but compatible arguments for an element of randomness have been put foward by March (1976) and Day (1984).) Is it not possible to find some means of constraining the imagination, both of scientists and entrepreneurs, while not imposing any absolute prohibition on what might appear to be the wildest flights of fancy?

Popper (1972(a), p. 13) himself draws attention to the advantages which scientists normally derive from the existence of a well-defined problem-situation: yet if all knowledge is provisional, and therefore problematical, how do these definitions emerge? Popper recognises the problem: "every test of a theory...must stop at some basic statement or other which *we decide to accept";* these should be "statements about whose acceptance or rejection the various investigators are likely to reach agreement" (Popper, 1972(a), p. 104). However, he chooses to emphasise the permeability of such frameworks rather than their persistence (Popper, 1970, p. 56). For an extensive treatment of the significance of frameworks in the growth of knowledge, we must turn to Lakatos' (1970) discussion of scientific research programmes. A research programme contains a "hard core" of unchallenged propositions which permit many variants; the best example in economics (because it is the easiest to define) is the general equilibrium research programme, which requires the analyst to seek the equilibrium properties of a system of optimising economic agents, in an economy the characteristics of which can otherwise be specified according to the analyst's fancy, provided only that the specification is complete. (As Hahn (1973) has shown, the equilibrium may be defined in terms of theories and policies rather than prices and quantities.)

Such a research programme is not imposed; it gains adherents on the basis of the expectations of those who join, perhaps supplemented by evidence of its apparent success, and may lose adherents for similar reasons. A major attraction is the ease of communication between those who share a single analytical framework and who use similar concepts — though the degree of precision, even within the hard core, should not be exaggerated. Those who do not find the programme congenial may join another, or try to develop one of their own; self-exclusion from an "invisible college" has obvious drawbacks, but may also have advantages, and the outsider may produce a significant contribution to knowledge.

That each of us should operate within the loosely-specified constraints of a "research programme" is probably an inevitable consequence of the confrontation between our bounded rationality and the myriad interconnections of the universe; our imagination has to be constrained in order to be effective. As G. K. Chesterton remarked, "a man must be orthodox upon most things, or he will never even have time to preach his own heresy". Organisations too need their own orthodoxy if they are to keep within a single scheme of action the variety of people that they need to make them effective. A part of this orthodoxy, in organisations of any size, is likely to be something that may be called a corporate strategy, which attempts to specify the criteria (some of which may be in qualitative terms) which are to be used in evaluating opportunities for new business. The classic discussion is by Ansoff (1965).

For our purposes research programmes and corporate strategies have the following merits. First, they ensure that if the first hypothesis was in the correct general area, there is a good chance that future hypotheses will be less readily refuted. Second, they promote a degree of harmony between the ideas and actions of different individuals, and even a certain predictability about the ideas and actions of groups with other research programmes or strategies. They facilitate the identification of people and of organisations with complementary and with rival interests, thus offering a partial solution to the problems identified by Richardson, and providing a basis for formal or informal arrangements which might also help to solve them. There can, however, be no guarantee that either will not break down; a string of successes or of failures is not conclusive. Pilkingtons, for example, encountered repeated and expensive failures before they produced a workable — and highly profitable — float glass process: these failures might well have deterred less resolute entrepreneurs, and would very probably have led to the abandonment of the project had it been dependent on external finance.

Research programmes represent the kind of spontaneous order which seems, on the record, to promote the growth of usable and coherent scientific knowledge. Similarly constrained imagination appears to have similar merits in helping organisations (which embody more elements of spontaneous order than their formal descriptions often suggest) and economies to discover and exploit new knowledge. But if our knowledge consists of hypotheses which, however well corroborated, might yet prove false, it would be absurd to expect guarantees of success or of coherence. Indeed, it is not difficult to see how a research programme or strategy, the success of which depends in part on the selection of relationships to be investigated, might be brought to ruin by the reinforced neglect of other relationships which at some unsuspected point prove crucial. Lakatos argues that research programmes degenerate rather than collapse, but Kuhn's (1962, 1970) theory of scientific progress, to which Lakatos was in part reacting, postulates the overthrow of a ruling paradigm when repeated failures to find unrefuted applications of its central concepts accumulate to produce a crisis. Repeated failures to find a profitable application of a particular corporate strategy, despite all attempts at amendment by the exercise of constrained imagination, may similarly lead to crisis, and the disintegration of the coalition which was constructed on the expectation of its success. The old theories can no longer be made to support credible conjectures which yield expectational profit.

Profit, Expectations and Coherence   **31**

Breakdown

We may imagine two ways in which this situation may arise. In the first, an enterprising organisation encounters a string of experimental failures, and is faced with the apparent need to find a new basis for its business, with all that this implies for intra-organisational (and extra-organisational) relationships and the reconstruction of a viable coalition. In the second, an organisation which has settled into a comfortable set of routines, buttressed by a theory (possibly ill-formulated) of business success which serves to soothe the indolent imaginations of its managers, realises, gradually or suddenly, that these routines are failing to produce their accustomed results. Resolutional losses appear.

Now the failure of well-corroborated routines through outside disturbance is an essential feature of Schumpeter's theory of development. The theories which maintain the stability of input prices and thus enable entrepreneurs to calculate their expectational profits are subverted by the innovations which that stability facilitates. Innovation destroys the procedural rationality of the circular flow, and in doing so makes impossible the calculation which is necessary for the planning of new enterprises. Entrepreneurial imagination is no longer productively constrained, and finds no way of discriminating between the multitude of possible sequels of any new venture, no way of bringing the possibilities to a focus, no way of calculating any kind of plausible expectational profit, no way of recognising any incentive to action. Therefore no action is taken; and the innovative boom degenerates into depression.

The collapse of confidence which marks the Schumpeterian depression is remarkably similar in character and in its effects to the failures which Professor Shackle has consistently argued are at the heart of Keynes' theory of unemployment. Its causes, however, are very different. Shackle's (1972, Chapter 37) argument is based on the impossibility of foreknowledge, and the consequent impossibility of any calculable basis for investment. Savings represent the postponement of consumption, but savers do not wish to commit themselves to any particular form or timing of this postponed consumption. For the economy to be in balance, no more resources must be devoted to current consumption than are required to meet current demand; therefore, as long as net saving is positive, some resources must be allocated to future demand, by creating the capital stock necessary to meet it. But no one can know what will be the pattern of future demand, and therefore no one can know what outfit of capital will be appropriate. The amount and pattern of investment depends on the imagination of entrepreneurs; but, in the absence of futures markets, the conjectures from which they compute their expectational profits (or the marginal efficiency of capital) cannot be tested for several years.

These expectational profits may, however, be revised, on the basis of whatever new data or new ideas may be deemed relevant. The more conscious are entrepreneurs of the flimsiness of their conjectures, the more susceptible they are likely to be to anything which appears to cast doubt upon them. Particular reliance, Keynes (1937) argued, may be placed on what appear to be the opinions of others who might be thought either wiser or better informed: the state of long-run expectations is in considerable measure a reflection of that mysterious but crucial thing called "business confidence" — a proposition, incidentally, given some emphasis (in his usual unemphatic way) by Marshall. Investment plans are thus liable to be revised, in either direction, long

32   Journal of Economic Studies 12,1/2

before it is possible to calculate any resolutional profit. Upward revisions may not cause too much difficulty, since resource constraints will limit what can be accomplished (though one should not be complacent about the possibilities); but downward revisions may leave very few projects which show an expectational profit — either because the appraisals generally record an expectational loss, or because there seems to be no adequate theory on which to base any appraisal at all. The calculations which Schumpeter deemed essential to entrepreneurial action cannot be made. "We simply do not know" (Keynes, 1937, p. 214).

Despite these similarities, there is a crucial difference between Schumpeter's analysis and that which Professor Shackle attributes to Keynes. It is the difference between systematic and kaleidic effects. As in Kuhn's theory of scientific revolutions, the collapse of order in Schumpeter's model is a necessary stage in the growth of knowledge — though it must be recognised that in Kuhn's formulation it is the decay of an orderly paradigm which provides the incentive for novel conjectures, whereas for Schumpeter the novel conjectures destroy the order. But for Shackle and Keynes, however, collapse can occur at any time, in response to any exogenous shock; since expectations can have no secure foundations, any event which causes us to enquire about the foundations is potentially destructive of order.

This difference is encapsulated in the contrasting relationships between business cycles and unemployment. Schumpeter explains unemployment by his theory of the business cycle; Keynes explains the phases of the business cycle — which are not closely integrated — by applying a general theory of unemployment. If Keynes, in Professor Shackle's (1972, p. 429) phrase, developed an economics of disorder, Schumpeter argued that disorder was an inevitable stage in the movement to a new kind of order, embodying more effective knowledge.

The establishment of this new order, embodying the knowledge generated by the wave of innovation, requires a process very different from the creative destruction to which Schumpeter gave such attention; entrepreneurial disruption must be complemented by reintegration. "The economic system needs rallying before it can go forward again; its value system needs reorganising" (Schumpeter, 1934, p. 217). Who is to reorganise it? Those who were competent to manage the routines of the circular flow are disoriented, and in need of guidance (p. 79); but the innovators themselves are no less dependent on already-established values to provide the correct basis for those accurate calculations without which enterprise is impossible (pp. 235-6). Yet we are assured that the necessary reintegration will take place (p. 243). How far Schumpeter's belief in the ability of the market economy to achieve something approximating to a competitive general equilibrium was founded in his admiration for Walras and how far it depended on some kind of empiricism need not be discussed here. What we are offered is a combination of theoretical necessity (p. 243) and situational determinism (p. 40). His argument for equilibration is open — as his theory of innovation is not — to Richardson's criticisms of competitive theory; it is also incompatible with a Popperian view of knowledge. A powerful critique of this element in the Schumpeterian system has recently been offered by Day (1984), whose conclusion that "the whole idea of an equilibrium is fundamentally incompatible with wise behaviour in an unfathomable world" (p. 68) clearly aligns him with Professor Shackle.

Now this objection to Schumpeter's use of equilibrium does more than cast doubt upon his theory of business cycles. It threatens to undermine his theory of innovation.

Profit, Expectations and Coherence **33**

For unless the economy is in a state of equilibrium which embodies true knowledge, then the "accurate calculations" on which entrepreneurs depend turn out to be no more than examples of the "pretty, polite techniques" for hiding our ignorance of which Keynes (1937, p. 215) was so scornful.

Progress and Coherence
Is innovation, then, like investment, a matter of animal spirits, subject to kaleidic change? In part, it must surely be so — as must, for similar reasons, the growth of knowledge to which it is related. Conjectures necessarily go beyond the evidence; the more potentially fruitful they are, the slighter their apparent support. As Professor Shackle has argued for so long, we create possible futures in our imagination. Yet is is perhaps fortunate that most of us, most of the time, have no wish to exploit, or even to face "the teasing of mystery and doubt" (Shackle, 1967(a), p. 288) but seek protection in existing theory. Just as essential nutrients can be poisonous if taken to excess, so may a multitude of diverse conjectures lead not to the growth of knowledge but its disintegration. Constructive imagination requires permeable constraints. Coherence and progress, in both science and the economy, appear to be dependent on a kind of loosely-organised disorder — a mixture of collaboration and competition, within a framework which is normally accepted but open to challenge at any time, and always subject to unsuspected, and sometimes demoralising, shocks. It is perhaps not surprising that we have no very satisfactory models of either.

References
Ansoff, H. I., *Corporate Strategy*, New York, McGraw-Hill, 1965.
Casson, M., *The Entrepreneur: An Economic Theory*, Oxford, Martin Robertson, 1982.
Day, R. H., "Disequilibrium Economic Dynamics", *Journal of Economic Behaviour and Organisation*, Vol. 5, 1984.
Hahn, F. H., *On the Notion of Equilibrium in Economics*, Cambridge, Cambridge University Press, 1973.
Keynes, J. M., "The General Theory of Employment", *Quarterly Journal of Economics*, Vol. 51, 1937.
Kirzner, I. M., *Competition and Entrepreneurship*, Chicago, University of Chicago Press, 1973.
Kirzner, I. M., *Method, Process and Austrian Economics*, Lexington, Massachusetts, D. C. Heath, 1982.
Kuhn, T. S., *The Structure of Scientific Revolutions*, Chicago, University of Chicago Press, 1st ed. 1962, 2nd ed. 1970.
Lakatos, I., "Falsification and the Methodology of Scientific Research Programmes", in I. Lakatos and A. Musgrave (Eds.), *Criticism and the Growth of Knowledge*, Cambridge, Cambridge University Press, 1970.
March, J. G., "The Technology of Foolishness", in J. G. March and J. P. Olsen, *Ambiguity and Choice in Organizations*, Universitetsforlaget, reprinted in D. S. Pugh (Ed.), *Organization Theory*, Harmondsworth, Middlesex, Penguin, 1976.
Nelson, R. R. and Winter, S. G., *An Evolutionary Theory of Economic Change*, Cambridge, Massachusetts, Harvard University Press, 1982.
Popper, K. R., "Normal Science and its Dangers", in I. Lakatos and A. Musgrave (Eds.), *Criticism and the Growth of Knowledge*, Cambridge, Cambridge University Press, 1970.
Popper, K. R., *The Logic of Scientific Discovery*, sixth impression, London, Hutchinson, 1972(a).
Popper, K. R., *Objective Knowledge*, Oxford, Oxford University Press, 1972(b).
Richardson, G. B., *Information and Investment*, Oxford, Oxford University Press, 1960.
Richardson, G. B., "The Organisation of Industry", *Economic Journal*, Vol. 82, 1972.
Schumpeter, J. A., *The Theory of Economic Development*, Cambridge, Massachusetts, Harvard University Press, 1934.
Skinner, A. S., "Adam Smith: An Aspect of Modern Economics", *Scottish Journal of Political Economy*, Vol. 26, 1979.

[8]

How Economists can Accept Shackle's Critique of Economic Doctrines without Arguing Themselves out of their Jobs

by Peter E. Earl and Neil M. Kay
University of Tasmania and Heriot-Watt University, Edinburgh, respectively

Introduction

The methodology of mainstream neoclassical economics deals with knowledge deficiency problems in a deterministic manner and as "refinements to the theory of economic action rather than rudiments of it" (Coddington, 1975, p. 151). For Shackle (1972), such an approach to the subject is unacceptable, since its deterministic nature is fundamentally at odds with his argument that, to be meaningful, choice must make a difference to the unfolding skein of events. Central to his view of the nature of choice is clearly a rejection of the concept of equilibrium and of the assumptive fiction that co-ordination is achieved, on a once-and-for-all basis, via the costless efforts of an omniscient auctioneer. If choices are meaningful in Shackle's sense, the skein of events contains many surprises, many incentives for agents to rethink their views of things and change their behaviour. For example, the workings of a multiplier process falsify expectations and these surprises may then spark off euphoric or depressing super-multiplier effects. In markets for financial assets, "bulls" and "bears" cannot both be right in their predictions, while in product markets the creative exercise of marketing and research and development personnel's imaginations may continuously send out waves and backwashes in keeping with Schumpeterian notions of creative destruction. If one accepts Shackle's alternative starting point, one must sacrifice notions pertaining to "given" preferences and technologies and, with them, the stable functions upon which IS-LM macro models (see Shackle, 1982(a)) and orthodox value theory are built.

Few economists have been prepared to begin their analyses by focusing on the origins of choosers' beliefs and how they change, and then to use these choice-theoretic foundations as a basis for the study of non-equilibrium dynamics. Instead, the received wisdom has been that Shackle's contribution is eloquently presented but unduly nihilistic and, ultimately, self-denying. This article considers the validity of the conventional charge against Shacklean work by asking whether unpredictability and novelty are destructive of economic theorising in general, or whether we can make sensible statements about a world in which Shacklean notions of surprise and uncertainty are pervasive, even paramount. Our position is that it is, in fact, possible to reconcile a lack of faith in the usefulness of much model building based on a deterministic or probabilistic view of the world, with a belief that it is possible to develop useful explanatory theories of economic behaviour. Central to this reconciliation is a Shackle-inspired view of how one should see the role of the economists, and it is to this that we shall first proceed.

Predictability and Policy Formation
It was very much with Shackle's (1967(a), 1972, 1973(c), 1974(a)) "fundamentalist" interpretation of Keynes' vision in mind that Coddington (1983, p. 61) made the following observation about the kind of Pandora's box opened for economic science by "root and branch" adherents to a subjectivist position:

> If subjectivist logic is followed to the point of becoming convinced that there is nothing for economists to do but to understand certain (praxiological) concepts, then the only problem that remains is that of subjugating one's conscience long enough to draw one's salary in exchange for imparting this piece of wisdom. One could, of course, having got into this state of mind, spend a good deal of time and energy in trying to convince those who engage in macroeconomics, econometric model building, general equilibrium theory and so on, of the folly of their ways. But, that task accomplished, there would be nothing left but for the whole profession to shut up shop.

A similar stance concerning the policy contribution of fundamentalist Keynesians is taken by Cross (1982), who characterises, via a "non-diagram", the position of those economists who emphasise the unpredictability of events. The "non-diagram" shows a point in space depicting the current configuration of variables, with arrows leading off in all directions to depict what may happen next; there are no lines representing particular functional relationships.

It is by no means obvious that the pursuit of a subjectivist position has to be quite so "indiscriminately destructive" (Coddington, 1983, p. 50) as it is often taken to be. In particular, it is not obvious that, if one allows the future to be unknowable before its time and undetermined by past events, one has necessarily to jump to the polar opposite from perfect foresight and proclaim that we can say nothing about anything. The Shacklean perspective certainly does involve a rejection of the notion that economists should seek to make *single-line* predictions of what *will* happen. However, it does not deny that an economist might be able to contribute to the process of policy formation by providing insights on the *range of things* that *could* happen. To be sure, economists might frequently be surprised by what does happen in actuality, but they may be serving a useful role if they are less bemused and make less costly errors of advice concerning economic matters than would someone who lacked their special expertise.

It would appear that the economist who has accepted the Shacklean perspective can contribute to the process of policy formation in a variety of ways, all of which have a good deal in common with the functions served by those strategic thinkers in large corporations whom Jefferson (1983) has characterised as "scenario planners". The economist can actively attempt:

(1) to *highlight* the areas of uncertainty and delimit the bounds of unknowledge, given the existing structure of the system, so that the policy makers can have some appreciation of what disasters they might have to cope with or what opportunities they might be able to grasp (providing they make advance preparations) if they implement particular changes;

(2) to *propose improvements* to the design of the system so that it is better able to cope with dangerous threats and creative opportunities as they materialise;

(3) to *discover* ways of modifying or eliminating the incidence of surprises in the environment.

The economist seeking to undertake these tasks has only to admit defeat in situations where he is unable to discriminate between rival possibilities with a satisfactory degree of confidence in his own judgemental processes, so that far too many things seem to be equally difficult to disbelieve as potential sequels to policy choices. (Of course, how many believable sequels are "far too many" to be tolerable will vary according to how open-minded and able to live with the reality of uncertainty the economist is and/or who his paymaster happens to be.) The obvious question that follows from this is: "How often should we expect the utter defeat of such an economist, who faces up to Shackle's vision of the scheme of things and does not shunt knowledge problems aside in a cavalier manner in order to make tightly specified predictions?". The answer is inevitably uncertain, but in the following sections of this article we hope to provide a basis for concluding that quite often the Shacklean economist may end up with something constructive to say.

Surprise, Uncertainty and Emergence
Quite how unpredictable the subject matter of economics appears to be will vary according to the level of abstraction at which the economist attempts to make sense of it. Economic sub-systems, like smoke particles in a demonstration of Brownian Motion, may be moving around in a manner which seems to lack any pattern, yet higher-level economic sub-systems, like a puff of smoke drifting through the air, may be more stable and manageable and consequently explicable. For example, one could well imagine that an economist might end up "failing to see the wood for the trees" if he sought to arrive at conclusions about possible sales in a market by looking at the behaviour of individuals who were each adapting in a complex manner to their own, individually perceived views of the environment. However, if the economist confined himself to market-level data (in the manner of, say, Houthakker and Taylor, 1970) he might succeed in avoiding bewilderment in respect of possible future developments in that market.

In other disciplines, there has been considerable debate from an instrumentalist standpoint about the relative merits of reductionism and holism (cf., Koestler and Smithies, 1969; and Hofstadter, 1979, pp. 310-36). This is a debate from which economists have generally excused themselves, despite the emerging crisis in the profession. We view this as unfortunate, since the issues this debate raises may help indicate real opportunities for economic analysis and scenario construction.

Despite its professed concern with developing predictive models, traditional economic analysis remains, in principle if not always in practice, firmly and exclusively reductionist in treating as axiomatic the notion that the behaviour of the world can be described from the bottom upwards, in terms of aggregates. Shackle has rightly argued that the legitimacy of this approach is highly questionable, particularly in the context of attempts to understand speculative markets where traders are trying to outguess each other's behaviour. However, the important point to be recognised in this connection is not so much that widespread crowd behaviour in the market place undermines traditional economic analysis, but that the "problem" of non-decomposability can be a starting point for *novel questions* and possib.e solutions. Thus chemists do not have constantly to bear Heisenburg's Uncertainty Principle in mind, ecologists do not have to incorporate physio-chemical relations in their models, and a gravitational model of the solar system can safely ignore the complexity and variety of the natural world on earth.

Such a holistic perspective has already been adopted by structuralists and systems theorists in their model building in the other social sciences, yet most economists have tended to avoid anything which threatens "bottom up", aggregative models and decomposability. Neoclassical economists seem to be prepared to confine themselves to the questions which suit their methodology instead of displaying a willingness to embrace alternative methodologies that "reach the parts their own cannot reach". But one *can* grasp the nettle of indecomposability by employing non-reductionist methodologies — for example, we have made attempts to show how systems or structuralist approaches can provide insights on resource allocation questions that recognise the pervasiveness of unpredictability and uncertainty at lower levels. This work has encompassed consumer budgeting processes and the evolution of preferences in a social setting (Earl, 1983(a), (b); 1984(a)), corporate and organisational evolution and innovation (Earl, 1984(b); Kay, 1979, 1982, 1984), and monetary policy (Dow and Earl, 1982, 1984). Within these hierarchical research programmes it becomes apparent that, at higher levels, new questions, concepts and issues emerge, displacing those associated with lower levels. It is, therefore, only natural that new theoretical approaches and models should also emerge, displacing those associated with lower levels.

Scenario Writing with Keynesian Uncertainty
Even after attempting to analyse problems at a variety of levels, the economist may, nonetheless, still feel that it is desirable (for example, in order to avoid oversights and spot potential for kaleidic change) to try to understand behaviour in the context of unpredictable change at the level at which such change takes place. If this level concerns that of individual decision makers, the economist should not be unduly perturbed if he happens to recall Keynes' famous comment to his critics on what he meant by "uncertainty":

> The sense in which I am using the term is that in which the prospect of a European war is uncertain, or the price of copper and the rate of interest twenty years hence, or the obsolescence of a new invention or the position of private wealth owners in the social system in 1970. About these matters there is no scientific basis on which to form any calculable probability whatever. We simply do not know. (Keynes, 1937, p. 214; see also Keynes, 1936, pp. 161-2 concerning "animal spirits" and investment behaviour.)

Shackle's rejection of expected utility theory and his emphasis on the flimsy expectational foundations of many decisions was, of course, both affected by, and is often juxtaposed with, this passage. It is easy to read from it the suggestion that people often have to take decisions while lacking *any reasons* for believing less in some possible sequels than in others. In such situations people are unable to form useful potential surprise curves, let alone probability distributions, and even Shackle's theory of deliberation in the face of uncertainty breaks down.

But all is not lost in such contexts. The possibility that decision makers may be unable to choose rationally does not necessarily ensure that the *economist* cannot offer reasoned advice which concludes that wide ranges of conjectured sequels should not be taken seriously. In fact, the recent work of Heiner (1983) leads us to the view that the behaviour of economic agents may be *less* surprising (at least to an economist familiar with contributions to the literature of behavioural theory such as those by Simon (1957, 1969, 1979) and Steinbruner (1974, chapter 3)), the greater the uncertainty with which they have to deal.

The basis for Heiner's rather paradoxical-sounding contention is as follows. Suppose that decision makers are very highly informed about the structures of the choice problems. If this is the case, they can confidently select complex, tailor-made solutions to them, on the basis of very detailed chains of reasoning. The economist trying to comprehend and anticipate their behaviour will not be able to obtain, far less handle, all the idiosyncratic information enjoyed by the multitude of his subjects. Consequently, it will seem to him that the successive choices of individuals lack consistency. Now consider situations where decision makers face choice-problems of great complexity and uncertainty: here, they will have no basis for choosing *particular* complex solutions. Rather (as Keynes, 1937, p. 214, himself was quick to recognise), their choices will tend to be made at a rather high level of abstraction, using tried and trusted *general* "recipes for success". The repeated use by individuals of such "programmes", for dealing with situations in which they "simply do not know", will enable the economist to discern some degree of consistency between their successive choices, which may provide a basis for fairly confident advice about what they could and could not reasonably be expected to try to do. In so far as the economist has access to resources for fieldwork investigations of how his subjects may be segmented into groups with common sets of programmes for dealing with complex problems, he should be able to construct useful scenarios about the bounds to possible market-level behaviour.

Choice environments that preclude "rational" choice clearly pose major problems for orthodox forms of economic analysis. However, it would appear from the foregoing discussion that such problems can be overcome by making a switch in methodology in the direction of behavioural research and studying the procedures decision makers actually use for coping with Keynesian uncertainty.

Organisational Strategies for Coping with Surprise and Uncertainty
It might well be argued that a knowledge of decision-making units' repertoires of action programmes is of limited use to the scenario-writing economist who cannot successfully anticipate the environmental shocks with which the decision makers will have to deal. Even the most creative scenario writers may on occasion recognise that they are being asked to deal with environments that are full of surprises — actual events which they fail to consider as possibilities. However, an inability to specify or define stimuli in advance does not necessarily mean that the economist cannot draw up scenarios concerning how particular systems may fare, and which policy measures might usefully change their fortunes. The economist should at least be able to classify and order environments in terms of key characteristics — for example, stability/turbulence, static technology/dynamic technology — before considering ways in which the decision makers might seek to cope with different patterns. Even though their individual

events may be unpredictable, different kinds of turbulent environments may display particular regularities or patterns, signalling the need for appropriate system design or procedure if the decision maker is to operate and survive in his own particular turbulent environment. Thus although the economist may, like his subjects, be unable to predict the unpredictable, at a higher level of abstraction it may be possible to expect the unexpected, as Boulding (1968) has suggested.

The task of the economist preparing for surprise and reacting to it in respect of environments that are classified in one way or another as "surprise rich" may be likened to that of policy makers called upon to deal with aspects of mental illness. People with mental disorders may act unpredictably and thereby seem a menace to the rest of the community; their unpredictability may actually be the only consistent feature of their personalities. But individual societies still manage to evolve *specific* social, legal, psychiatric and police systems and procedures to deal with such problems. Likewise, while speculative behaviour in financial markets may be directionally unpredictable, economic advisors standing on the sidelines may still be able to devise policies — such as "lifeboat" buffer loan agreements between the Central Bank and major clearing banks, and deposit insurance schemes — to deal with the kinds of problems, such as the failure of financial intermediaries, in which it is prone to result.

The economist may have a good deal to learn from the study of how organisations, like societies, develop devices and methods for dealing with surprising events. One method is to design the system deliberately so as to enhance its prospects for adapting to change in a flexible manner. Burns and Stalker (1961) explicitly recognise Shackle's work on potential surprise as a precursor to their own which is concerned with the appropriateness of different organisation designs for coping with alternative environments. In the light of case study investigations, they argue that "organic systems" (characterised by continual adjustment and re-definition of tasks, "authority" residing in expertise rather than hierarchical position, and predominantly lateral rather than vertical communication and delegation of authority and control) tend to be more appropriate for rapidly changing conditions that generate fresh problems and unforeseen circumstances. By way of contrast, a mechanistic system (characterised by precise specialisation and division of labour and vertical hierarchical relationships emphasising superior/subordinate responsibilities) may be more suitable for stable conditions. Child (1977, p. 90) sees matrix management systems (discussed in detail in Child, 1977, chapter 4) adopted by many modern firms as potentially enjoying many of the advantages of the "organic" system described by Burns and Stalker. Such findings have an obvious significance for the economist called upon to comment on a possible rescue plan for a "lame duck" corporation: if it has a mechanistic structure and the environment is turbulent, the chances of saving it may be slim in the absence of a major restructuring operation, and established practices may be something the existing personnel would find very hard to abandon.

Another broad strategy commonly employed for coping with turbulent environments is to devise methods of localising and limiting the danger posed by external threats, even if the source or form of the threat cannot even be approximately specified in advance. If individual sub-systems can be decoupled from the overall system without threatening the latter's integrity or survival, then this may form the basis of system design in such environments (and, if it does not, the economist may consider proposing incentives, regulatory changes, or direct intervention to redesign the system accordingly). Following Simon (1969), we would expect that, after a period of environmental turbulence, the surviving systems would be found to be those that had exhibited a good deal of decomposability. However, since decoupling is not without its costs, we would only expect to find organisations adopting decoupling strategies, in areas where previously they had sought the benefits of integration, at the time of the onset or expectation of a period of turbulence.

The following rather disparate collection of examples should help clarify what we mean by decoupling, as well as indicating how common it is. First, we note that in some cases the development of revolutionary political parties has been characterised by the adoption of a cellular system, in which small groups of activists operate independently without clear knowledge of the identity of members associated with other cells. Even if one cell is uncovered and broken up, their self-contained and limited knowledge means that the survival of other cells may not be directly threatened by exposure. The development of modular production systems is a related strategy in so far as it facilitates decoupling and reassembly: the progressive upgrading of a system of hi-fi "separates" (as distinct from a "music-centre") and the adaptability of a module-based degree course are cases in point, for they permit the decision maker to change direction in response to changing circumstances as time unfolds; he or she is not locked into an inflexible strategy. The conglomerate strategy may provide similar advantages in the managerially controlled firm: the decomposability of a strategy based on unrelated product markets means that both divestment of old divisions and formation of new divisions may be undertaken in isolation without strategists having to be overly concerned with any relation of the part to the whole. Thus the conglomerate may exploit the flexibility and adaptability features of modular design. It is commonplace to argue that a diverse collection of product markets helps generate earnings stability by averaging out the performances of various differently fluctuating but ongoing activities. Less widely appreciated, however, is the fact that the decomposability of a conglomerate firm means that if any part of its operations is threatened — say, with obsolescence — the unrelatedness of the part with the whole limits the possibility that the rest of the system also will be threatened. Thus the conglomerate may limit the damage posed by external threats to sub-systems, just as in the case of the political cell system.

It may seem paradoxical to identify desirable survival properties associated with some decomposable systems, in view of our argument that non-decomposability may be an important feature of economic systems. In fact, the conglomerate is a special case, and usually decomposability will only have limited applicability in its description: for example, the absence of product-market linkages between groups may facilitate decoupling of individual divisions, while the existence of linkages between product markets within divisions may inhibit decoupling of individual products. The conglomerate is typically a complex multi-level organisation whose system description may alter as we move between levels.

Further, the conglomerate is only one type of diversified system that may be set up — with or without the participation of the economic policy maker — to deal with turbulent environments. For example, Rumelt (1974) describes the development of the "related-linked" strategy which has recently become significant in US industry. An example of this kind of strategy would be a manufacturer of industrial clothing who diversified into ladies' clothes and then into toiletries and cosmetics. In the first move, there are likely to be technological links (shared production techniques, R & D, etc) while the second move is more likely to exploit marketing links (e.g., shared distribution channels, advertising and image). Thus the firm is built around a series of market or technological links between groups of products and yet no single link dominates the corporate strategy. While decoupling may be inhibited due to these linkages, the diversified nature of such a strategy should, as in the conglomerate, help to localise and limit most external threats (see Kay, 1982, 1984, for further discussion).

Organisation design is, therefore, an important device for dealing with unstable and unpredictable environments. We would hope that, as he seeks to piece together scenarios and policy advice, organisational matters are rarely far from the economist's mind (or, for that matter, the corporate planner's). Consider, for example, how monetary policy acquires an altogether different complexion once it is seen not merely in terms of debates about the appropriate type and size of money supply target, but also from the perspective concerning the structure of links between the financial institutions involved in the process of credit creation. Once one recognises the layered nature of modern financial systems — where one bank's assets are another's liabilities, and where scrambles for liquidity can be self-cumulating — it becomes less easy to countenance the withdrawal of lender-of-last-resort facilities as a means to achieving a monetary base target. The organisational perspective thus helps in the generation of cautionary scenarios, yet it may help also to provide justifiable grounds for optimism — for example, a layered financial system *might* turn out to be sectorally segmented in a way which ensured, say, that industrial production and employment were largely immune from a property market crash (see further, Dow and Earl, 1982, chapters 11 and 12).

Organisations seeking to maintain flexibility when confronting a turbulent environment have yet other defence mechanisms that protect and insulate them from unpleasant shocks: they can hold cash, engage in multiple sourcing of inputs, lease rather than buy, and avoid long-term contracts. These kinds of behaviour can be anticipated in alert organisations and promoted in sleepy or impulsive ones. As Loasby (1967) warns, flexibility and adaptability may be impaired if formal planning leads to an over-enthusiastic commitment of resources; it may be rational to defer some decisions until the future unfolds, and devices such as the above may enhance responsiveness in unpredictable environments. One would expect organisations confronting treacherous but foggy landscapes either to make tentative explorations in a variety of directions (see Waddington, 1977) and avoid crucial, large-scale experiments until they can see how the land lies, or, like Eisenhower, to utilise the "delay principle" (see Ansoff, 1979, p. 53) and defer decisions altogether until all essential information is available or the fog has cleared. The economist should not be ashamed to offer policy advice that involves similar kinds of behaviour: procrastination can have its efficiency advantages.

Anticipating Surprise
The previous section was concerned with ways in which economists, like economic systems themselves, may seek to prepare for surprises and react to them. The decision-making systems were those portrayed as passive in the face of external developments; they did not actively attempt to change or eliminate unpredictable developments in

42   Journal of Economic Studies 12,1/2

their environments, though their strategies might facilitate the generation and development of benign surprises internally (e.g., a firm's structure may be such that it creates a conducive atmosphere for R & D). Our essential theme was that system design can be adjusted to cope better with creative opportunities and dangerous threats as they materialise.

However, another line of attack is to focus on policies to modify or eliminate the incidence of surprises. For example, cartelisation and collusive or co-operative behaviour are means by which economic systems may be able to pre-empt future dangers of competitive attack. Cyert and March (1963) describe the process of neutralising competitors' threat as one of creating a "negotiated environment". Uncertainty, surprise and threat are bargained away. Much of the descriptive literature on monopoly behaviour can be interpreted in this fashion, displaying a richer and more complex decision-making process than is typically contained in neoclassical models of monopoly and oligopoly. By recognising the prevalence of such attempts to preclude surprises, the economist is not merely able to narrow down the range of possible occurrences in the contexts in which the attempts are taking place, but is also able, once more, to pursue similar approaches in the kinds of policies he recommends.

In fact, at the level of government policy making, many proposals can be interpreted as intentionally reducing the possibility of unpleasant or destabilising surprises. Friedman's development of monetarism can also be, at least partly, interpreted as intending to reduce the surprise potential of environments faced by economic decision makers. Friedman sees stable monetary growth as a means of engendering confidence and predictability by eliminating this area as a major source of possible surprise and instability. (However, his failure to examine the structure of relationships between monetary institutions results in his blindness to the possibility that monetary base control could actually run counter to the stability of the monetary system.) Indexation and indicative planning are two other policy measures that have been at least partially justified in similar fashion in so far as they deal with potential sources of ignorance and uncertainty.

Successful pre-emptive policy "strikes" are, of course, contingent upon creative thinking about what could happen. It is here that many economists would tend to highlight the nihilistic message in Shackle's critique of deterministic model building; for he seems to suggest that, although creative thinking can only take place within the limited set of reference points that decision makers *already* have at their disposal, the number of new possibilities which they could nonetheless dream up is immense. In his most recent book, Shackle makes this point particularly vivid by likening the reference points to alphabetic elements and then noting (1979(a), p. 21) that a small set of alphabetic elements can generate a huge dictionary. From this standpoint, it would seem unreasonable to hope that the economist (or the corporate planner) would be very successful in trying to anticipate the creative thoughts of decision makers. There would appear much scope for missing ideas that came to their minds and for becoming paranoid about those that did not (the latter would be a stronger possibility the more that decision makers actually behaved in a programmed manner and themselves avoided trying to dream up possible scenarios before choosing).

A possible way round this problem emerges in the recent work of Ansoff (1979), who has developed an analysis of corporate response to strategic surprises (novel, unexpected, rapidly developing environmental threats having a potentially significant effect on the organisation's performance) based partly on the earlier work of Cyert and March. He argues that many potential strategic surprises could be avoided or better dealt with if organisations develop techniques to recognise and act on "weak signals" from the environment. Ansoff's work implies that the degree of potential surprise associated with many developments could be reduced if devices for recognising and amplifying weak signals (early hints and clues) can be introduced. The analyst might then be more confidently able to pin down the channels down which creative thinking could be proceeding. For example, Ansoff points out that in the early 1940s there was a general sense of expectation of important break-throughs and developments in electronics; the early post-war period made it clear to experts that the break-through would materialise as the transistor; and so on. Recognition of weak signals at an early stage would allow the organisation to prepare for subsequent development, just as exploration can be made safer with the aid of scouting parties.

Ansoff's analysis is interesting, though he does not really deal with the problem that weak signals of impending shocks are easier to identify with the benefit of hindsight. *Ex ante* anticipation of future shocks requires sorting out significant signals from background noise, and this trick is not easily achieved. For example, it is easy to detect weak signals in the aerospace industry in the early post-war period to the effect that the future of commercial aviation lay in VTOL and SST developments, less easy to detect that jumbo jet travel would soon dominate.

Cognitive and Strategic Barriers to Kaleidic Thoughts and Actions

Shackle's emphasis on the potential for discontinuous shifts in economic systems — potential which arises from the creative powers of human minds — seems to rest uneasily with the inertia that one observes in much individual and organisational behaviour. In some degree, this may be explained by the use of programmed decision methods instead of deliberative approaches to choice; by simple procrastination instead of abrupt reactions to perceived environmental changes; by the existence of constraining long-term contracts (other than those which are so onerous in the face of a disturbance that they involve bankruptcies — see Minsky, 1975); and, more generally, by the existence of various forms of slack which help make the system "shatter-proof" and dampen the effects of disturbances which might otherwise have been amplified (cf., Leijonhufvud, 1973).

In this section we wish to emphasise two further possible explanations of inertia, an appreciation of which may enable the economist better to argue when and where discontinuous shifts of behaviour might, and might not, be reasonably expected.

First we note that decision makers will have strong incentives to resist changes wherever they are dealing with highly integrated systems that are highly specific in their purpose. The costs of change when such systems are threatened with obsolescence will be such as to make worthwhile attempts to force the environment back into conformity with the system's capacities. If such Procrustean efforts fail, of course, the non-decomposability of the obsolete system then guarantees precisely the kind of revolutionary, kaleidic shift discussed in Shackle's work.

For example, for someone who has an old car that is becoming increasingly prone to unreliability, a decision to make a commitment to the purchase of a new one may

44   Journal of Economic Studies 12,1/2

be revolutionary in nature. Often it will follow a long period during which expensive repairs are made to the old car because each time an individual part wears out it threatens to immobilise the car, both physically and as a saleable item. Each repair involves the decision maker in staking his judgemental capabilities on the possibility that further breakdowns are not just around the corner. The business history literature is full of parallel examples of periods of last-ditch stands, followed by revolutionary upheavals (see Earl, 1984(b), chapter 5). An especially pertinent case involving a highly integrated production process concerns the Ford Motor Company at the time of the obsolescence of the Model T. In his attempt to keep the product viable, once he conceded that further price cuts no longer increased market penetration in a profitable manner, Henry Ford reluctantly went against his own principles and advertised it. When eventually production was abandoned and the changeover to the Model A and a general policy of frequent model changes was undertaken, the 18-month disruption involved $200 million losses for Ford, 60,000 workers being laid off in Detroit, with 15,000 machine tools being replaced and another 25,000 totally rebuilt. In the process, too, many of the workers' skills were rendered obsolete in so far as they related to the task idiosyncrasies (cf. Williamson, 1975) of producing the Model T rather than those of coping with assembly-line methods in general. But despite the far-reaching physical upheaval entailed in Ford's belated attempt to match his production system with a more turbulent, styling-dominated market, forces of inertia remained. As Selznick (1957, p. 110) points out, only after World War II was an in-depth reorganisation completed; initially, necessary changes in orientation and in the hitherto lowly status of sales and public relations functions failed to materialise.

The mention of Henry Ford's "principles", and of the difficulties his company had in achieving changes in orientation relates to our second point: the fact that a creative mind can throw up many fantastic new potential hopes and fears, even from a limited collection of existing perspectives, does not mean we should jump to the conclusion that such a mind will deem them *believable* conjectures. Central to Shackle's potential surprise analysis is an assumption that choosers seek to discriminate between rival possible sequels on the basis of how easily they can be disbelieved — that is to say, according to the grounds they can imagine for arguing that events could not happen. In the potentially kaleidic mind a tension therefore exists, between creative processes that open up possibilities and creative processes that, by throwing up possible objections, seek to close off possibilities. In the midst of this there appears to be a problem of infinite regress: objections to possible sequels are themselves possible sequels that must be able to stand up to objections if they are not to be disbelieved.

For his part, Shackle has not, so far as we are aware, devoted much attention to the means by which degrees of disbelief come to be assigned to particular sequels, nor to the infinite regress problem we have just raised. Rather, he has preferred to take potential surprise curves as already existing in the minds of decision makers, though only as tentative constructs, possibly ripe for imaginative revision. This has left the path wide open for critics such as Coddington (1983, chapter 4) who make accusations of nihilism after characterising Shackle's (and other fundamentalist Keynesians') analyses using the ideas of "the spontaneous and erratic workings of individual minds...to drive a wedge between behaviour and circumstances" (Coddington, 1983, p. 53).

A natural counter to this charge, and one which deals with the infinite regress problem, is to argue that assignments of degrees of disbelief can be traced back to a self-imposed hierarchy of *rules* according to which the decision maker organises his view of the world. That is to say, individual minds are to be seen, not as erratic, but as *judgemental systems* for processing creative suggestions. On the surface, behaviour may at times seem without consistency, but it is actually constrained by an underlying set of procedures. If the economist can access the structures of judgemental systems employed by representative members of segments of the decision-making population, he may be able to infer which possibilities they would find unbelievable if they imagined them. Thence he could narrow down the bounds of their possible choices and anticipate, with some degree of confidence, their inertia in particular areas.

This view of the mind as a system of judgemental rules which also generates creative suggestions subject to an existing set of reference perspectives is one which we take from the work of the psychologist George Kelly (1955). Like Shackle, Kelly is at pains to depict choice as a forward-looking, theory-testing exercise, with choices being made amongst images that decision makers construct for themselves. Kelly (1955, p. 59), too, emphasises that people have a finite number of blinkers through which they attempt to make sense of the world. But he goes beyond Shackle when he stresses that an individual's theories are interrelated in ways which are relatively immovable, so that any newly imagined ways of construing events are tested for admissibility (rather like submissions in a courtroom proceeding) against these prior tenets. As he (1955, p. 20) puts it, "the structure we erect is what rules us". New thoughts that threaten to destroy existing expectations will be deemed inadmissible, unless, that is, a failure to admit them would actually clash with the maintenance of expectations that have been assigned an even higher ranking in the person's hierarchy of ideas. (In the latter case, the new ideas would be admitted at the cost of the rejection of the lower level notions that they contradict.)

If a person's expectations and theories are related in this hierarchical manner, with one notion often being used as a judgemental reference point for many others, then the spill-over effects of admitting a particular new notion may be considerable. The situation is rather akin to that which a neoclassical economist would face if he had to give up the notion of maximising behaviour as one of the central, "hard-core" assumptions of his research programme. (Lakatos' 1970, well-known hard core/protective belt separation in his view of *scientific* research programmes is very similar to Kelly's view of the use of a hierarchy of ideas by an *individual* seeking to form expectations in everyday life. In both cases some notions are deemed to have priorities over others, for maintenance in the face of anomalies.) Thus we would expect that the more subordinate implications are attached to a particular notion (or "construct", in Kelly's terms), the more a person will resist accepting new ideas that entail his changing the notion. This has been found to be the case in work by Hinkle (1965) and Crockett and Meisel (1974) where subjects' attitudes were investigated using developments of research techniques pioneered by Kelly. These research techniques (described in detail in Adams-Webber, 1979) could equally well be used by economists seeking to uncover the bounds of their subjects' abilities to believe new notions and thence their resistance to making kaleidic shifts of behaviour (see Earl, 1984(a), for some suggestions of how these techniques might be applied, and some contexts in which they might be particularly revealing).

46   Journal of Economic Studies 12,1/2

In fact, some of these techniques are already in use in market research.

A Kelly-inspired view of expectations does not preclude the notion that people will make Shacklean shifts of outlook as a result of creatively exercising their imaginations. But it does suggest that such changes — and associated changes of outward behaviour — will occur mainly at the sub-system level. Ideas with really dramatic damaging implications for a person's outlook will only be admissible if a *failure* to admit them would, by virtue of the higher level contradictions this entailed, result in even more alarming implications. Otherwise, they will tend to be ruled "out of court" as "unbelievable". Thus, for example, most of us may find it easier to imagine we might select tea instead of coffee, than to imagine we might one day find ourselves in the dole queue (particularly if we are tenured academics) or choose to give up our possessions and opt for a monastic way of life. (What would "the world be coming to" if universities failed to honour academic employment contracts?) Thoughts that contradict our beliefs concerning social institutions or our own self-images will be particularly hard to accept as serious possibilities, for so much of our daily outlook is contingent on these core constructs.

To conclude this section it is instructive to note that Kellian psychologists have analysed thought-disordered schizophrenia as being due to successive attempts by sufferers to introduce decomposability into their judgemental systems. By severing links between ideas, they seek to reduce the implications of expectational falsifications in a surprising world. Unfortunately, such a policy leads to completely inconsistent thinking if applied repeatedly: lacking any anchor points — any principles — for forming beliefs, the sufferer believes one thing one moment, another the next. In his outlook he is as flexible as corporate planners who have sought to deal with the possibility of unpleasant environmental surprises by moving in the direction of a conglomerate activity set or, in the extreme, to becoming simple portfolio investors who only own parts of any production system. Such planners can make rapid and kaleidoscopic changes of activities via the stock market; they are not constrained by linkages when they want to shed interests. But, taken to extremes, strategies that pursue decomposability can result in confusion rather than the ability to deal with surprises. An individual suffering from thought-disordered schizophrenia often finds himself at the mercy of events due to the fluidity in his outlooks. His mind is the prototype of the "spontaneous and erratic" mind in Coddington's critique of subjectivism, while, as Adams-Webber (1979, p. 66, emphasis added) observes, "the experience of such |a person|, in so far as we can imagine it, must seem hopelessly *kaleidoscopic*". Investors, whose eagerness to diversify is on a par with the ability of schizophrenics to take on new perspectives, often encounter analogous problems: the more activities in which they are involved, the less insight they can have into any of them. This, coupled with their reluctance to exploit scope for synergy (or, in the "portfolio investor" extreme, to direct operations at all) means they may be unable to generate performances which match those achieved by specialists, even if the business environments in which they participate are in some degree turbulent (see further, Earl, 1984(b), pp. 115-19).

Conclusion

From the standpoint of conventional economics, it is not easy to see Shackle's emphasis on the centrality of ignorance and uncertainty in economic affairs as providing anything other than a means whereby economists might argue themselves out of their jobs. A Shacklean adherence to a hard line on the non-quantifiable nature of uncertainty and the pervasiveness of ignorance and surprise naturally leads to an emphasis on the unpredictablity of economic behaviour. In turn, recognition of unpredictability subverts the principle and practice of economic model building that has evolved as the accepted basis for modern economic analysis.

From the standpoint of behavioural economics, Shackle's critique of orthodoxy seems to serve a constructive, not nihilistic role. It clears the ground for alternative approaches to pattern finding and theory building by economists, who, we have argued, may use the following escape routes as means to delimit the bounds of possible sequels to particular policy and environmental disturbances:

(1) *holistic* analysis where higher level systems are more stable than sub-systems;

(2) the practical study of *procedures* employed by decision makers as bases for choice in situations of Keynesian uncertainty;

(3) attempts to classify environments by type (e.g., "surprise rich", "surprise poor") and then to analyse the relation between system and environment;

(4) recognition that decision-making units do not simply react to unpredictable change in their environments but may actively develop methods of neutralising their environments, creating predictability, order and control out of potential chaos;

(5) attempts to assess the extent and structure of linkages between physical structures, and between ideas, for these constrain what can be undertaken and thought, and provide a basis for anticipating either inertia or kaleidic shifts and the amplification of disturbances.

The first escape route leaves much or all of the uncertainty behind at lower levels while the remainder may, at best, enable policy makers actively to exploit the opportunities presented by unexpected developments, or at worst, permit a damage limitation exercise. These escape routes all approach the problem laterally rather than directly: instead of attempting to predict the unpredictable, they find devices which permit the uncovering of behaviour relations and patterns in human activity.

References

Adams-Webber, J. R., *Personal Construct Theory: Concepts and Applications,* Chichester, Wiley, 1979.

Ansoff, H. I., *Strategic Management,* London, Macmillan, 1979.

Boulding, K., *Beyond Economics,* Ann Arbor, University of Michigan Press, 1968.

Burns, T. and Stalker, G. M., *The Management of Innovation,* London, Tavistock, 1961.

Child, J., *Organization,* London, Harper and Row, 1977.

Coddington, A., "Creating Semaphore and Beyond", (Review of G. L. S. Shackle: *Epistemics and Economics*), *British Journal for the Philosophy of Science,* Vol. 26, 1975, pp. 151-63.

Coddington, A., *Keynesian Economics: The Search for First Principles,* London, George Allen and Unwin, 1983.

Crockett, W. H. and Meisel, P., "Construct Connectedness, Strength of Disconfirmation and Impression Change", *Journal of Personality,* Vol. 42, 1974, pp. 290-9.

Cross, R., *Economic Theory and Policy in the UK,* Oxford, Martin Robertson, 1982.

Cyert, R. M. and March, J. G., *A Behavioral Theory of the Firm*, Englewood Cliffs, New Jersey, Prentice-Hall, 1963.

Dow, S. C. and Earl, P. E., *Money Matters: A Keynesian Approach to Monetary Economics*, Oxford, Martin Robertson, 1982.

Dow, S. C. and Earl, P. E., "Methodology and Orthodox Monetary Policy", *Economie Appliquée*, Vol. 37, 1984, pp. 143-63.

Earl, P. E., "The Consumer in his/her Social Setting: A Subjectivist View" in Wiseman, J. (Ed.), *Beyond Positive Economics?*, London, Macmillan, 1983(a).

Earl, P. E., *The Economic Imagination: Towards a Behavioural Analysis of Choice*, Brighton, Wheatsheaf, 1983(b).

Earl, P. E., *The Corporate Imagination: How Big Companies Make Mistakes*, Brighton, Wheatsheaf, 1984(a).

Earl, P. E., "A Behavioural Analysis of Choice", unpublished doctoral dissertation, University of Cambridge, 1984(b).

Heiner, R. A., "The Origin of Predictable Behaviour", *American Economic Review*, Vol. 73, 1983, pp. 560-95.

Hinkle, D. N., "The Change of Personal Constructs from the Standpoint of a Theory of Implications", unpublished doctoral dissertation, Ohio State University, 1965.

Hofstadter, D., *Gödel, Escher, Bach: An Eternal Golden Braid*, Hassocks, Sussex, Harvester, 1979.

Houthakker, H. S. and Taylor, L. D., *Consumer Demand in the United States: Analyses and Projections*, second edition, Cambridge, Massachusetts, Harvard University Press, 1970.

Jefferson, M., "Economic Uncertainty and Business Decision Making", in Wiseman, J. (Ed.), *Beyond Positive Economics?* London, Macmillan, 1983.

Kay, N. M., *The Innovating Firm: a behavioural theory of corporate R & D*, London, Macmillan, 1979.

Kay, N. M., *The Evolving Firm: strategy and structure in industrial organisation*, London, Macmillan, 1982.

Kay, N. M., *The Emergent Firm: knowledge, ignorance and surprise in economic organisation*, London, Macmillan, 1984.

Kelly, G. A., *The Psychology of Personal Constructs*, New York, Norton, 1955.

Keynes, J. M., *The General Theory of Employment, Interest and Money*, London, Macmillan, 1936.

Keynes, J. M., "The General Theory of Employment", *Quarterly Journal of Economics*, Vol. 51, 1937, pp. 209-223.

Koestler, A. and Smithies, J. R. (Eds.), *Beyond Reductionism*, London, Hutchinson/Radius Books, 1969.

Lakatos, I., "Falsification and the Methodology of Scientific Research Programmes", in Lakatos, I. and Musgrave, A. (Eds.), *Criticism and the Growth of Knowledge*, London, Cambridge University Press, 1970.

Leijonhufvud, A., "Effective Demand Failures", *Swedish Journal of Economics*, Vol. 75, 1973, pp. 27-48.

Loasby, B. J., "Long Range Formal Planning in Perspective", *Journal of Management Studies*, Vol. 4, 1967, pp. 300-8.

Minsky, H. P., *John Maynard Keynes*, New York, Columbia University Press, 1975.

Rumelt, R. P., *Strategy, Structure and Economic Performance*, Cambridge, Massachusetts, Harvard University Press, 1974.

Selznick, P., *Leadership in Administration*, Evanston, Illinois, Harper and Row, 1957.

Simon, H. A., *Models of Man*, New York, Wiley, 1957.

Simon, H. A., *The Sciences of the Artificial*, Cambridge, Massachusetts, MIT University Press, 1969.

Simon, H. A., "Rational Decision Making in Business Organizations", *American Economic Review*, Vol. 69, 1979, pp. 493-513.

Steinbruner, J. D., *The Cybernetic Theory of Decision*, Princeton, Princeton University Press, 1974.

Waddington, C. H., "Stabilisation in Systems", *Futures*, Vol. 9, 1977, pp. 139-46.

Williamson, O. E., *Markets and Hierarchies: Analysis and Antitrust Implications*, New York, Free Press, 1975.

[9]

Shackle's Theory of Decision Making under Uncertainty: Synopsis and Brief Appraisal

by J. L. Ford
University of Birmingham

Introduction

In recent years Professor Shackle's numerous, highly imaginative and original works on the role of expectation and uncertainty in the modelling of economic behaviour have at last become more widely acknowledged. However, still relatively little attention is paid to one of his seminal and earliest studies, that concerned with his own theory of expectations and individual decision making under uncertainty, work on which was begun and published in the 1930s and completed in 1949 with the appearance of the first edition of *Expectation in Economics*. Thereafter, until the early 1960s, his theory received a modest amount of interest. However, it tended to become neglected; reference rarely appears to it in books or papers on expectation, even in those papers discussing decision making under uncertainty (see, as one of the latest examples, G. O. Schneller and G. P. Sphicas, 1983). The literature has been dominated by the risk-based, expected utility approach to decision taking[1].

I have attempted in a recent book (Ford, 1983) to redress the balance and in so doing to consider what historical literature there exists on Shackle's theory. In this article I obviously cannot cover the material and ideas presented there. Rather, I have endeavoured to provide: a brief outline of Shackle's theory; a summary of some problems that seem to occur with it, and my proposed alternative approach, the Shacklesque, or, as it has been called rather grandly, the Fordian, model; a summary of the ability of Shackle's model to solve problems tackled by the use of the expected utility theorem; and a brief comparison of Shackle's theory with the other theories of decision making under uncertainty. Even leaving on one side the possible deficiencies of Shackle's theory — and the sort of model I have suggested might take account of those deficiencies — what is useful is a comparison of the Shackle theory *per se* with the existing alternatives. In essence, apart from denying, except in special circumstances, the rational holding by an investor of a multi-asset financial portfolio, the Shackle theory appears to be as good as the expected utility approach and perhaps more intuitively sensible than the existing, competing, models that purport to analyse decision making under *uncertainty*, rather than under risk. We should note that we shall make no reference to the new work on risk theory, to replace the Expected Utility Theorem, embodied in Prospect Theory (Kahneman and Tversky, 1979) and Regret Theory (Loomes and Sugden, 1982). That comparison requires an extensive and hence a separate analysis. However, those "theories" too are risk-based (see |1| *supra*); and although the Shacklesque, Fordian, "theory" is effectively uncertainty-based, it is that theory, rather than Shackle's, which might be compared with the amendments of Expected Utility Theory, that are advocated in Prospect Theory. I say this despite the fact that Prospect Theory argues that individuals edit, or simplify, the risky prospects they face, in a way reminiscent of the telescoping, sifting of expectational outcomes on prospects (or strategies) suggested by Shackle's ϕ-function that we shall meet in the next section. Furthermore, as a corollary of the editing hypothesis, some irrationality of choice over risky prospects occurs, in respect of the axioms of Utility Theory used by Von Neumann and Morgenstern (1947) in their development of the Expected Utility Theorem, so that inconsistencies, intransitivities and the violation of (stochastic) dominance occur. In the Shackle theory, the use of the editing, ϕ-function, can also lead to those consequences.

But we have already said enough about a theory which we can do little more than mention here because of insufficient space. Let us move on expeditiously to the issues we are to consider.

An Outline of Shackle's Theory of Decision Making under Uncertainty
The approach advocated in the literature on decision making prior to the appearance of Shackle's theory (and in the vast majority of the literature that has emerged since that time) was founded on the use by the individual decision-making unit of probability (usually objective, frequently subjective) as a method of measuring the chances of occurrences of the potential outcomes of choices of action/strategies; and hence of helping describe "prospects". Thus, when considering, for example, the investment returns from the purchase of a particular piece of machinery, the decision taker (the entrepreneur) would have in mind, perhaps, a series of returns (discounted as appropriate) which, he believes, could possibly be generated from the use of the machinery. To each one of those prospective returns, or "outcomes", he is alleged to attach a probability of occurrence; the latter can be assigned directly or, as is normally the case in the literature, be allocated through the medium of "states of nature", "eventualities", or "states of the world". These last are alleged to be the generators of the economic conditions that will produce the imagined outcomes. In essence, to each state of nature there is, usually, assigned one outcome; to the state of nature the entrepreneur ascribes a probability; by implication that probability is attached to the relevant outcome. All the possible states of nature are known to him; that is, in technical language, he knows the universe of discourse. So, for each choice of action/prospect/strategy/investment, the entrepreneur knows the outcomes, the states of nature, and their probabilities. He is then able to select the strategy that best suits him; in effect, the one that maximises some objective. This might be an expected return or, as is the case in the orthodox literature, his *expected utility* (of return) developed by Von Neumann and Morgenstern (1947). That objective arises out of the set of axioms they have provided for rational decision making under risk|2|. Essentially these amount to the hypothesis that the individual decision taker has a (conventional) utility function over the outcomes. For each strategy or prospect, which is epitomised by the set of outcomes and their associated probabilities, to act rationally he must calculate an index (*I*) which is his *expected utility* from that strategy or prospect; so that:

Decision Making under Uncertainty 51

$$I_i = E(U_i) = \sum_{j=1}^{n} P_j U(a_{ij}); \quad \sum_{j=1}^{n} P_j = 1 \tag{1}$$

Here: i denotes strategy/choice of action; j refers to states of nature (n in toto); $U(\cdot)$ denotes utility; a_{ij} will be the outcome from pursuit of the ith strategy should the jth state of nature materialise; and P_j is the probability of occurrence of that state. The optimal strategy is the one that provides the highest $E(U_i)$.

Professor Shackle's approach is antipathetic to this "classical" model. It departs from it in three fundamental respects, namely: (1) it replaces probability by potential surprise; (2) it hypothesises that the individual decision maker will attempt to simplify, edit, the expectational elements from any strategy/prospect — an hypothesis allegedly based on psychological considerations. In the process of telescoping his expectations, Shackle maintains that the individual will consider gains and losses separately, being safety-first; again, another psychological insight. The ultimate outcome of the simplification procedure is that the individual will have epitomised the feasible set of outcomes from any particular strategy by just two monetary outcomes; the one encapsulating the possibilities of gain and the other those of loss. From the arguments he advanced under (1), Shackle's position is that there will be no meaning attached to a process whereby the outcomes of a strategy are weighted and summed (or where this is hypothesised to happen to utilities, as the case might be), since they are *rivals;* and (3) as a concomitant of (2), the Shackle schema replaces the ranking of strategies *per se* through expected utility, by a process which orders the pairs of competing (gains, losses) from the alternative strategies. Thus, in that schema, the selection of a strategy follows the evaluation of the competing expectational profiles; in the Expected Utility Theory they are inseparable.

These three differences (but (2) and (3), naturally, overlap) led to Shackle's theory being founded on three pillars: there is, indeed, a one-to-one mapping between the two triads. The pillars are, respectively: *the potential-surprise function; the ϕ,* ascendancy, or stimulus function; and *the gambler-preference function.* We shall now consider this apparatus, taking the pillars *seriatim.* So we commence with Shackle's strictures against the use of the probability calculus to portray decision taking under uncertainty and with the potential surprise function.

Shackle's position is predicated on his view that the reliance on probability (essentially objective, but partly, in his case, subjective) betrays a basic misconception of the nature of the decision-making process under *uncertainty.* The presence of uncertainty implies lack of knowledge; the application of probability suggests the existence of knowledge. Furthermore, the use of probability, relative frequency, in solving decision-making problems has, as a corollary, the view that the decision maker is involved in a multi-repeatable experiment against nature. Indeed, the contrary is usually the case in regard to decisions taken in an economic context. What might happen on the average, or for a large group of individuals taken collectively, has no relevance for the individual. Consider an individual endeavouring to select the best possible portfolio of financial assets. He will have a limited value of wealth. He stands to lose that wealth if he makes a totally wrong choice of portfolio. He might soon find himself "out of the game against nature" that is portrayed in the probabilistic conception of decision making. The chance of an infinitely repeatable investment of his wealth is, in an *unchanging* set of conditions, or could be, denied to him; he cannot rely on being able to trade on the relative frequencies of occurrence of particular yields on specified assets.

Those logical difficulties with the use of the probability calculus had not gone unnoticed in the statistical and philosophical literature. They figured prominently in two well known treatises, Venn's *The Logic of Chance* (1880) and more especially in various editions of Jeffreys' (1939) classic *Theory of Probability*. They had also been mentioned in Keynes's *Treatise on Probability* (1921). It is from picking up the thrust of their arguments that Professor Shackle re-emphasised the (seemingly) fundamental dangers inherent in automatic use of the probability calculus: also, the concept that he proposed as an alternative to probability as the linchpin of his own theory, namely *potential surprise,* seems to have as its antecedent the notion of surprise utilised by Venn.

The very fact that an "experiment" is being undertaken can destroy the circumstances in which it took place and make it impossible for it to be repeated. The situation where the investor has lost all of his wealth or had it altered by the "experiment" pertains to this. In addition, it is germane to point out that the general set of conditions present in the economy at any one investment point are not going to persist.

Shackle further deprecates the use of objective probability in the analysis of investment decisions because probability is a *distributional* variable. Thus suppose that at one time, n mutually exclusive states of nature are possible. If the investor now revises his expectations about those states and arrives at the conclusion that $n+1$, in effect, are possible, it is necessary for the probability of at least one of the n states of nature to be reduced to accommodate the extra eventuality. Why, Shackle asks, should an investor *have* to revise his estimate of any state of the world because another possible state emerges? Clearly there *is* a conundrum here. Even if we think of probability as *subjective* probability then the essence of this difficulty remains.

Since Professor Shackle says that objective probability is totally inapplicable to a non-seriable decision, such as any kind of investment decision, he argues that:

> ...the decision maker... is reduced to using *subjective* probability, which has no claims to be knowledge, which cannot offer any objective support to such constructions as the mathematical expectations, cannot vividly or meaningfully be used to arrive at a *weighted average* outcome, save when this phrase has a purely formal meaning and indicates no more than that an arithmetical procedure of multiplications and additions of the resulting products has been performed. For now we are brought face-to-face with the core of the matter: when the experiment is a non-divisible one, the hypotheses regarding its outcome are cut-throat *rivals,* denying and excluding each other. What, then, is the sense of *averaging* them? (Shackle, 1961(g), p. 60; italics in original.)

Shackle's own approach circumvents the "averaging problem"[3]. Consider an entrepreneur who is evaluating the best pieces of capital equipment, machinery, he should purchase. For each machine he sets out the outcomes (discounted returns, say), or payoffs, which he imagines he could obtain from the machine for a given financial outlay. Let us label the outcomes, r. These can be thought of as gains or losses relative to the financial outlay. Shackle always refers to gains and losses and so accordingly we shall largely do so. But yields, returns, can always be suitably re-defined so that they are "gains"/"losses".

Now, the degree of potential surprise (y) indicates the degree of surprise the investor would feel if a specified outcome turned out to be true. The size of degree of potential surprise, which reflects the individual's *degree of belief* in an outcome can range from zero to some (subjective, of course) maximum value, which would register complete *dis*belief in the *possibility* that the outcome to which it was assigned could occur.

Shackle devoted surprisingly little space in his original monograph (*Expectation in Economics,* (1949(a); 1952(a))) to the concepts of degree of belief and potential surprise and most of what he has written about them since merely reiterates his earliest observations. His views can be encapsulated in the following:

> It is only a man who feels very sure of a given outcome who can be greatly *surprised* by its non-occurrence. A degree of belief is not in itself a sensation or an emotion; but a high degree of belief is a condition of our being able to feel a high degree of surprise...we can use the degree of surprise which we judge would be caused to us by the non-occurrence of a given outcome...as an indicator of our degree of belief in this outcome. The range of possible intensities of surprise lies between zero and that intensity which would arise from the occurrence of an event believed impossible, or held to be *certain* not to occur. Within this range each one of us will find in his own past experience particular occurrences...each of which has caused him some degree of surprise, the memory of which remains with him vividly enough to serve, in conjunction with the event which caused it, as one of a series of fixed levels, not necessarily even spaced, providing together a scale of potential surprise...and |we shall| treat surprise as a continuous variable defined in a certain range, and subject to manipulation by the methods of the differential calculus... The measure so obtained is what we may call the *potential surprise* associated, by a particular person at a particular date, with the falsity of the answer or the non-occurrence of the outcome. (Shackle, 1952(a), p. 10.)

But then Shackle comes across a paradox and has to invert these notions so that we arrive at a concept of potential surprise related to the *occurrence* of an outcome:

> This formula, however, is not quite satisfactory for our purpose. In answer to any questions about the future, there will typically be in the mind of any one person a number of rival hypotheses, and amongst these there will be a subset of which each member is superior, as regards his degree of belief in it, to any hypothesis outside the subset, but of which no one member is superior to any other member. In this case he cannot attach any degree of surprise greater than zero to the falsity or non-fulfilment of any one particular member of this subset; for to do so would *ipso facto* mark this member off as claiming a higher degree of belief than any of the others. The most he can do is to attach nil potential surprise to the *fulfilment* of any member of the subset. But he *can* attach some positive degree of potential surprise to every hypothesis *outside* the subset, and by doing so he will express its inferiority, in the matter of the degree of his belief in it, to every member of the subset. And further, he can attach different degrees of potential surprise to different hypotheses outside the subset. It will be convenient, therefore, to invert our formula, and say that by assigning different degrees of potential surprise to the occurrence, rather than the non-occurrence, of different hypothetical outcomes, he assigns to these outcomes positions on a scale of belief. (*Ibid.*, pp. 10-11; italics in original.)

The notion of the "inner subset", or for continuous outcomes, the "inner range" indicates that rival hypotheses can have zero potential surprise attached to them. Nevertheless, Shackle's own inclination is to suggest that there will be only a few outcomes for, say, a particular investment, that will carry zero potential surprise.

The potential surprise function:

$$y = y(x) \tag{2}$$

where x denotes a positive or negative outcome/payoff, is drawn frequently by Shackle in the form of an inverted bell. There are, by the very nature of Shackle's approach, two branches for $y(\cdot)$. The latter can, naturally, assume any form over either its gain

54   Journal of Economic Studies 12,1/2

or its loss branch. However, out of an *exhaustive set* of rival hypotheses at least one must carry zero potential surprise (Axiom 9 of the Axioms by which Shackle has formalised his notion of potential surprise: Appendix to *Expectation in Economics*). But, as we say, in general, Shackle portrayed $y(\cdot)$ by a diagram such as Figure 1.

Figure 1.

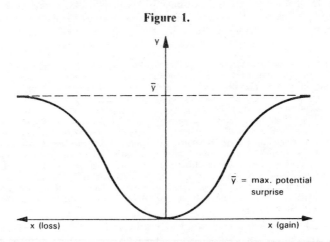

What now of the *ascendancy function* and the procedure by which $y = y(x)$ is encapsulated into one pair of (y,x) for each of its branches? Let gain = g and loss = l, then the ascendancy function indicates the power of an expectational element, namely pair of (g,y) or (l,y) to arrest the attention of the individual. It can be envisaged, according to Shackle, as a *stimulus function;* and he usually labels the function, the ϕ-function; so that:

$$\phi = \phi(x,y) \tag{3}$$

with x denoting either gain or loss. In general, Shackle assumes that properties of ϕ are as follows:

$$\delta\phi/\delta\chi > 0, \text{ for } x > 0; \; \delta\phi/\delta x < 0, \text{ for } x < 0, \; \delta\phi/\delta y < 0 \tag{4}$$

In effect, it is easier to work with loss as an absolute number, so that $\phi(\cdot)$ increases with loss, since Shackle himself uses the absolute value of loss in describing the gambler-preference map. We note that (3) implies that $\phi(\cdot)$ is the same over g and l: it need not be as Shackle has indicated. But it only serves to complicate notation by distinguishing ϕ_g from ϕ_l and adds nothing of substance.

    Thus, *ceteris paribus,* the higher is the gain on an investment the greater will be its power to attract the attention of the investor; and the larger is the loss on an asset the bigger will be its ascendancy in the mind of the investor. *Ceteris paribus,* as the potential surprise attached to a specified gain on an asset is increased, that gain will lose power to attract the investor's notice; this is the case likewise with an increase

Decision Making under Uncertainty   55

in the loss on an asset, since if the potential surprise on that loss falls there is less reason for the investor to pay attention to it, no matter what its magnitude happens to be.

Shackle makes the assumption that the ϕ-function is a continuous one. Therefore, for each possible level of ϕ we can derive a ϕ-indifference curve which traces out for us the combinations of (g,y) or (g,l) consistent with the attainment of that level of ϕ. The resultant indifference curves will have positive slopes in (g,y) or (l,y) space given the conditions contained in (4). We shall also assume, along with Shackle, that the second-order conditions are such as to permit us to construct the ϕ-indifference curves in the way we have done in Figure 2. On the latter we have also portrayed the potential surprise function; again, as with Figure 1, we have done so as if it were a continuous function (which it need not be). The functions for the gain and loss branches might or might not be identical.

Figure 2.

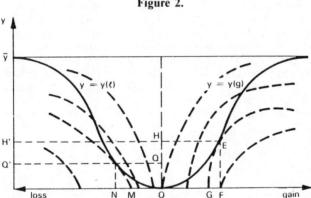

The *telescoping* of $y = y(g)$ and $y = y(l)$ each *into one element* is achieved by application of the ϕ-function, with the function being used as a "ϕocusing" device. In essence, the Shackle entrepreneur is alleged, as it were, to maximise his ϕ-function over gain and loss, separately, subject to the relevant branch of the potential surprise function. Thus consider Figure 2. At a point such as E the investor has maximised his ϕ-function. For at that point the highest value of ϕ has been attained *given* the constraint placed on it by the potential surprise function. The point E is an expectational element; it possesses a gain of OF and a degree of potential surprise equal to OH. That gain is labelled the *primary focus-gain* in Professor Shackle's theory. As we have intimated previously, it will have a concomitant primary focus-loss, namely ON, with an associated degree of potential surprise, OQ.

Those primary focus-values are, as their name implies, the gain/loss values on which the investor focuses his attention initially. They have a first claim on his mind; they represent, *according to Shackle,* the "best" that the investor can hope for and the "worst" that he has to fear. But they have attached to them a degree of potential surprise; or, in general, they will have. (Of course, there could be occasions when the gain and loss branches of the potential surprise function are coincidental with the horizontal axis of Figure 2.) The next step in the "ϕocusing", editing, process is one which removes the potential surprise element of the primary focus-elements. It is argued that the investor will need to have a *common base* upon which to compare the gains/losses from competing investment strategies. Therefore, he will find an equivalent gain/loss for each investment strategy where potential surprise has been discounted. Such equivalence is obtained by locating that gain/loss which is identical to the primary gain/loss in that it produces the same value of ϕ, but with zero potential surprise attached to it. Such a gain/loss is called the *standardised* focus-gain/loss, since the gain and the loss have been placed on the same, standard, footing. In Figure 2, the standardised focus-gain is provided by OG; at G the investor is on the same level of ϕ as he is at E, but there is now zero degree of potential surprise attached to OG.

The expectational elements for the investment/strategy have now been reduced to *two monetary values,* a gain and a loss. The analogue, but not, of course, the equivalent, counterpart in the expected utility probabilistic approach for, say, portfolio choice, is the telescoping of the probability of outcomes on the assets, to the relevant characteristics of those distributions, such as their means and variances.

The expectational elements on the investment have now been reduced to manageable proportions and to a comparable footing. The Shackle investor has reduced his $y(\cdot)$s to the equivalent of the payoff matrix for strategies utilised by the classical decision-making models (see below).

A procedure is now required by which the entrepreneur is able to rank the alternative pairs of (focus-gain, focus-loss). That task is accomplished by the introduction of the *gambler-preference function,* or its derivative, the *gambler-preference map.*

The gambler-preference function epitomises the investor's rankings of pairs of focus-values. From that function we derive indifference curves tracing out those combinations that produce the same level of "utility". In the Shackle schema the latter is only referred to implicitly as an indicator of preferences. But we can regard that indicator as some *"U"* or index. We may write:

$$U = U(G,L) \tag{5}$$

where:

$$\delta U/\delta G > 0; \; \delta U/\delta L < 0 \tag{6}$$

Here G and L denote, respectively, standardised focus gain and loss.

The gambler-preference indifference curves will assume the sort of form and shape as those illustrated in Figure 3. The curves are ranked (in ascending order) from the south-east to the north-west, by the hypotheses contained in (6). Points A and B might represent the focus-values from investing in either of two machines.

Although it seems from Shackle's presentation that he does expect the typical gambler-preference indifference curves to have the shape depicted in Figure 3, he wishes that each curve be not inextricably bound up with any other: each should be let free to express the individual's temperament (so that they are *not* strictly derived from a *given function*). Nevertheless, for a choice of investment strategy the curves must be

Decision Making under Uncertainty **57**

related, in some measure, if the individual possesses low risk-aversion, because Shackle propounds the view that the gambler-preference indifference curves are relevant only up to a barrier provided by the investable wealth of the individual:

> When the action-schemes being compared are investment schemes, the decision maker will have in mind some definite available sum of money which is the most he can dispose of on behalf of himself or those who have placed their wealth at his discretion. This sum we shall call his fortune. . . it is the most that he can lose. . . Thus at that point on the loss axis which corresponds to the decision-maker's fortune we erect, perpendicular to that axis, a barrier to the right of which the gambler-indifference curves would have no meaning. . . (Shackle, 1961(a), pp. 163-164.)

Figure 3.

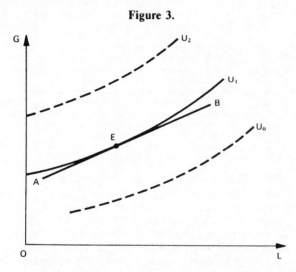

He considers two broad categories of investor, namely "the headlong gambler" and a person of more cautious temperament:

> For the more cautious temperament, any point which threatens total ruin as one of its possibilities, that is any point on the "barrier". . .is more repellant than any point whose threat is less than total ruin. No point on the barrier, that is to say, can be contained in any of his gambler indifference curves, which therefore must approach the barrier asymptotically. . . For the headlong gambler. . .there is no such restriction, his gambler indifference curves can meet the barrier at finite ordinates. (*Ibid.*, p. 164.)

The gambler-preference indifference curve that passes through the origin is accorded special status: it is used as a method of measuring *risk-preference:*

> The concept of the origin indifference curve leads us to a new and very simple definition of an individual's risk-preference, and enables us to measure the latter. A given individual in given circumstances will be able to name for any specific focus-loss a focus-gain such that if he is faced with this pair of focus-outcomes his situation seems to him neither more nor less desirable than if he had the assurance of experiencing neither gain nor loss. . . The ratio of the focus-less to its compensating focus-gain will in general be different when the focus-loss is different. The set of all such ratios obtained by varying the focus-loss, other circumstances remaining unchanged, is what we shall mean by the *schedule of gambler-preference* of the given individual in these circumstances. It is evident that this is simply the set

of ratios of abscissa to ordinate of all points on the origin indifference curve, when these ratios are placed in a one-one correspondence with the respective focus-losses concerned. (Shackle, 1952(a), p. 31.)

We note here that Shackle refers, oddly enough, to the concept of risk (in what he sees as an uncertainty situation) which is something that is an anathema to him. But setting that point aside, there is the question as to whether the gambler-preference function has a separate identity from the ϕ-function. In his summary explanation of the ϕ-function, in fact, Shackle indicates that the ϕ-function is possibly usurping the gambler-preference function in ranking the expectational characteristics of the investments such that it provides a choice of action by the entrepreneur:

> We decide on one particular course of action, out of a number of rival courses, because this one gives us, as an immediately present experience, the most enjoyment *by anticipation* of its outcome. Future situations and events cannot be experienced and therefore their degree of desirableness cannot be compared; but situations and events can be *imagined,* and the desirableness of these experiences which happen in the imagination can be compared. What gives imagined things a claim to be treated as the equivalents of future things? It is some degree of belief that the imagined things will take actual shape at the dates we assign to them... Thus the entity which gives us enjoyment by anticipation (or distress by anticipation) or, as I shall say indifferently, by imagination, has two sets of characteristics. The first set specifies or describes the situation or sequence of situations, saying what it would be like if it were to happen...the picture can consist, for example, in a meeting with an actual and living friend, or the conferment on us of some honour, or success in some attempt... The other set (of one member only) consists merely in our degree of belief that this picture will come true. But how is this degree of belief presented to our minds, and put on the same footing of concreteness, of capacity to influence our decisions, as the feelings aroused by the content of the picture? (*Ibid.,* p. 9.)

A Brief Critique of the Theory and a Suggested Alternative
During the late 1940s but especially during the 1950s and early 1960s literature appeared reasonably regularly, if not in large volume, on George Shackle's unique and highly original theory of expectation. I have attempted to offer an exposition and critical assessment of that literature and of Shackle's theory in the light of it in my recent book (in which a detailed bibliography will be found). I have also there advanced my own critique of his theory and suggested an alternative means of developing it to circumvent the alleged difficulties with it.

It is clearly not possible to recapitulate that material even in précis form. So, we shall limit ourselves to noting some of the points that have been or can be raised in an evaluation of Shackle's approach and his particular theory. These naturally concern the three pillars of his theory, especially the ascendancy or ϕ-function and the gambler-preference function. In the main the issues are these:

(1) In utilising the ascendancy or ϕ-function is it meaningful to replace primary focus-values by their standardised counterparts?

(2) Is the application of the ϕ-function wasteful of information on the feasible outcomes of any strategy?

(3) Is the ϕ-function really a "choice of strategy" function?

(4) As a corollary, is there a separate role for the gambler-preference function?

We can offer a comment on each of these. Point (1) is a key question. Standardising the focus-values so that allegedly "uncertainty" is removed and the same ascendancy-ϕ value is maintained does not, in fact, remove the uncertainty. The standardised

Decision Making under Uncertainty 59

focus-values will not, in general, carry zero potential surprise. When primary focus-values are replaced by standardised focus-values it is likely that the potential surprise function will be such that the individual is assumed to focus his attention on an outcome that carries other than zero potential surprise. It seems logically inconsistent to me to assume that the individual adopts such a procedure. It is a stronger one than that made by Roy Harrod that it is also hard to imagine how an individual would, via the primary focus-values, concentrate his attention on outcomes which (in general) would surprise him if they occurred. But that point itself leads us to counter Shackle's view that mutually exclusive rival outcomes should not be "averaged" by suggesting that the hypothesis that an individual concentrates his attention wholly on one of them, when only one can occur, is also untenable. No allowance is then made for the fact that indeed only one can materialise, and that, given there is uncertainty present, some kind of range should be used.

This leads on naturally to point (2). The application of the ascendancy or ϕ-function to the potential surprise function does not directly lead, of course, to the determination of the standardised focus-values, but it does so indirectly, and by selecting out one point on the potential surprise function, discarding all others. In effect, the ascendancy function does not encapsulate the information contained in the whole range of the potential surprise function. Hence, when two strategies are being evaluated by the gambler-preference function on the basis of focus-values, it is possible for a strategy to be chosen that is, as it were, almost totally dominated stochastically by the other. Shackle would repeat that this kind of consideration is not relevant. The outcomes for each strategy are rivals and the individual will simplify his expectational complex to one element of the many alternatives.

In a sense, the suggestion that the individual should utilise all the information contained in the potential surprise function is tantamount to saying that the ϕ-function should be replaced by a choice-of-strategy function such as a modified gambler-preference function and the latter be discarded. Point (3) is concerned with the question as to whether or not the ϕ-function is not, indeed, performing the role of choice-of-strategy in the Shackle schema. Shackle's alternative name, ascendancy or stimulus function, for the ϕ-function, and his own explanations of the function, lead to the view that the ascendancy function is a kind of utility function and not just a ϕocusing device. That itself has led to the view being expressed that strategies in the Shackle theory should be evaluated by the net ϕ-values (that for gain less that for loss) for the competing strategies.

But Shackle himself, though at times ambivalent on the nature of the ascendancy function and the comparative roles of the ascendancy and gambler-preference functions, will not agree to the use of net ϕ-values as the ranking criterion (see Shackle, 1961(a)). He sees that there is a need for a separate gambler-preference function, that that function captures different elements of what he calls "attitudes to risk" of the individual, and that the ascendancy function *is a focusing,* telescoping or editing function.

If the point is taken that the whole of the potential surprise function would be relevant to choice of action, then the editing role played by the ϕ-function disappears and so too do the concepts of focus-values. So two possible difficulties are removed simultaneously. But the ϕ-function has to be replaced by an amended *U*- or gambler-preference function. My own suggestions here are that potential surprise be mapped into what we might call "subjective probabilities". It is assumed that the individual has a utility function over gains and losses (which he considers separately, *à la* Shackle; and which might be of different forms). To act rationally, he should evaluate the net expected utility from the gain and loss branches, choosing that strategy which promises the highest, positive, net value, or what I call Action Choice Index.

In this suggested model (axiomatised *à la* Von Neumann-Morgenstern) the so-called subjective probabilities sum to one for both gains and losses, and so only in case of, say, no losses on all strategies would the suggested net expected utility criterion produce the same choice of strategy as the conventional expected utility approach.

The suggestion had previously been made in the literature especially by Krelle (1957), that potential surprise (y_i) can be mapped into subjective probability (π_i). Thus let:

$$\pi_i = \frac{\bar{y}-y_i}{\sum\limits_{i=1}^{n}(\bar{y}-y_i)} \quad ; \quad \bar{y} = \max y \tag{7}$$

where the y_i pertain to a potential surprise function for a particular strategy; then $\Sigma\pi_i=1$ and the mapping of y into π is isomorphic. Note that these "subjective probabilities" are, indeed, only evaluated after the individual has specified his potential surprise functions. It is not being argued that he does, will or should rely directly on subjective probability estimates of the chances of success of the imagined outcomes. In that sense it is not so vulnerable to the criticisms levelled at it by Professor Shackle. But his point still stands that since π_i is a distributional variable an extra imagined outcome with an associated degree of potential surprise, must alter all the π_i for the pre-existing outcomes. Also, of course, in the Fordian model, an averaging process is being employed, and Shackle's possible psychological insight regarding the simplification of expectational data is ignored. But the axiom that the individual has regard to the "range" of feasible outcomes, imagined by himself not given by a *deus ex machina*, seems no less acceptable than one which states that he will select one only of those outcomes as encapsulating, say, the gains on a strategy.

Axioms, of course, are designed to be positive statements, though they are often stated on *a priori* grounds. A comparative evaluation of the competing models, naturally, would have to be accomplished by a testing of their axioms and predictions.

A Summary of Some Applications of the Shackle Theory to Decision Models Hitherto Founded on the Expected Utility Theorem

The developments in Prospect Theory (see Kahneman and Tversky, 1979) and of Regret Theory (see Loomes and Sugden, 1982), are too recent to alter the fact that almost all of the models that have been utilised to evaluate the choice of strategy in a variety of situations which are characterised by uncertainty have adopted the probabilistic expected utility framework as the method of analysis. As a sample of the numerous decision models available we might mention those concerned with: portfolio choice; consumer search; labour search; labour supply; two or multi-period consumption-loan decisions; the purchase of insurance; and output choice for firms under demand or price uncertainty.

Decision Making under Uncertainty **61**

In *Choice, Expectation and Uncertainty* (1983) I have considered models such as these along the lines suggested by Shackle's approach *per se*. That is to say, I have ignored any of the seeming inconsistencies and deficiencies in the Shackle theory, of the kind which we have noted above, and I have used Shackle's own model to analyse the selection of the optimal strategy for economic agents in those types of uncertain environments. As a consequence, it has been possible to demonstrate that the Shackle theory can offer a solution just as readily as can applications of the expected utility theorem. However, in the case of portfolio choice the Shackle theory can, in general, only account for a diversified portfolio over two, not several, assets. Again, except in special circumstances, it can explain the holding of money, seen as a "riskless" asset, alongside only one other asset.

We cannot consider all of these models here but we should perhaps refer to two. Let us take the simplest possible versions of a portfolio selection problem and of a consumption-saving model.

We consider the portfolio selection problem first and we make the following simplifying assumption: we are concerned with only the asset portfolio of an individual investor; the model is one based on choice of portfolio one period at a time; financial assets are divisible; there are no transaction costs involved in asset sales and purchases; there is zero inflation; and there is no taxation on investment returns of any kind. We suppose that the investor is concerned with obtaining the highest return on his wealth. Alternatively, we could, of course, hypothesise that he was interested in end-of-period wealth and he would be concerned with the gains/losses around his existing wealth that competing portfolios offered.

According to the Shackle schema he will construct potential surprise functions for the positive returns ("gains") and for the negative returns ("losses") per monetary unit of investment in each of the available financial assets[4]. He will reduce those to a standardised focus positive return and negative return for asset A, say, g_A and l_A respectively. These will be scaled-up by his total wealth (W) to produce the total standardised focus-values, G_A and L_A. The G_i, L_i are compared for all possible assets via the U- or gambler-preference function. One such comparison can be effected in respect of the (G_i, L_i) for every asset. But it is possible that a *combination* of the assets could yield a higher U-indifference curve than could any one of them. The issue then becomes one of determining if an efficient investment frontier over (G,L) can exist consisting of more than two assets.

In deriving that frontier the value of G, for example, can be envisaged as a weighted average of the g_i, with the weights being the values of the holding of the relevant assets. Thus for two assets, A and B, we would have:

$$G = g_A x_A + g_B x_B \tag{8}$$

$$L = l_A x_A + l_B x_B \tag{9}$$

where x_A and x_B denote the money values of the holdings of assets A and B, respectively. The efficient investment frontier for two assets would be obtained by the investor's maximising G subject to a given level of L and of wealth (W), where:

$$W = x_A + x_B \tag{10}$$

In the case of only two assets, naturally, the solution of the optimum values of x_A and x_B is trivial and follows from solving the two constraints L and W. We should also note that we can definitely write equations (8) and (9) as combinations of comparable focus-values if the degree of correlation between comparable focus-values on the assets is unity (see Egerton, 1960 and Ford, 1983).

The efficient investment frontier is linear:

$$G = \left[\frac{g_A - g_B}{l_A - l_B}\right] L + \left[\frac{g_B^l A - g_A^l B}{l_A - l_B}\right] W \tag{11}$$

Now, consider Figure 3. The frontier might assume the position taken up by AB; with A, for example, denoting the pair of total focus-values that would obtain if all of the investor's wealth were to be placed in asset A. The point E would represent the optimum (G,L); and it would imply a unique allocation of wealth across assets A and B. So, diversification is possible.

But if we now include a third possible asset, C, that can be purchased, we find that the investor has a linear efficient frontier for investment in assets A and C, and for investment in assets B and C.

Suppose the focus-values on asset C are higher than those on asset B. The picture can then be depicted by Figure 4.

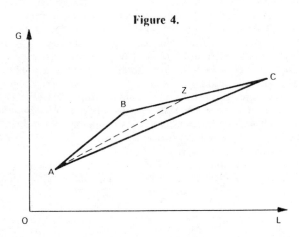

Figure 4.

Three assets can only be held within the triangle ABC on Figure 4, such as along AZ. But all points in the triangle are inefficient: they are dominated by points on the ABC boundary; for given L a higher G can be obtained on that boundary than inside it (and hence on AC). The fact that assets only have *two* characteristics in the Shackle model and that the frontier is linear in asset holdings excludes multi-asset diversification. The results of analysing portfolio choice using the expected utility criteria are sufficiently well known for us not to have to repeat them here.

In concluding our comments on portfolio selection and the Shackle model we should make the following remarks. The method we have adopted to examine asset choice in the confines of the Shackle framework is the one used by Dr R. A. Egerton (1956, 1960). There is an alternative approach, which is based on the investor's evaluating the *focus-values* for every feasible *portfolio*. Such an approach means that the potential surprise function for each asset is "scaled-up" by the value of the holding of the asset; and for any given *y* the "scaled-up" potential surprise curves are added to produce the potential surprise curve for the given portfolio and hence for the given level of wealth. This method is the one adopted by Shackle himself (*Expectation in Economics,* chapter 4) and it leads to the same investment frontiers and the same degree of asset diversification as in our analysis.

So Shackle himself was well aware of the limitations of his theory in respect of asset choice. The deficiencies of this aspect of his theory were highlighted by Sir Charles Carter (1950) in his review article of *Expectation in Economics* in the *Economic Journal.* Shackle tried to counter these criticisms in the second edition of his book by suggesting that characteristics of assets other than their focus-values must be considered by investors who hold multi-asset portfolios; alternatively, he argued that investors might adopt the "safety-first" strategy of A. D. Roy (1952) and minimise the chance of occurrence of a disastrous portfolio return. The first point, *ex hypothesi,* implies that Shackle's own theory is an incomplete one; and the second will *not* permit "spreading of risks" to occur in the Shackle schema *per se.* The Roy criterion is based on the probability calculus; and in the Shackle theory the only way that the notion of a disaster rate of return can be incorporated is via the gambler-preference function which should then include some variable such as the ratio between focus-loss and wealth (see Ford, 1983).

Finally, one interesting point is that the method Shackle uses to determine the focus-values on a portfolio, implies that the degrees of potential surprise apply, as it were, to a given contingency or state of nature. Otherwise, the potential surprise functions could not be summed laterally. So he is assuming that the focus-gains on assets are perfectly correlated; so too are the focus-losses.

We must move on expeditiously to offer a brief exposition of a two-period consumption model using the expected utility approach and that advocated by Shackle. Thus take this simple model (Sandmo, 1970). An individual possesses a utility (U) function which depends upon his consumption (C) in the current period, C_1, and in the next period, C_2. In period 1 the individual's income consists solely of earned income, Y_1. In period 2 his income will be equal to his earned income, Y_2, plus the yield (r) on his saving undertaken in period 1, S_1. He is assumed to spend all of his income in period 2, hence:

$$C_2 = Y_2 + (Y_1 - C_1)r \tag{12}$$

Y_1 and Y_2 are certain but r is random, with known probability density function, $f(r)$. Then the conventional solution to the choice of C_1 is that the individual is assumed to maximise the expected value of utility subject to (12). Thus:

$$E|U(C_1, C_2)| = \int_a^b U(C_1, Y_2 + (Y_1 - C_1)r)f(r)dr \tag{13}$$

where a to b is the range of the yield on saving. Writing U_i for $\delta U/\delta C_i$ the first-order condition for a maximum of $E(U)$ with respect to C_1 is:

$$E(U_1 - rU_2) = 0 \tag{14}$$

For the sake of illustration, let:

$$U = C_1^2 C_2 \tag{15}$$

The first-order condition for the maximisation of $E(U)$ becomes:

$$2Y_2 + 2Y_1 E(r) - 3C_1 E(r) = 0 \tag{16}$$

$$\therefore C_1 = \frac{2(Y_2 + Y_1 \bar{r})}{3\bar{r}} \tag{17}$$

where $\bar{r} = E(r)$; and at the value of C_1 given by (17) the second-order condition for a maximum of U obtains, so that C_1 is optimal. We also have sensible *a priori* results in that:

$$\delta C_1/\delta Y_1 > 0; \; \delta C_1/\delta \bar{r} < 0 \tag{18}$$

A *ceteris paribus* increase in current income, at constant opportunity cost of future in terms of current consumption, induces our individual consumer or household to spend some of the increased income on increasing his current purchases, since those increased purchases will not reduce his future consumption ($\delta C_1/\delta Y_1$ is less than unity).

In applying the Shackle schema to the choice of C_1 we have to posit that the consumer would seek to maximise the utility he believes he would have from the available range of current consumption. The only unknown is the yield on saving (r), that would be provided by the standardised focus-gain (focus-positive return) on saving, rather than by $E(r)$. Let that focus-value be denoted by g. Then applying the Shackle paradigm we would say that the consumer will:

$$\max_{C_1} \; U = U(C_1, C_2) \tag{19}$$

$$\text{s.t.} \; C_2 = Y_2 + (Y_1 - C_1)g \tag{20}$$

Given g, the consumer chooses that value of C_1 that would maximise his U-curve if the *yield on S_1 that did materialise happened to be g.* Such a focus-value, recall, would occasion zero degree of potential surprise for the consumer. If we assume that the exact form of the U-function is that contained in equation (15) the optimal level of C_1 can be discovered and it is similar to that obtained from expected utility approach, namely:

Decision Making under Uncertainty **65**

$$C_1 = \frac{2(Y_2 + Y_1 g)}{3g} \tag{21}$$

Again we see that if the anticipated opportunity cost of C_1 rises because there is an increase in g, C_1 will be reduced.

It is possible, naturally, for g to turn out equal to $\bar{r}$ in which case two individuals with the same U-function would select, optimally, the same level of current consumption and saving. But the seeming similarity between the expected utility and the Shackle approaches here arises because of the specific form of the U-function we have used. Consequently only the mean value of the yield affects C_1 in the expected utility framework, which would not have been the case had the U-function been non-linear in C_2, as the reader can confirm readily.

Shackle's Theory and the Classical Criteria for Decision Making under Uncertainty
Several models have been propounded in the literature as descriptions of the procedures individuals might adopt in formulating decisions they must take under uncertainty rather than risk, and of the decision criteria which they finally adopt to choose between competing strategies. Four of these approaches have produced what are commonly known as *classical* decision criteria: these are the proposals emanating from (1) Wald, the *maximin* criterion, derived from Game Theory; (2) Hurwicz (1951), the Index of Pessimism-Optimism; (3) Savage (1951), the Minimax Hypothesis of Subjective Loss; and (4) Laplace, the Principle of Insufficient Reason.

It seems apposite, therefore, also to effect a comparison between these criteria and Shackle's theory *per se,* even though this has partly been done by Ozga (1965). Since a comprehensive exposition of the criteria can be found in several places (see, for example, Luce and Raiffa, 1958), and we need merely to summarise how these criteria would be applied by any individual, let us take a simple concrete example. Consider then Table I, which we can regard, initially, as a pay-off matrix from alternative strategies (S_j), which might be the discounted returns over the lifetime of an investment that the entrepreneur conceives as possible. The columns (α_j) represent the possible "states of nature" as the entrepreneur sees things. In his mind, three possibilities occur; to none of them, however, can he attach any probability of occurrence.

Now consider the four classical decision criteria under uncertainty. The *Wald criterion per se* does not require us first of all to transform the pay-offs into utilities. That criterion states that the individual will concentrate his attention on the lowest pay-off for each strategy. Then the strategy is selected that promises the largest minimum outcome. Thus, in respect of Table I, S_1, S_2 and S_3 are characterised by 4, -2 and -3 respectively.

Table I.

	α_1	α_2	α_3	Wald	Hurwicz	Savage	Laplace
S_1	4	4	4	4*	4	14	4
S_2	-2	12	5	-2	12-14a	13	5
S_3	-3	3	18	-3	18-21a	9*	6*

The Hurwicz hypothesis is that the individual will calculate an index for each strategy which is, in effect, a linear combination of the worst and the best outcome promised by each strategy across the alternative states of nature. To evaluate the index again the numbers in Table I do not necessarily have to be cast in terms of utilities. So, taking them as given, and letting the weight assigned to the lowest pay-off for any strategy, *i*, be *a* we have that:

$$H_i = a \, \text{Min}_{ij} + (1-a)\text{Max}_{ij} \qquad (22)$$

Therefore, the values for H_i for $i = 1, 2, 3$ are as presented in Table I; and the choice of strategy will depend upon the value that the entrepreneur attaches to the coefficient *a*. If he is relatively pessimistic he will attach a higher value to *a;* to the extent that should his $a = 1$ then he is ultra-pessimistic.

The Savage criterion is founded on the supposition that the entrepreneur will select the strategy which minimises the maximum loss he believes he can attain. For the three strategies these are 14, 13 and 9 respectively.

The Laplace criterion reduces to one whereby each state of nature is given an equal *probability* of occurrence; in a sense we have moved away from the uncertainty framework, in which the entrepreneur is alleged to have no prior information about the states of the world. To invoke the Laplace criterion we can use either the pay-off matrix in numerical form or we can translate the outcomes into their utility equivalents. In general, the literature adopts the latter procedure; so that using the Laplace criterion reduces the choice of strategy to the one which maximises expected utility. In making the entry under the Laplace column in Table I, we have assumed that either the entrepreneur employs the pay-offs in calculating expected values or that utility equals pay-off; so that for negative pay-offs there is disutility.

If $0 \leq a \leq 2/3$, then strategy 3 is the optimal strategy under the Hurwicz criterion so that Table I informs us that application of the classical criterion would, apart from that of Wald, lead to strategy 3, indeed, being the optimal strategy to adopt. The Wald criterion, however, is not one that would appeal to intuition. It pays no attention to the profile of returns across the various, competing, states of nature. Thus, in terms of Table I, we observe that it is only in the first state of the world that strategy 1 dominates strategy 2. Indeed, if we had set the lowest loss on strategy 2 as a gain of 4, the Wald criterion would inform us that the entrepreneur would be indifferent between strategies 1 and 2; and yet, in terms of stochastic dominance, strategy 2 clearly dominates strategy 1. The Savage criterion suffers from similar, myopic deficiencies. The Hurwicz index does at least take cognisance of the *range* of outcomes on each and every feasible strategy, but the Laplace criterion is the one that makes most use of the information contained in the pay-off matrix.

We have noted how the Shackle schematic does not give full recognition to the expectational information contained in a pay-off matrix. But let us see how the Shackle apparatus would lead to the entrepreneur's choosing one of the three available investment strategies. In Shackle's approach we would have to view the construction of the pay-off matrix in an intrinsically different manner from that used hitherto.

Thus, to recapitulate the essentials of his approach, we would first envisage the entrepreneur imagining that he has three different types of machine he could purchase.

Decision Making under Uncertainty **67**

He is of the opinion that for each of them three outcomes are possible; these are the numbers contained in Table I. Now, to each of the numbers there will be assigned a degree of potential surprise at their occurrence; these degrees will fill the void left by the fact that decision taking under complete ignorance admits of no usable likelihoods of occurrence for the relevant outcomes. The pay-offs in Table I, when set out in classical form, have no other attributes except the $1/\Sigma\alpha_j$ in the case of the Laplace criterion.

For each strategy, the pair of pay-offs (degree of potential surprise) have to be reduced to two numbers, by the ϕ-function, namely the standardised focus-loss and focus-gain. Now, to render the Shackle model as close as possible to the classical models, let us assume, initially, that the entrepreneur believes that all the outcomes are not only perfectly possible but carry *zero* degree of potential surprise.

In that case, the process of telescoping the expectational elements for each strategy must result in the entrepreneur's focusing his attention on the best and the worst outcomes in Table I. Thus, for strategy 1, this will mean that the standardised (here, equals the primary) focus-gain is 4; the standardised focus-loss is zero, *ex hypothesi*, since strategy 1 promises to produce no losses. The standardised focus-values are as follows: strategy 1, 4 and 0; strategy 2, 12 and -2; and strategy 3, 18 and -3. The ϕ-function here selects the end of the ranges of outcomes.

These focus-values on the investment alternatives have now to be ranked. The Shackle procedure, we recall, is effectively to combine each pair of focus-values into an "index", via the application of the gambler-preference function. The latter implies a set of gambler-indifference curves: they balance any focus-gain against any focus-loss. In short, they (or more strictly the gambler-preference function) provide weights for the respective focus-values. That simple observation permits us to see the likelihood of *equivalence between the Hurwicz index and the Shackle index of choice.* Exact equivalence, of course, for any two entrepreneurs with identical pay-off matrices rests upon the equivalence of the Hurwicz coefficient of optimism and the weight attached to focus-gain in the Shackle index.

Lack of knowledge of the outcomes forthcoming from investment strategies in the Shackle paradigm does not, as we know, imply that the entrepreneur attaches a zero degree of potential surprise to each and every outcome. If he does not do so the Shackle model will not necessarily produce the same optimal strategy as that predicted by the Hurwicz criterion. It will, naturally, still lead to a situation where the entrepreneur considers only the "best" and the "worst" outcomes for each strategy and then weighs them in his mind through the gambler-preference map. However, except fortuitously, the presence of non-zero degrees of potential surprise associated with the outcomes in Table I will not lead, for example, to the highest gain for a particular strategy being the standardised focus-gain. The presence of the second possible characteristic of any expectational elements in the Shackle schematic can mean that the focus-value matrix assumes a different form from that where each element in Table I is assumed to carry zero potential surprise.

Where the feasible outcomes do possess a degree of potential surprise, the Shackle schematic does take account (even if it does not do so as comprehensively as we suggested it should earlier in this article) of the *range* of outcomes. So that it is somewhat more in tune with intuition than the Wald, Savage and possibly the Hurwicz criterion.

Additionally, Milnor (1954) has proposed nine axioms which should be satisfied by a theory of decision making under uncertainty. He has shown that the Wald, Hurwicz and Savage criteria cannot satisfy all the axioms. However, in certain conditions (such as when the gambler-preference function is linearly additive in G and L), the Shackle theory can meet all of Milnor's axioms[5].

Concluding Remarks

The theory of decision making under uncertainty that George Shackle has advanced is one of the most seminal theories in economics, *per theory*, to have been developed in the last 40 years or so. It is a theory that is elegant, imaginative and challenging. It is pre-eminently a theory which endeavours to place the theory of decision making under uncertainty in a realistic framework.

We might disagree with the explicit and implicit behavioural axioms upon which the theory is founded. But the notions that economic agents cannot rely on probability in taking decisions under uncertainty and that they do simplify (somehow or other) the imagined prospects on the alternative strategies open to them, have much to commend them. However, whether we accept them or not we find that the Shackle paradigm will, almost universally, permit all forms of decisions under uncertainty to be solved, and so it stands comparison with the orthodox approach.

The Shackle decision criterion also compares favourably, in particular circumstances, with the classical decision criteria. In general, we can suggest that it is more intuitively appealing than they are.

However, arguably, there are problems with the Shackle schema. At times decision makers do appear to be acting illogically. Amendments to the scheme to remove those inconsistencies do permit a theory to be constructed which preserves part of Shackle's alleged insights into the axioms of human behaviour (including the notion that individuals are loss-averters) but which is more in keeping with the letter of the Expected Utility Theory (Ford, 1983, chapter 5).

Naturally, empirical evaluation of the relevant axioms and of the respective predictions will be needed before a complete evaluation of the competing models can be effected. The recent laboratory experiments on the axioms of Von Neumann-Morgenstern have indicated that choices can reveal various kinds of inconsistencies or irrationalities (see Kahneman and Tversky, 1979). Therefore, it is possible that Shackle's theory, which seems to reveal similar attributes, will prove to be tenable.

Notes

1. This is so despite the development of Prospect Theory (see Kahneman and Tversky, 1979) and of Regret Theory (see Loomes and Sugden, 1982). But in any case, these two "theories" are very much of the same lineage as the Expected Utility Theory, being founded on the probability calculus; despite the fact that the Loomes-Sugden paper carries the word "uncertainty" in its title.

2. On these see, for example, Von Neumann and Morgenstern (1947), Luce and Raiffa (1957), Hey (1979), and Ford (1983).

3. We draw attention to the fact that the averaging process will apply to outcomes or the "utility" of outcomes in the traditional approach. When drawing attention to the limitations of that approach Shackle has tended in all his writings to take as an example the application of it to the question of the appropriate investment in physical capital and to do so by taking the choice criterion prevalent in the literature at the time he published his seminal work on expectation, namely "choose that

Decision Making under Uncertainty   **69**

investment which promises the greatest expected returns". But, equally, and more generally, the criticism of the "averaging process" entailed there, applies to the notion that utilities attach to outcomes and it is expected utility across investments that is being maximised. Clearly, also in that situation, should utility be a linear function of outcomes, the decision maker is, effectively, choosing the strategy that promises (*à la* Bernouilli) the highest expected return.

4. We note once more that the analysis can be developed in terms of positive/negative returns or gains/losses. In this portfolio model we have adopted the more common procedure of working in terms of returns per unit of wealth invested in an asset: so that the choice of portfolio has to be made by reference to *total* positive/negative returns. The latter being scaled-up values of the focus-returns on the relevant asset; the scalar being the level of wealth invested in the asset. However, we have continually referred in parentheses to the parallel concept in Shackle's presentation of his theory and have retained "gains", "losses" on the gambler-preference diagram.

5. This assertion requires a comprehensive analysis to support it which cannot be attempted in this paper. For some further analysis, see Ford (1984).

References

Carter, C. F., "Expectation in Economics", *Economic Journal,* Vol. 60, 1950, pp. 92-105.

Egerton, R. A. D., "Safety-first or Gambler-preference and the Holding of Assets", *Oxford Economic Papers,* Vol. 8, 1956, pp. 51-59.

Egerton, R. A. D., *Investment Decisions under Uncertainty,* Liverpool, Liverpool University Press, 1960.

Ford, J. L., *Choice, Expectation and Uncertainty,* Oxford, Basil Blackwell, 1983.

Ford, J. L. S., "G. L. S. Shackle's Theory of Expectations: A Critical Overview", paper prepared for Shackle Conference, Guildford, 1984.

Hey, J. D., *Uncertainty in Microeconomics,* Oxford, Martin Robertson, 1979.

Hurwicz, L., "Optimality Criteria for Decision Making under Uncertainty", Cowles Commission, Discussion Paper, 1951.

Jeffreys, H., *Theory of Probability,* Cambridge, Cambridge University Press, 1939.

Kahneman, D. and Tversky, A., "Prospect Theory: An Analysis of Decisions under Risk", *Econometrica,* Vol. 47, 1979, pp. 263-291.

Krelle, W., "Review of G. L. S. Shackle, *Uncertainty in Economics",* *Econometrica,* Vol. 25, 1957, pp. 618-19.

Loomes, G. and Sugden, R., "Regret Theory: An Alternative Theory of Rational Choice under Uncertainty", *Economic Journal,* Vol. 92, 1982, pp. 805-824.

Luce, D. R. and Raiffa, H., *Games and Decisions,* New York, John Wiley and Sons, 1957.

Milnor, "Games against Nature" in Kalish, G. K., Thral, R. M., Coombs, C. H. and Davis, R. L., *Decision Processes,* New York, Wiley, 1951.

Ozga, S., *Expectations in Economics,* London, Weidenfeld and Nicolson, 1965.

Roy, A. D., "Safety-first and the Holding of Assets", *Econometrica,* Vol. 20, 1952, pp. 431-449.

Sandmo, A., "The Effect of Uncertainty on Saving Decisions", *Review of Economic Studies,* Vol. 37, 1970, pp. 353-360.

Schneller, G. O. and Sphicas, G. P., "Decision Making under Uncertainty: Starr's Domain Criterion", *Theory and Decision,* Vol. 15, 1983, pp. 321-336.

Venn, J., *The Logic of Chance,* 3rd edition, London, Methuen, 1880.

Von Neumann, J. and Morgenstern, O., *The Theory of Games and Economic Behaviour,* second edition, Princeton, Princeton University Press, 1947.

[10]

The Possibility of Possibility

by John D. Hey
University of York

It is now over 35 years since Professor Shackle published his masterly *Expectation in Economics,* therein formalising and synthesising his innovative work of the previous decade. Since then, though in varying degrees, controversy has raged over the relevance of his ideas for economic theory, and over the relevance of economic theory for economic life.

This essay* is confined to one small part of Professor Shackle's work, though possibly a part which has become one of his trademarks: that is, his work on *possibility* and *potential surprise*. At the same time, this work characterises neatly the particular nature of Professor Shackle's thinking, and illustrates simultaneously the appeal of that thinking and the frustration experienced by those who fall prey to that appeal.

Possibility as an *uncertainty-variable* (to use Professor Shackle's own, eminently appropriate terminology) has an immediate intuitive appeal. Intuition also favours it over *probability* as an uncertainty-variable, especially in view of the latter's association with statistics and mathematics. However, frustrations set in when one tries to formalise one's intuition about possibility, and, moreover, when one attempts to distinguish this formalisation from a similarly formalised version of probability. Relying on theoretical arguments alone one is often driven to the conclusion that either possibility and probability are one and the same (in that there is a one-to-one mapping between them), or that possibility is an all-or-nothing characteristic, therefore being subsumed in terms of richness by probability. However, Professor Shackle and others would disagree.

Over the past 35 years, and particularly so over the 20 or so years since the first edition of *Decision, Order and Time in Human Affairs* was published, the conventional wisdom in economics has moved on (though not necessarily progressed) significantly, despite effectively ignoring Professor Shackle's contributions. This conventional wisdom now essentially accepts that the appropriate uncertainty-variable is *subjective probability (as expressed through preferences amongst uncertain choices)*. This reflects a fundamental shift from the view of 20 years ago.

The reasons for this shift lie partly in the increased use of mathematics and axiom-based theories, and partly in the now almost universal acceptance of the notion that,

*I am indebted to Professor George Shackle, Professor Steve Littlechild, Dr Frank Stephen and to participants in the George Shackle Conference held at the University of Surrey on the 7th and 8th of September 1984 for helpful comments.

since tastes and beliefs inevitably influence choice, then the study of choices can reveal the tastes and beliefs that lie behind them. Thus, the conventional wisdom would argue that one can determine the "uncertainty-variable" which influences choice simply by examining the choices which are made. Furthermore, and most crucially, if choices are made in a "consistent" manner then the "uncertainty-variable" which emerges has all the characteristics of probability. Hence the current predominance of subjective probability as the "correct" uncertainty-variable. It is interesting to note that, even in the second edition of *Decision, Order and Time* (published in 1969), Professor Shackle makes only passing reference (p. 104) to "subjective probability, |as| represented by the views of Ramsey, de Finetti and Savage", and no works of these authors are cited in his bibliography.

Let me be more specific. The conventional wisdom in economics accepts that Subjective Expected Utility (SEU) theory is the "correct" way of describing, and hence predicting, choice under uncertainty. SEU theory has two components: a utility function, defined over the final consequences; and a probability function, defined over the "states of the world". Both components are subjective; both reflect the individual's choice in uncertain situations: the utility function reflects the individual's assessment of the worth of the final consequences; the probability function reflects the individual's assessment of the relative likelihood of the various states of the world.

To save space, let me assume that the individual's utility function has already been determined. (The ways of doing this are already well documented in the literature; see, for example, Hey, 1984.) All that remains is to determine the individual's probability function. To do this, one proceeds as follows: let S be some "state of the world", for which one wishes to discover the individual's subjective probability evaluation. Let $\overline{S}$ denote the complement of S: that is, $\overline{S}$ happens whenever S does not, and *vice versa*. Let $P(S)$ denote the individual's subjective probability evaluation of S. Then one confronts the individual with a choice of the following form:

	S	$\overline{S}$
C_1	1	0
C_2	p	p

where the table entries indicate the *utilities* gained by the individual if the relevant (choice, state-of-the-world) pair obtains. Thus, if the individual chooses C_1, then he or she will get utility 1 if S occurs and utility 0 otherwise; while if the individual chooses C_2, then he or she will get utility p regardless of whether or not S occurs.

One then asks the individual to specify the value of p at which he or she is indifferent between C_1 and C_2; let us call this p^*. Then, presumably, for $p > p^*$, C_2 is preferred to C_1; while for $p < p^*$, C_1 is preferred to C_2. It seems reasonable to assume that such a p^* exists: for if $p = 0$ then C_2 "clearly" is not preferable to C_1, while if $p = 1$ then C_1 "clearly" is not preferable to C_2.

One can then conclude that $P(S) = p^*$. (Since the expected utility of C_1 is $1 \times P(S)$ $+ 0 \times P(\overline{S}) = P(S)$, and the expected utility of C_2 is p. At $p = p^*$ these are equal, since at $p = p^*$ the individual is indifferent between C_1 and C_2. Thus $P(S) = p^*$, if the individual's choice is determined by expected utility. Note, in passing, that this also implies that $P(\overline{S}) = 1 - P(S) = 1 - p^*$, for otherwise the utility of choice C_2, for $p = p^*$, would not equal p^*, which would be absurd.)

Of course, the inferred "probability" must be *context-free*. Thus, if the individual is subsequently asked to determine the value of q, call it q^*, at which he or she is indifferent between D_1 and D_2 in the following choice:

	S	$\overline{S}$
D_1	$a+b$	a
D_2	q	q

then q^* must equal $a + bp^*$ (for otherwise $P(S)$ would be inferred as p^* in the first situation, and as $(q^*-a)/b$ in the second). In a sense this requirement rather trivially follows from the fact that the (Von Neumann-Morgenstern) utilities are unique only up to a linear transformation.

That the inferred "probabilities" do have the properties of probabilities, (thereby justifying the removal of the inverted commas) can be seen fairly easily. Consider, for example, the addition rule for mutually exclusive events. Let S_1 and S_2 be mutually exclusive, and let S_3 denote the residual state of the world $(\overline{S_1 \cup S_2})$. Suppose $P(S_1)$ and $P(S_2)$ are determined as p^*_1 and p^*_2 respectively using the method described above. Thus the individual is indifferent between C_1 and C_2 and between D_1 and D_2 where

	S_1	$S_2 \cup S_3$
C_1	1	0
C_2	p^*_1	p^*_1

	S_2	$S_1 \cup S_3$
D_1	1	0
D_2	p^*_2	p^*_2

Now consider the choice between E_1 and E_2 as given by

	$S_1 \cup S_2$	S_3
E_1	1	0
E_2	q	q

Let $q = q^*$ be the value at which the individual is indifferent between E_1 and E_2. One can argue that $q^* = p^*_1 + p^*_2$ as follows: choice E_1 is clearly the same as having *both* C_1 and D_1 but the individual is clearly indifferent between having both C_1 and D_1 and C_2 and D_2; now the latter is equivalent to having $p^*_1 + p^*_2$ whatever happens — which is the same as E_2 with $q = p^*_1 + p^*_2$. Thus $P(S_1 \cup S_2) = q^* = p^*_1 + p^*_2 = P(S_1) + P(S_2)$; which is the addition rule for mutually exclusive events.

Furthermore, it is apparent that "rational" behaviour requires that $0 \leq P(S) \leq 1$ for all S, with the equalities holding only if the individual believes that S is certain either not to happen or to happen.

The conclusion, of course, is thus that subjective probabilities are simply things which emerge from rational individual choice. Thus no theorising about what is the "correct" uncertainty-variable is needed. In other words, most of the frantic early debates on the subject were unnecessary.

What would Professor Shackle make of all this? He could deny the *consistency* requirements (the "definition" of "rational" behaviour) by arguing that choice is too complex. He could deny the *existence* requirement by arguing that real life is too vague. I suspect, however, he would dismiss the very framework of analysis. In particular, I would imagine he would be very unhappy about the "state of the world" $\overline{S}$, which necessarily constitutes a *residual hypothesis*. In his *Decision, Order and Time,* he specifically states that "the essential condition for the use of a distributional uncertainty variable is that the list of suggested answers should be complete without a residual hypothesis" (Shackle, 1961(a), p. 49).

Professor Shackle's preferred uncertainty-variable is, of course, *possibility*, or, equivalently, *potential surprise* (the two being inversely related). He specifically dismisses the use of *probability* (whether objective or subjective) largely but not solely on the grounds that probability is a distributional variable, and thus necessarily inconsistent with the existence of a residual hypothesis.

Before the current conventional wisdom (as described above) became generally accepted, there were numerous theoretical discussions concerning possibility and probability and their relationship (if any). I do not intend to add to this extensive literature in this article. Nor do I intend to speculate further as to how this literature might have differed if Professor Shackle had published his *Expectation in Economics* some 30 years later, except to point out that the current conventional wisdom would regard much of the *theoretical* discussion as being unnecessary or irrelevant — the key issues being essentially empirical.

Remarkably, there has been precious little empirical work on the specific question of the "correct" uncertainty variable. It is the purpose of this article to attempt to remedy this deficiency. In a sense, the "obvious" way to investigate this question — at least as viewed from the modern viewpoint — would be to investigate whether individuals can make consistent rational choices under uncertainty, and whether their subjective probabilities can indeed be inferred from these probabilities. This could, however, be regarded as unfair to Professor Shackle and his supporters, particularly in that it would very much be an *indirect* test of the key question. So I decided to take the bull by the horns and enquire *directly* into possibility and probability, and their relationship.

I adopted an "experimental" approach for this enquiry. The experiment reported on in this article was one of a series carried out with funds provided by the Innovation and Research Priming Fund Committee of the University of York. I am most grateful to this Committee for their support. Subjects were paid volunteers, all students from the University of York. The amount received varied between £2 and £10 for a three-quarter-hour-or-so session; payment was linked to their answers, as described below.

The "experiment" was performed at a computer terminal, linked to the University's mainframe; the subject was alone in the terminal room. A total of 16 subjects performed the experiment, each of whom was sent the instructions some time in advance of the time at which they were to perform the experiment. (These instructions are reproduced in the Appendix to this article. It will probably clarify the following discussion if this Appendix were read before proceeding further with the main text.) Subjects came to my office at pre-arranged times, and there was ample opportunity for subjects to question me before they performed the experiment. Some took more advantage of this than others.

As can be seen from the Appendix, the experiment involved three separate *uncertain situations:* the first was that of the weather on York campus the following day; the second was that of the subject's "employment status" in June of the year following graduation; the third was that of the Prime Minister of the UK in June 1989 (that is, a year after the latest possible date of the next General Election). In each uncertain situation, there were several possible outcomes (specified by me in the first two situations and by them in the third).

The purpose of the experiment was to get the subjects to appraise the uncertainty involved in each situation in *four different ways;* the first three being (1) possibility, (2) potential surprise and (3) probability and the fourth being (4) the minimum selling price of a lottery ticket. The ultimate objective of the experiment was, of course, to see whether these four different ways were one and the same, or whether, as Professor Shackle would assert, that (1) and (2) say the same thing, but something different from what (3) and (4) mutually say. More fundamentally, I was intrigued to know whether the subjects could, indeed, appraise the uncertainty in these four different ways. To encourage them in their efforts, I told them that their payment would be linked to their answers, but I did not specify the nature of this link. (In fact, their payment depended on their answers to the lottery ticket question in Uncertain Situation 1 and on the weather on York campus the day after they did the experiment.)

Let me be more specific. Consider, for example, Uncertain Situation 1, the weather on York campus at noon the following day. I followed *The Times'* categorisation and invited the subjects to consider the eight mutually exclusive and exhaustive categories: cloud, drizzle, fair, fog, rain, snow, sun, thunder. Subjects were then asked to assess each of the eight categories in each of the four ways mentioned above.

First, they were asked to specify, on a scale from 0 to 9, how possible they thought each outcome was: 0 was to signify completely impossible, 4 or 5 as moderately possible and 9 as perfectly possible (note the use of Professor Shackle's term), with intervening numbers signifying intervening possibilities. Second, they were asked to specify, again on a scale from 0 to 9, how surprised they would be if each outcome were to occur: 0 was to signify complete absence of surprise, 4 or 5 moderate surprise;

9 total amazement, and so on. Third, they were asked to specify, again on a scale from 0 to 9, how probable they thought each outcome was. Finally, they were asked to specify the minimum amount for which they would sell a lottery ticket (which would yield £10 if the outcome were to occur and £0 otherwise). The answers for this, of course, should (did) lie between 0 and 10. Full details are given in the Appendix.

Subjects were also invited, if they felt unable to answer any of the questions, to enter a negative number rather than a number between 0 and 9 (or 10). *None of the subjects exercised this option.* In other words, all the subjects indicated that they understood the questions and felt able to answer them. This caused *me* more surprise than anything! (This *may* have been a consequence of the vaguely-specified reward structure: on this, see later.)

In Uncertain Situation 2, there were seven possible outcomes, one of which was a *residual hypothesis*. None of the subjects mentioned any difficulty in coping with this residual category.

In Uncertain Situation 3, the subjects themselves were asked to specify the list of possibilities. They were specifically asked to keep the list to a reasonable length and to include a residual "catch-all" category. None of the subjects mentioned any difficulty in constructing this list or in coping with the residual except for one foreign student (subject 12) who commented that her "knowledge regarding British policy is rather weak"; nevertheless she answered all the questions. The length of the list of possibilities varied from five (subject 12) to 18 (subject 1).

To summarise: subjects were asked to specify, for each of the outcomes in each of the three uncertain situations, (1) the possibility, (2) the potential surprise and (3) the probability (all on an integer scale from 0 to 9 inclusive) and (4) the minimum selling price of a lottery ticket (on a continuous scale from 0 to 10). A typical set of answers (subject 9) is shown in Table I.

Before proceeding to an analysis of the results, it may be useful at this stage to make a few general comments about the experimental design.

First, the choice of Uncertain Situations: I wanted these to be spaced at different points in time, so that I could assess the impact of time on the subjects' responses. The idea behind this was the intuitive notion that uncertainty appears to be greater the more distant in time is the resolution of the uncertainty. Thus, there is very little uncertainty about the possibilities for weather tomorrow, rather more about the possibilities for employment some one to three years hence, and much more about the possibilities for the UK Prime Minister in 1989. (The experiments were conducted in June 1984.) The actual choice of Uncertain Situations was quite difficult: I wanted to choose situations which were reasonably familiar and meaningful to the subjects, but I also wanted to avoid the "moral hazard problem". This relates specifically to the "minimum selling price of a lottery ticket" question: clearly if the occurrence of the possibilities is (partly) under the control of the subject then the question becomes rather meaningless. In fact, this is partly a problem with Uncertain Situation 2, though only one subject seemed to notice that. (In her comments, at the end of the experiment, subject 7 remarked: ". . .the prices to sell tickets for confused me as in the second situation I could deceive the person I'm selling it to".) I suppose I could have "personalised" the Uncertain Situations, and made them specific to the subject, but that would have complicated matters enormously.

Table I. Raw Answers of Subject 9

	(1)	(2)	(3)	(4)
Uncertain situation 1				
cloud	5	2	5	2.00
drizzle	3	3	4	3.00
fair	4	2	5	3.00
fog	1	8	2	0.50
rain	4	4	3	3.00
snow	0	9	1	0.10
sun	7	1	6	4.00
thunder	0	7	2	0.25
Uncertain situation 2				
employed	4	4	5	3.00
in HM forces	0	9	0	0.05
registered unemployed	1	8	1	1.00
self-employed	6	3	6	6.00
student	3	7	2	2.00
unregistered unemployed	2	2	3	1.00
other	1	6	3	1.00
Uncertain situation 3				
Thatcher	5	5	5	4.50
Kinnock	2	6	3	3.00
Steele	4	5	4	3.00
Owen	3	6	2	2.00
Some other member of Labour party	7	2	7	7.00
Some other member of Tory party	3	7	5	3.50
Some other member of Alliance	2	7	2	1.00
A member of some other party	1	8	1	0.50
Someone else	1	8	0	0.25

(1) possibility   (2) potential surprise
(3) probability   (4) minimum selling price of lottery ticket.

Second, the choice of questions and the mode of the required responses: in a sense I wanted to make the three questions (possibility, potential surprise and probability) symmetrical, so that no biases were inbuilt. But this may be regarded as inappropriate. In particular, it would be argued that I should have asked for a specific number to represent probability, so that I could have tested the proposition that the probabilities summed to one. This criticism appears to miss the point — since the "probability" question does not reveal the subject's subjective-probability-as-expressed-through-preferences-amongst-uncertain-choices; for this latter is revealed through the minimum selling price question. Rather the "probability" question tests whether subjects can rank possibilities in terms of *how probable they think they are;* this is quite different from "subjective probability" as specified above. However, if the conventional wisdom is correct, then one would hope that there is some strong connection between these two things; for instance, it would be very odd if a subject had a lower minimum selling price for an event that he or she thought more probable.

Further, it could be argued that it is not sensible to rank the possibility, or potential surprise, of the residual hypothesis ("some other outcome"). This may be true, but none of the subjects specifically said so, and none refused to do the required ranking.

Of course, it may have been the case that subjects felt obliged to answer all questions, including those they really thought were unanswerable, (despite being repeatedly invited to decline to answer any question), because of the vaguely specified reward structure. As can be seen from the Appendix, subjects were simply told: "Your payment will depend upon your answers to the questions, so it is in your interest to be as careful as possible in your answers. All will be revealed after the experiment." The reason why I linked the reward to their performance was obviously to provide an incentive for careful responses. The reason why I was rather vague was because the only sensible way to make this link was through their answers to the minimum selling price question in Uncertain Situation 1. (In practice, I chose one of the possibilities at random, chose "lottery" or "minimum selling price" at random, observed the *actual* weather at noon the next day, and paid them accordingly.) However, if subjects had actually known this, then they might have restricted their careful responses to this one question on the one Uncertain Situation. This would not have been satisfactory. However, as it stood, subjects may well have misinterpreted the reward structure to mean that their payment would be larger if all questions were answered and if their answers were consistent. I appreciate that there is a problem here, but I am not sure what one can do about it (except dispensing with any incentive mechanism).

In the written instructions I discouraged any attempt at consistency (among the responses to the four questions) by insisting that each question be answered independently. (See the Appendix: "I appreciate that these various ways of appraising uncertain situations overlap; but please consider these one at a time, trying to banish thoughts of the others".) This was reinforced in the experiment itself by *not* displaying to the subject the responses on the four questions simultaneously. (After the responses on *each* question, the set of responses for *that* question were displayed; and the subject invited to change any he or she wished to change.) As far as I know, none of the subjects kept a written record of their responses. So any conscious attempt at consistency by the subjects would have had to rely on conscious memory: this would have been very difficult indeed.

One major drawback of my experimental design was that the uncertain situations were "static"; that is, the various possibilities were fixed once-and-for-all. It would have been particularly interesting to explore (a) the effect of changing information, and (b) the effect of changing the list of possibilities (by, for example, being more precise about the "residual hypothesis"), on the subjects' responses. This would have enabled some much stronger tests of Professor Shackle's theories to be implemented. Unfortunately, the difficulty of incorporating such changes into the experimental

78 Journal of Economic Studies 12,1/2

design detered me from trying; but this is clearly an important next step in further experiments.

Now let us turn to the results. Some general comments about the responses may be of interest before we turn to a detailed statistical analysis.

(1) Recorded values of *possibility* ranged over all integral values between and including 0 and 9, except for one subject (no. 6) whose values were all *either* 0 *or* 9. (Subject 6 thus follows Professor Carter in thinking that all outcomes are either impossible or perfectly possible; on this, see Shackle's discussion in chapter 11 of *Decision, Order and Time*.)

(2) Just three out of nine subjects who somewhere gave a 9 for possibility *always* simultaneously gave a 0 for potential surprise. (This is in marked contrast to Professor Shackle's assertion on p. 76 of *Decision, Order and Time* that "perfect possibility is...unequivocally represented by zero potential surprise in all instances".)

(3) In contrast, seven out of 11 subjects who somewhere gave a 0 for possibility *always* simultaneously gave a 9 for potential surprise. (Again this is something that intuition would suggest, for surely, if something you regard as impossible were actually to occur, you would be totally amazed. Not so with 4 of my subjects!)

(4) Only one of the 16 subjects entered a 0 for potential surprise for at least one of the outcomes in each uncertain situation; five subjects had at least one zero in two situations; seven had at least one zero in just one situation; and three subjects had no zeros for potential surprise anywhere. (This goes sharply against Shackle's axiom 9 which states that "at least one member of an exhaustive set of rival hypotheses must carry zero potential surprise", Shackle, 1961(a), p. 81.)

(5) For all subjects and in each uncertain situation the *sum* of the minimum selling prices always exceeded 10, sometimes by a considerable margin. Perhaps they were all risk-lovers, but I doubt it. (On this, see later.)

The above points suggest quite clearly that there was some considerable semantic confusion, or, at least, considerable differences in interpretation amongst the subjects. This rather neatly reflects similar confusions in the early literature.

Now let us turn to a more systematic analysis. In essence, Professor Shackle's point is that possibility and potential surprise are very closely (and inversely) related, and *possibly* that probability and minimum selling price of lottery ticket are closely related, but that the first pair is not related to the second pair. One obvious way to examine this is to inspect the correlation matrix of these four indicators. Table II presents the relevant matrices for subject 9 (whose raw scores were given in Table I).

All the signs in Table II are as expected. The correlation between possibility and potential surprise is higher than that between possibility and probability in situation 3 but not elsewhere. Similarly, the correlation between possibility and probability is lower than that between probability and minimum selling price in situation 3 but not elsewhere. Clearly Table II does not contain any dramatic evidence to suggest that Professor Shackle's views are correct.

Table II. Correlation Matrices of Subject 9

Uncertain situation 1 (8 observations)

	(1)	(2)	(3)	(4)
(1)	1.0	−0.93	0.93	0.90
(2)	−0.93	1.0	−0.97	−0.92
(3)	0.93	−0.97	1.0	0.86
(4)	0.90	−0.92	0.86	1.0

Uncertain situation 2 (7 observations)

	(1)	(2)	(3)	(4)
(1)	1.0	−0.66	0.89	0.97
(2)	−0.66	1.0	−0.82	−0.57
(3)	0.89	−0.82	1.0	0.86
(4)	0.97	−0.57	0.86	1.0

Uncertain situation 3 (9 observations)

	(1)	(2)	(3)	(4)
(1)	1.0	−0.95	0.91	0.94
(2)	−0.95	1.0	−0.84	−0.92
(3)	0.91	−0.84	1.0	0.96
(4)	0.94	−0.92	0.96	1.0

Overall (24 observations)

	(1)	(2)	(3)	(4)
(1)	1.0	−0.82	0.89	0.90
(2)	−0.82	1.0	−0.83	−0.67
(3)	0.89	−0.83	1.0	0.88
(4)	0.90	−0.67	0.88	1.0

(1) possibility (2) potential surprise
(3) probability (4) minimum selling price of lottery ticket.

An analysis of all the subjects is presented in Tables III and IV. Table III reports correlations between possibility and the other three uncertainty-variables for each subject over all three uncertain situations. (The data were pooled; the number of observations for each subject is indicated in the table.)

A glance at Table III will reveal that the correlation between possibility and potential surprise was higher than that between possibility and probability for seven of the 16 subjects, and was lower for eight of the 16 subjects. Again, this is hardly conclusive evidence in support of Professor Shackle's position. Table IV looks at this comparison in more detail. Again, the evidence does not support Professor Shackle. (In situation 1, $r_{(1)(2)}$ is greater than, equal to and less than $r_{(1)(3)}$ for 3, 3 and 9 of the subjects respectively (ignoring subject 14 who was clearly confused). In situation 2, the corresponding figures are 8, 2 and 6; and in situation 3, 7, 1 and 8.)

Table III. Overall Correlations of Possibility with the Other Indicators

Subject no.	$r_{(1)(2)}$	$r_{(1)(3)}$	$r_{(1)(4)}$	n
1	− 0.94	0.92	0.91	33
2	− 0.95	0.85	0.80	25
3	− 0.92	0.92	0.91	28
4	− 0.88	0.87	0.79	23
5	0.92	0.90	0.87	26
6(a)	− 0.33†	0.39*	0.49*	22
7	− 0.83	0.92	0.93	24
8	− 0.84	0.78	0.81	23
9	− 0.82	0.89	0.90	24
10	− 0.82	0.92	0.89	24
11	− 0.65	0.93	0.81	21
12	− 0.86	0.87	0.93	20
13	− 0.93	0.87	0.88	32
14(b)	− 0.43*	0.42*	0.40*	22
15	− 0.93	0.98	0.96	24
16	− 0.85	0.87	0.87	24

r_{ab}: correlation coefficient between a and b

(1) possibility
(3) probability

(2) potential surprise
(4) minimum selling price of lottery ticket.

*significant at 5 per cent level.
†*not* significant at 5 per cent level.   All rest significant at one per cent level.

(a) subject whose values for (1) were either 0 or 9.
(b) subject clearly showed confusion in situation 1 (see Table IV).

A comparison of the results in the three uncertain situations revealed no obvious pattern. As I remarked earlier, I had deliberately chosen the three situations so that they were spaced at different points in time — with Uncertain Situation 1 being the nearest and Uncertain Situation 3 the most distant. I had hoped that some pattern in the responses would emerge; to be specific, I had expected that the correlations between the four uncertainty-variables would be greatest in Uncertain Situation 1 and least in Uncertain Situation 3 — reflecting the increasing uncertainty with time. But no such pattern emerged. Indeed, the correlation matrices were broadly similar in each of the three Uncertain Situations — see, for example, Table II (though I did not carry out any formal tests of the proposition that they were the same). Because of this similarity, I save space below in reporting the results of analyses using *pooled data;* that is, data on the three Uncertain Situations combined. The number of observations varies from subject to subject, because the number of possibilities in Uncertain Situation 3 varies from subject to subject.

Table IV. Correlations of Possibility with Potential Surprise and Probability

Subject no.	Situation 1		Situation 2		Situation 3	
	$r_{(1)(2)}$	$r_{(1)(3)}$	$r_{(1)(2)}$	$r_{(1)(3)}$	$r_{(1)(2)}$	$r_{(1)(3)}$
1	− 0.95	0.98	− 0.95	0.90	− 0.93	0.91
2	− 0.97	0.85	− 0.99	0.99	− 0.97	0.93
3	− 0.97	0.97	− 0.81*	0.89	− 0.95	0.97
4	− 0.97	0.90	− 0.97	0.90	− 0.77*	0.76*
5	− 0.97	0.94	− 0.95	0.97	− 0.96	0.94
6(a)	− 0.78*	0.90	0.00(c)†	0.00(c)†	0.00(c)†	0.00(c)†
7	− 0.88	0.96	− 0.95	0.97	− 0.74*	0.84
8	− 0.76*	0.88	− 0.98	0.65†	− 0.80	0.88
9	− 0.93	0.93	− 0.66†	0.89	− 0.95	0.91
10	− 0.87	0.96	− 0.97	0.95	− 0.87	0.89
11	− 0.91	0.94	− 0.92	0.96	− 0.75*	0.85*
12	− 0.91	0.98	− 0.93	0.74*	− 0.69(d)	0.14(d)†
13	− 0.98	0.98	− 0.93	0.92	− 0.93	0.72
14(b)	0.77(b)*	−0.70(b)	− 0.99	0.95	− 0.93	0.96
15	− 0.98	0.99	− 0.97	0.98	− 0.90	0.96
16	− 0.91	0.92	− 0.93	0.87	− 0.83*	0.93

For notes other than (c) and (d) see Table III.
(c) No variation in values for possibility.
(d) Overseas subject with poor knowledge of British politics.

It is clear from the various analyses described above that, in general, all four uncertainty-variables are very closely related. The natural question to ask, therefore, is whether they are in fact all saying the same thing. The obvious statistical technique to investigate this question is principal components analysis. This I performed for each of the subjects for each of the three uncertain situations and for the three situations pooled. To save space, I report below merely the results for the pooled observations; those for the three uncertain situations separately were very similar. (I will gladly provide details to any interested reader on request.)

Table V. Principal Components Analysis for Subject 9 (Pooled Data)

	PC1	PC2	PC3	PC4
Eigenvalues	15.14	1.61	0.43	0.23
% eigenvalues	86.96	9.27	2.48	1.29
Eigenvectors	− 0.51	− 0.24	0.68	− 0.46
	0.58	− 0.76	− 0.03	− 0.28
	0.48	0.16	0.73	0.47
	−0.42	− 0.58	− 0.05	0.70

The principal components analysis was performed on the raw data. An example is given in Table V, which reports the results for the pooled raw data for subject 9. This is the same subject to whom Tables I and II related.

Table V reveals that, for subject 9, the first principal component accounts for almost 87 per cent of the total variance of the four uncertainty-variables, the second principal component accounts for over nine per cent, and the last two for just two per cent and one per cent respectively. So all four uncertainty-variables are *almost* all saying the same thing, though it does appear that there may be *two* messages emerging from the four indicators.

A formal test of the hypothesis that there are "really" only k significant principal components ($k = 1$ or 2) is given in Dhrymes (1970), to which the reader should refer for further details. The test requires the construction of a variable which has a chi-squared distribution with five or two degrees of freedom under the null hypothesis that there are "really" only one or two "significant" principal components. Table VI reports the observed values of these variables for the 16 subjects using pooled data.

Table VI. Test Statistics for the Hypothesis that there are k Significant Principal Components

Subject	k 1	2
1	9.2	0.5
2	31.4**	11.9**
3	9.5	0.3
4	9.1	1.2
5	1.9	0.1
6	34.6**	0.2
7	12.1**	0.6
8	7.5	4.2
9	21.1**	2.1
10	18.4**	4.0
11	23.6**	3.0
12	5.5	0.6
13	8.2	3.9
14	50.7**	11.5**
15	19.1**	1.6
16	11.7*	8.0**

**significant at one per cent level.
*significant at 5 per cent level.

Table VI shows that, for seven of the 16 subjects, only the first principal component is "significant". Thus, for these seven, all four uncertainty-variables are saying the same thing. In particular, possibility, potential surprise and probability are simply alternative ways of expressing the subjects' assessment of the uncertainty present in the three situations. Moreover, these three are a good guide to choice since the minimum selling price of the lottery ticket is highly correlated with all three.

Of the remaining nine subjects, six have two, rather than one, "significant" principal components (though for subject 7 the second is significant at merely the five per cent level); the remaining three subjects apparently have three "significant" principal components.

Let me begin by looking at those six subjects with two "significant" principal components (subjects 6, 7, 9, 10, 11 and 15). For subject 6 it is quite clear from an inspection of the relevant correlation matrix, that it is *possibility* which essentially forms the second principal component, the first being mutually formed from the other three uncertainty-variables. In this instance, the reason is not hard to find: it may be recalled that this subject had just 0s and 9s as values for possibility. So possibility for this subject is different, but only in that it is less "rich". For the other five subjects (7, 9, 10, 11 and 15) the correlation matrix reveals clearly that the second principal component is formed primarily by *potential surprise,* the first being mutually formed from the other three uncertainty-variables. For subject 9, this can be confirmed from Table II. Thus, for these five subjects, possibility and probability are effectively saying the same thing (which is different from potential surprise), and both are a good guide to choice (through their high correlation with the minimum selling price).

Finally, let me look at the three subjects (2, 14 and 16) who appear to have three "significant" principal components. For subject 2 the correlation matrix suggests that the first principal component is derived from all four indicators, with the second and third being derived from the residuals of the pairs (possibility and potential surprise) and (probability and minimum selling price) respectively. This case is the nearest to that suggested by Professor Shackle. No clear pattern emerges for subject 16, while subject 14 appears to have been very confused (or perhaps a trifle drunk), as Tables III and IV will confirm. Perhaps not too much should be read into the results for subject 14!

Unfortunately, lack of space precludes detailed reporting of various other analyses I performed. However, I would be happy to supply the raw data and details of other analyses to interested readers on request. The general impression is, however, accurately conveyed by the above summary.

Let me begin my concluding remarks by noting that what surprised me the most about the experiment was the fact that *all* the subjects answered *all* the questions. Let me emphasise that they were repeatedly given the opportunity to refuse to answer a question if they felt unable to answer or if they felt that they did not understand the question. So it is, indeed, surprising that no one took up this opportunity. I appreciate that subjects do not like to appear stupid, but it was made clear to them that there were no correct answers and that it was perfectly acceptable not to give an answer.

I also made it clear that they should answer each question independently — that is, they should, for example, try to empty their minds of all considerations other than possibility when answering the possibility question. Of course, I cannot judge how successful they were at doing this; or, indeed, if such a thing is possible. When invited to comment (on the computer) at the end of the experiment, four of the subjects specifically said that they found it difficult to distinguish between possibility and probability. But that in itself is interesting.

In a sense, the very fact that all the subjects answered all the questions (even those relating to a residual hypothesis) seriously undermines Professor Shackle's position. His position is further weakened by the fact that, for seven of the 16 subjects, all four uncertainty variables seemed to be saying the same thing. Moreover, most of the remaining nine subjects had potential surprise as standing alone from the other three, so the experiment does little to confirm Professor Shackle's position.

How does the conventional wisdom emerge from this analysis? The fact that all subjects answered the minimum-selling-price question appears to confirm the *existence* of subjective-probability-as-expressed-through-preferences-amongst-uncertain-choices. However, the experimental design did not permit the testing of whether the implicit "probabilities" were context-free, nor whether they indeed had the properties of probabilities. To do this, one would need to ask composite questions of various kinds. Moreover, one would also need to find the utility function of the subjects; this would complicate matters considerably. Implicit in much of my discussion above is the assumption that subjects are approximately risk-neutral in the range of £0 to £10. But this assumption is clearly inconsistent with the assertion that the implicit "probabilities" do, indeed, have the properties of probability given that for *all* the subjects, in each uncertain situation, the sum of the minimum selling prices always exceeded 10, sometimes by a considerable margin.

So the experiment casts doubt on both the conventional wisdom and on Professor Shackle's position, though in my opinion the damage to the latter is the greater. Some of the observations can clearly be rationalised in terms of a random error term, though the greatest evidence against Professor Shackle's position is the fact that all the subjects answered all the questions. This may, however, be the fault of the vaguely-specified reward structure. This could be improved in future experiments, which should also extend the analysis to include changing information and changing possibilities. Such further experiments look promising.

At this stage, it seems I should conclude: possibly possibility, probably probability. Is this surprising?

References
Dhrymes, P. J., *Econometrics,* New York, Harper and Row, 1970.
Hey, J. D., "Decision under Uncertainty", in F. Van der Ploeg (Ed.), *Mathematical Methods in Economics,* Wiley, 1984.

Appendix

Uncertain Situations

Thank you for agreeing to take part in this simple "experiment". Its purpose is to attempt to discover the way that people perceive and describe uncertain situations. The "experiment" should not take more than three-quarters of an hour of your time. Your co-operation is greatly appreciated.

The "experiment" is conducted at a computer terminal, which is simple to operate. I will tell you how to operate the terminal in due course, but first I will describe the basic structure of the "experiment".

The "experiment" involves three separate *uncertain situations.* The first is that of the weather on York campus at noon tomorrow (that is, the day after you perform the experiment); the second is that of your "employment status" in June of the year following your expected graduation from York; the third is that of the Prime Minister of the UK in June 1989 (that is, a year after the latest possible date for the next General Election). For each of these three uncertain situations, there are obviously a variety of possible outcomes (these are discussed below). You will be asked to appraise these possible outcomes in three different ways: namely (1) their possibility, (2) their potential for surprise, and (3) their probability. In addition, you will be asked to indicate for how much you would wish to sell lottery tickets whose prizes depend on the actual outcomes. I will discuss these in more detail below, but first I will describe the three uncertain situations and their respective possible outcomes.

Uncertain Situation 1: The weather on York campus at noon tomorrow (that is the day after you perform the experiment)
To describe the various possible outcomes, I follow *The Times* in adopting the following categorisation:

1. cloud
2. drizzle
3. fair
4. fog
5. rain
6. snow
7. sun
8. thunder.

In reporting the weather at a particular place at a particular time, *The Times* uses *one and only one* of the above categories. Thus the above eight categories are to be understood as *mutually exclusive* and *exhaustive*. You are to follow the practice adopted by *The Times*. (If you are unhappy about this, or do not understand what it means, please discuss it with me *before* you do the experiment.)

Uncertain Situation 2: Your "destination category" in June of the year following your expected graduation from York
To describe the various possible destinations, I follow the Department of Employment in adopting the following categorisation:

1. employed
2. in HM Forces
3. registered unemployed
4. self-employed
5. student
6. unregistered unemployed
7. other.

In reporting a person's "destination category" at a particular time, the Department of Employment uses *one and only one* of the above categories. Thus the above seven categories are to be understood as *mutually exclusive* and *exhaustive*. You are to follow the practice adopted by the Department of Employment when considering *your* "destination category" in June of the year following your expected graduation from York. (If you are unhappy about this, or do not understand what it means, please discuss it with me *before* you do the experiment.)

Uncertain Situation 3: The Prime Minister of the UK in June 1989 (that is, in June of the year following the latest date for the next General Election)
In this situation, *you* will be asked to list the various possibilities. You should proceed as in the other two situations, and provide a list of *mutually exclusive* and *exhaustive* possibilities. I would suggest starting with specific names, (such as "Thatcher", "Kinnock", "Steele", "Owen", etc); then moving on to non-specific members of specific political parties, such as "some other member of the Labour Party", "some other member of the Conservative Party", etc); concluding with the very general "someone else". (Do not insert

quotation marks.) You will be given the opportunity to revise your list until you are satisfied with it. (If you wish to alter (or delete) a particular entry, the computer will ask you to specify the entry number and then to enter the altered entry (which will be nothing if you wish to delete the entry). If you wish to add an additional entry, the computer will ask you to specify the new entry number and then to enter the new entry.) Please ensure that your list is such that *one and only one* of the list can be the Prime Minister of the UK in June 1989. (If you are unsure about this, or do not understand what it means, please discuss it with me *before* you do the experiment.)

For each of the uncertain situations, you will be asked for your views on the following:

(1) *How POSSIBLE you think each outcome is*
You will be asked to express this on a scale from 0 to 9: 0 (zero) should be used to indicate that you regard that outcome as COMPLETELY IMPOSSIBLE; 9 (nine) should be used to indicate that you regard that outcome as PERFECTLY POSSIBLE; intermediate integers should be used to indicate intermediate possibilities: thus, for example, 4 or 5 should be used to indicate that you regard that outcome as MODERATELY POSSIBLE; 1, 2 and 3 for less than moderately possible; and 6, 7 and 8 for more than moderately possible.

If, for any outcome, you feel unable to indicate how POSSIBLE you think that outcome is, then enter ANY NEGATIVE INTEGER.

(2) *How SURPRISED you would be if each outcome were to occur*
You will be asked to express this on a scale from 0 to 9: 0 (zero) should be used to indicate that you would NOT BE SURPRISED AT ALL if that outcome were to occur; 9 (nine) should be used to indicate that you would be TOTALLY AMAZED if that outcome were to occur; intermediate integers should be used to indicate intermediate degrees of surprise: thus, for example, 4 or 5 should be used to indicate that you would feel MODERATE SURPRISE if that outcome were to occur; 1, 2 and 3 for less than moderate surprise; and 6, 7 and 8 for more than moderate surprise.

If, for any outcome, you feel unable to indicate how much SURPRISE you would feel if that outcome were to occur, then enter ANY NEGATIVE INTEGER.

(3) *How PROBABLE you think each outcome is*
You will be asked to express this on a scale from 0 to 9: 0 (zero) should be used to indicate that you regard that outcome as COMPLETELY IMPROBABLE; 9 (nine) should be used to indicate that you regard that outcome as COMPLETELY CERTAIN to occur; intermediate integers should be used to indicate intermediate probabilities; thus, for example, 4 and 5 should be used to indicate roughly fifty-fifty probability; 1, 2 and 3 for less than fifty-fifty probability; and 6, 7 and 8 for more than fifty-fifty probability.

If, for any outcome, you feel unable to indicate how PROBABLE you think that outcome is, then enter ANY NEGATIVE INTEGER.

(4) *How much you would sell lottery tickets for*
Consider a particular outcome of a particular uncertain situation: say, rain on York campus at noon tomorrow. Consider a lottery ticket which pays you £10 at noon tomorrow if the outcome occurs (that is, if it is raining on York campus at noon tomorrow) but £0 otherwise. *Imagine you have been given such a ticket.* Now ask yourself what is the *smallest* amount of money for which you would be willing to sell this ticket (with payment at noon tomorrow). Call this £x. Then you presumably are indifferent between (1) the prospect of definitely having £x at noon tomorrow, and (2) the prospect of having £10 at noon tomorrow if it is raining then and £0 otherwise. The computer will ask you to determine the appropriate value of x. Note carefully that there is no objectively correct answer: simply respond with *your* value of x. (Do not enter a £ sign). Presumably if you think that rain tomorrow is relatively unlikely, then the lottery ticket is relatively worthless and so your value of x is relatively low; but if you think that rain tomorrow is quite likely, then your value of x will be quite high. But the precise value of x is entirely up to you.

You will be asked to specify the relevant value of x for *each* outcome in each uncertain situation. Do remember that, for each outcome you are being asked: "What is the *smallest* price for which you would sell a lottery ticket which you have been given which pays you £10 if the specific outcome occurs and £0 otherwise". Note: all the relevant payments are to be made at the time of the resolution of the

uncertainty (that is, at noon tomorrow in Uncertain Situation 1, in June of the year following graduation in Uncertain Situation 2, and in June 1989 in Uncertain Situation 3).

If, for any outcome, you feel unable to indicate this minimum selling price, then enter ANY NEGATIVE
number.

I appreciate that these various ways of appraising uncertain situations overlap; but please consider these
one at a time, trying to banish thoughts of the others. So, when you are considering the POSSIBILITY
question, concentrate solely on HOW POSSIBLE you think the various outcomes are. Likewise for the
other questions.

If you have any doubts as to what I am asking you to do, please check with me *before* you do the experiment. You will get an opportunity to comment on the experiment at the end, but by then it may be too late!

The above describes the structure of the experiment; below I describe the practical details.

PRACTICAL DETAILS
The experiment is conducted in the Terminal Room of the Department of Philosophy (Derwent C004).
I am most grateful to the Department of Philosophy for permission to use this room.

When you are seated comfortably, switch on the computer terminal (a rocker switch at the back of the
machine at the bottom right). Press RETURN. When the machine has warmed up, type

LOG 15055,14504

and then press RETURN. (Carefully note the difference between the letter O and the number 0; in these
instructions, the number zero is typed Ø). The computer will then respond with a message which ends with

PASSWORD:

Now type in

EXPTS

and then press RETURN. Note that the word EXPTS will not actually appear on the screen; this is for
security reasons.

The computer will now respond with lots of information of no relevance to this experiment. Ignore it.
When the information has been printed, and the computer finally types a . (full stop), type in

RUN EXPTG

and then press RETURN. The experiment has now begun. (If, at any stage, you make a typing mistake, use the

key (situated at the lower right of the keyboard) *before* pressing RETURN. Each time you press — the
computer backspaces one character; so backspace the appropriate number of characters, then type in the
correct entry (and then press RETURN).

The operation of the experiment itself is explanatory. The three situations are presented in order, and
the four types of questions asked for each. At the end, you will be invited to type in any comments. The
programme will then automatically terminate.

Finally, type

/ENDG

wait a few moments until the machine reports that "EXPERIMENTS has logged off", and then switch
off the computer.

Your payment will depend upon your answers to the questions, so it is in your interest to be as careful
as possible in your answers. All will be revealed the day after the experiment. Please come to my office
to get paid.

Summary
    (1)   Read this document carefully in advance. Bring these instructions with you when you come to
           do the experiment.
    (2)   Start the experiment by following the instructions in the PRACTICAL DETAILS above.

(3) The program explains things as it goes along (but refer back to these instructions if necessary). Take your time.

(4) After the experiment is finished, type /ENDG and switch off the computer.

(5) Come to my office (Alcuin D201C) the day after the experiment to get paid.

I am very grateful to you for taking part in this experiment. If you would be interested in learning about the outcomes of this and other experiments, do let me know.

Thank you very much.

[11]

Professor Shackle and the Liquidity Preference Theory of Interest Rates

by Peter G. McGregor*
University of Strathclyde

Introduction

Professor Shackle has long maintained both the originality of the liquidity preference theory of interest rates and its paramount importance for macroeconomics. He has argued, for example, that:

> The greatest innovation in Keynes's great trilogy of the *Treatise*, the *General Theory* and the epilogue in the *QJE*, is his theory of the rate of interest. (Shackle, 1974, p. 54.)
>
> "Liquidity preference" is an explanation of the level of interest-rates which relieves them of their duty or their competence to equalize the full-employment intended saving flow with the full-employment intended net investment flow, and leaves them free to be "too high" for this equalization, so that there is general heavy unemployment as there was in the 1930s; or to be "too low" for this equalization, so that there is a persisting rise of the general price-level, as there has been from 1945 to 1965. (Shackle, 1967, p. 207)|1|.

This view of the liquidity preference theory of interest contrasts markedly both with that expressed in recent contributions to monetary theory and with that implicit in modern mainstream macroeconomics. Indeed, the latter appears, at least, to afford the interest rate "maladjustment", to which Shackle refers above, no central role, and instead gives primary emphasis to the degree of wage and price flexibility|2|. However, a number of recent articles of a more specialist monetary theory orientation might be construed as heralding a re-awakening of concern with, and renewed assertion of the importance of, the theory of interest. The remarkable feature of these contributions by Kohn (1981(a), (b)), Laidler (1984), Leijonhufvud (1981) and Tsiang (1980, 1982) is, though, their universal support for a loanable funds (LF) theory of interest. It seems that the liquidity preference theory of the rate of interest is now widely regarded as either unimportant, incorrect or both.

This article seeks to provide a critical evaluation of Shackle's account of the liquidity preference theory of interest in the light of recent contributions to macroeconomics and monetary theory. Our concern is consequently with only a small part of Shackle's

*The article as a whole, and the second and fourth sections in particular, draw liberally on the product of joint research undertaken with Andrew Bain, who was initially approached to be co-author of this article. His response reflected, I hope, a combination of pressure of other work and modesty, rather than caution. I am indebted to him for encouragement and for extensive comments on, and detailed discussion of, many aspects of my work in this area. I am also grateful to participants in the 1984 Scottish Economists' Conference (especially Geoff Harcourt and Alistair Dow) for helpful comments on an earlier version.

90   Journal of Economic Studies 12,1/2

extensive contributions to economics, although this is a part of his work which is fundamental to his distinctive vision of the macro-economy. Thus, whilst the liquidity preference theory of interest is, in Shackle's view, but one manifestation of the pervasive influence of (non-probabilistic) uncertainty[3], its impact on the propensity to consume and the marginal efficiency of capital[4] would be a matter of much less concern for macroeconomics in the absence of interest rate maladjustment.

The second section of this article attempts to clarify the basis of the debate on interest theory. It is argued there that much of the dispute centred on the question of the immediate effects of changes in productivity and thrift on the rate of interest, i.e., it concerned *impact interval* interest theory[5]. However, different theorists have, often implicitly, employed different definitions of, for example, "the impact interval" and "the rate of interest", so we seek to avoid possible confusion by acknowledging these differences and recognising their possible analytical significance.

The three subsequent sections of the article analyse Shackle's impact interval interpretation of liquidity preference (LP) theory. The first of these sections is concerned with the accuracy of Shackle's interpretation of Keynes' interest theory. The latter two are concerned with the two key elements of Shackle's interpretation: the stock-flow issue and the role of expectations, respectively. Our basic argument is that Shackle has succeeded, where others have not, in combining and motivating elements identifiable in Keynes' writings into a coherent, logically consistent, instantaneous interval liquidity preference theory of the bond rate. Nevertheless, some doubts are expressed concerning the universal applicability of Shackle's theory, and we suggest that it is perhaps most usefully employed in conjunction with an apparently conflicting theory, depending on circumstances.

Whilst the crux of the debate on interest theory, on the present interpretation, is the behaviour of interest rates over some impact interval, the importance attributed to any interest rate maladjustment in such an interval depends on its likely persistence. The sixth section of the article takes up this issue, and, in particular, addresses the question of whether wage and price flexibility can correct any interest rate maladjustment and thereby provide at least partial support for mainstream macroeconomics' comparative neglect of interest theory. This proves to be critically dependent on the source of interest rate maladjustment, a fact which leads us to accept Shackle's, but reject Leijonhufvud's (1981), logic for placing the interest rate at the very centre of the macroeconomic stage. Brief concluding remarks are presented in the final section.

Preliminaries
The debate on theories of interest was concerned primarily with the immediate effects of changes in productivity and thrift on the rate of interest. The notion that interest rates could, and indeed would, adjust so as to equalise "the full employment intended saving flow with the full employment intended net investment flow" was the heart of the "classical" theory of interest. In this theory interest rate adjustments ensured continuous equality of *ex ante* saving and investment flows. LP theory is commonly interpreted (following the emphasis of Keynes' *General Theory*) as denying any immediate influence of either *ex ante* saving or investment flows on interest rates[6]. LF, in contrast, implies that disturbances to both productivity and thrift push interest rates in the direction envisaged in "classical" theory, but fail to call forth an exactly

compensating change in the other components of aggregate demand over the impact interval.

This outline raises a number of questions concerning the precise definition of terms and assumed institutional contexts. The remainder of this section attempts to identify and clarify these potential sources of confusion.

First, there is some evidence that the nature of the "market" on which interest is presumed to be determined varies among contributors to the debate. LF theory appears to have its roots in the context of a Wicksellian model of interest rate determination. Here, "the" interest rate is that on bank loans and the source of any maladjustment is inelasticity of banks' expectations (Ackley, 1957; and Leijonhufvud, 1981). Market forces ultimately punish and so lead to a correction of such maladjustment (Leijonhufvud, 1981).

In Shackle's view of LP theory, however, "the" interest rate (to anticipate our subsequent discussion of this issue) is that on (long-term) bonds. In contrast to the Wicksellian system the interest rate reflects the price of a continuously marketable asset with capital value uncertainty. Shackle's assumed market structure seems *a priori* to offer far greater opportunities for speculation to drive the interest rate away from its "natural" level and, perhaps, keep it there. Specifically, the presumed dominance of pre-existing bond stocks over the flows stemming from plans for new saving and investment provides a vehicle for maladjustment which cannot be matched merely by bankers' inelastic expectations.

This does not, in itself, validate rejection of LF theory on the grounds of its inapplicability to anything other than rudimentary financial systems, but it does suggest that there are possible dangers in failing to link arguments to a specific, explicitly stated institutional context. Thus there seems to be a tendency among LF theorists to think in terms of the determination of the interest rate on loans, rather than in terms of the determination of actual bond prices. For a given institutional structure this, of course, makes no difference at all, but in view of the origins of the two theories, and in particular their associations with different types of assets, in practice it may have contributed a little to the confusion which is sometimes apparent in the literature.

Theorists have also differed in their definitions of the impact interval over which interest theory is to be considered. Hahn (1955), for example, draws attention to both the *finance* and *expenditure* intervals. The former refers to the period over which the finance for planned expenditures is raised, but expenditures are not yet implemented. The latter includes the interval over which implementation of plans occurs, but prior to the operation of the induced multiplier effects on income and their feedback onto financial markets. Shackle[7] has seemed to reject such period (i.e., discrete-time) analysis in favour of an *instantaneous interval* analysis. As we show subsequently, the choice among these intervals can have a very significant bearing on the results obtained. Consequently, we also consider the question of which impact interval it is appropriate to adopt.

Contributions to the interest theory literature have often discussed the determination of "the" interest rate without explicitly stating the precise nature of the asset which is the focal point of their analysis. Consequently, authors have occasionally seemed to differ quite markedly in their implicit assumptions concerning the term to maturity of the "representative" financial asset. Nor can this difference be resolved by appeal to, for example, the expectations theory of the term structure: over impact intervals, at least, the notion of a perfectly integrated set of financial markets seems untenable (and many would dispute its relevance over much longer intervals). As illustrative of the significance of this point, it is worth drawing attention to the existence of what we take to be two quite distinct LP theories of interest[8]. One theory, apparent in Hahn (1955), Rose (1957), Edwards (1966) and Grossman (1971) emphasises the implications for interest theory of the need to use the loan market to finance *unanticipated* savings and investment flows, as well as their planned counterparts, over the expenditure interval. Either these authors had interest rates on short-term bills in mind when they constructed their theories or the latter must be rejected as wholly unconvincing: the long-term bond market hardly seems an appropriate vehicle for financing unanticipated income flows. Long-term bonds are particularly unsuited to playing the role of a "financial buffer"[9].

Shackle, in contrast, like Kahn (1954) explicitly concerns himself with an LP theory of the interest rate on long-term bonds. Furthermore, not only does the maturity of the chosen asset differ, but so too does the impact interval to which the analysis relates. As noted above, Shackle adopts an instantaneous interval of analysis, in general, in preference to what he perceives to be the arbitrary nature of period analysis. The roots of both LP theories can be found in Robinson (1951). In the remainder of this article we confine ourselves to a consideration of the LP theory of bond interest rate determination. However, we allow for a variety of impact intervals because of our view that these significantly influence choice among competing theories.

Having cleared the ground of a number of possible sources of confusion, we are now in a position to proceed to a critical evaluation of Shackle's interpretation of LP theory. First, we consider the extent to which Shackle's views constitute a valid interpretation of Keynes' own writings on interest theory. Second, we provide a critical evaluation of Shackle's view of interest. The crux of this theory is that bond prices, and hence interest rates, are determined in what he describes as a *speculative* market, in the sense implied by the following quotations:

> The price which traces the play of a speculative market is *inherently restless,* its movements are in some degree self-generating. (Shackle, 1974, p. 57, my emphasis.)
> |H|e (i.e., Keynes) brought in not only the speculative bond market "determining", or tossing up and down, the long-term interest rate, but the notion of liquidity preference itself, which embraces the whole gamut of influences: speculative, political, diplomatic and even fashionable, which bear upon men's thoughts, emotions, imaginations and resolves. Keynes showed that interest is a *psychic* phenomenon, in a meaning wholly overshadowing time preference. (Shackle, 1974, pp. 60-61.)

The bond market is "speculative" in the sense that it is *dominated* by speculative activity which has the effect of generating considerable fluctuations in the bond rate of interest. Speculation is clearly viewed as destabilising in its effects, "tossing up and down" the bond rate irrespective of the level of any "natural" rate of interest. The elements of the theory are spelt out by Shackle:

> The interest rate arises from *uncertainty* about the future prices of the bonds given by borrowers in exchange for loans; it depends upon the valuation of *stocks* rather than flows; it balances the conflicting views, about the imminent movement of those bond prices, entertained by *two camps* within the group of holders or potential holders of these bonds. (Shackle, 1967(a), p. 154.)

The lender of money on the bond market "cannot know at what price the bond will be saleable at a future date, and he cannot know at which date he may wish to sell it" (Shackle, 1967, p. 203). This uncertainty is ultimately at the root of the speculative dominance of the bond market. However, uncertainty *per se* does not account for speculative dominance: this requires, in addition, the two other elements referred to by Shackle in the above quotation. The stock-flow issue and the nature and role of expectations are discussed in the fourth and fifth sections respectively.

Shackle on Keynes on Interest

Shackle[10] has often argued that Keynes' theory of interest rate determination as expounded in the *General Theory* and in his subsequent *Economic Journal* contributions (Keynes, 1937(a), (b)) was flawed by its dependence on the appeal to the *ex post* equality of savings and investment flows as a major element in its critique of classical interest theory.

It is perhaps worth noting that (an admittedly somewhat speculative) alternative interpretation exists[11]: that Keynes in these passages was seeking to draw attention to classical and loanable funds theories' apparent neglect of the need to finance all expenditure flows, whether planned or not. For consider the response of a world of commodity price rigidity to an increase in planned saving destined for the loan market. If the fulfilment of all planned expenditures is ensured by inventory adjustments, then over the expenditure period firms have to finance the unintended accumulation of stocks which is generated by the disturbance. If this unanticipated flow is financed on the same basis as the intended flow interest rates are unaffected by the disturbance over the chosen impact interval. This, at its simplest, is the basis of the literature referred to earlier stemming from Robinson (1951), Hahn (1955) and Rose (1957).

Tentative supporting evidence for this view is offered by the fact that Keynes did not appear to be hampered by the *ex ante/ex post* "confusion" in the creation of his theory of income determination, as Shackle himself has noted. Thoroughgoing confusion on this issue would have precluded the development of a theory which asserted that an increase in saving generated a fall in income which corrected the initial savings-investment gap.

Shackle (1974(a), p. 12) notes that Keynes, at least on one notable occasion, had appeared to grasp the essence of the *ex ante* concept of saving and investment. The interpretation offered above provides a possible alternative to Shackle's view that Keynes had intuitively grasped the significance of the distinction at one point, but neglected it elsewhere.

Nevertheless, even if this view were to be wholly accepted, it is of no assistance in the development of an LP theory of the *bond* rate: as already noted, the bond market seems an unlikely vehicle for financing unanticipated expenditures; the expenditure interval would be considered too long (at least by Shackle) to facilitate appropriate analysis of the bond market.

Shackle's interpretation of Keynes' theory is consequently based primarily on Keynes' *Treatise*. Thus he writes that:

It [i.e., Keynes' theory of the rate of interest] is presented in fullest, freshest and liveliest colours, and almost in its completed form, in the *Treatise*. It does not emerge there all in one place and in one piece, but seems to take shape under our eyes in Keynes' thought. (Shackle, 1974(a), p. 54.)

As Shackle's (1974(a)) subsequent quotations from the *Treatise* illustrate, many of the elements of a liquidity preference theory of the bond rate are present therein. However, it is Shackle who combines and motivates these elements into a coherent theory of bond rate determination. To Shackle must go a significant part of the credit, and responsibility, for the theory that ultimately emerges from his reading of the *Treatise*|12|.

Stocks versus Flows|13|
Ex ante investment and saving flows manifest themselves in the bond market as *increments* to the total supply and demand for bonds respectively. Shackle has repeatedly argued|14| that these increments are small relative to outstanding stocks of bonds over the appropriate interval, and that their influence may consequently be entirely swamped by the influence of the latter with obvious consequences for both the classical and LF theories of interest. In the present section this "stock-flow" issue is examined in some detail.

The analysis is divided into two main parts which deal with discrete and continuous time respectively. The former category covers both finance and expenditure interval analyses, whilst the latter relates exclusively to the instantaneous interval. In adopting the discrete/continuous time distinction, the analysis reflects the emphasis of recent literature concerned with the appropriate formulation of asset market equilibrium in macroeconomic models|15|. However, as will become apparent, our analysis attributes far greater significance to this distinction than the current literature affords it, and indeed we attempt to show that the choice of impact interval can be critical in determining results.

Period Analyses
It has already been suggested that this is not a part of Shackle's perspective of LP theory, but a brief review is nevertheless essential to an appreciation of Shackle's position|16|.

Over the finance interval, LF results are assured provided that *ex ante* flows are at least partially financed in the bond market as Hahn (1955) had clearly recognised. However, Shackle often argues as if an increase in saving was likely to be entirely "money financed", in which case LP results hold|17|. As will become clearer in section six below, for Shackle a critical feature of money in a world of uncertainty is that it permits deferment of choice — it facilitates avoidance of specific commitment. If, as Shackle presumes, increased saving often reflects increased caution in the face of an uncertain future, money is the ideal vehicle for effecting the decision and the "all money financing" case takes on considerable practical relevance. Even if mixed money-bond financing is considered, finance interval analysis seems to offer a fairly weak foundation for LF theory since casual empiricism suggests that it has no real world counterpart: no neat finance-expenditure distinction is apparent in the real world|18|.

The literature postulating a *finance constraint* (by which is meant a *money* constraint) on expenditures claims to validate LF results over the expenditure interval (for the case with at least partial bond financing of disturbances)|19|. This literature, based upon a Robertsonian period analysis, effectively constrains finance interval behaviour to extend to the expenditure interval as a whole by ruling out post-finance interval access to asset markets. This restriction, in our view, is generally unwarranted and leads to an over-mechanical theory of money and of other asset markets, which is critically dependent on the presence of a Robertsonian consumption lag[20].

Foley (1975) proposed another discrete time (expenditure interval) formulation of asset equilibrium which ensures LF results, namely the *end of period* concept of equilibrium. Here asset prices adjust, at the beginning of the period, to equate end-of-period demands and supplies, which reflect the influence of *ex ante* saving and investment flows for the coming interval. As Buiter (1980) has argued, this concept of equilibrium implies that asset markets are in the nature of one-period forward markets. The concept consequently seems to us to be of little use in providing a theoretical basis for an LF theory of *bond* rates[21].

The end-of-period asset equilibrium is contrasted to the (expenditure interval) *beginning-of-period* concept of equilibrium in asset markets (Foley, 1975). Here asset prices are viewed as adjusting so as to ensure that transactors are content to hold beginning-of-period asset stocks. This formulation lends itself to a spot market interpretation[22], and precludes any influence for *ex ante* saving and investment flows and so is held to represent an LP theory of interest. This latter property, however, reflects neglect of the need for transactions balances related to planned expenditures over any finite interval (given restricted asset market access over the interval). The LP character of this concept of asset equilibrium does not, in general, survive a corrected specification.

A third possible discrete time rational for an LF theory of bond rates can be derived from consideration of the implications of the existence of financial buffers which act as "shock absorbers" in the financial system. Laidler (1984) was first to draw attention to this possibility, although his arguments were apparently not intended to be confined to bond interest rates and the precise rationale for the LF result is not spelt out (and tended to be linked, unnecessarily, to a Robertsonian analysis). Our view is that this argument is at best applicable to bond (or, at least, non-buffer) rates, and that its force derives from the way in which financial buffers facilitate transitory beginning-of-period portfolio shifts and insulate non-buffer markets from undesigned income and expenditure flows which arise over the interval. This renders feasible a *spot* market interpretation of LF theory which is not tied to any particular formulation of the consumption function[23].

This brief review of period analyses of asset markets offers little support for the notion that saving and investment plans have no impact on current interest rates: flows are important in a discrete time context[24]. The one important exception to this is where such flows find their initial impact in money holdings alone. In view of his judgement as to the source of many major macroeconomic disturbances, this is an exception which we suspect Shackle would wish to emphasise. However, Shackle's position in any case seems to imply rejection of all period analyses in favour of an instantaneous interval approach, a point illustrated by the following comment on Tsiang's (1956) finance constraint article:

> We feel bound to say that this statement betrays a misunderstanding of the *methodology* of liquidity preference theory. That theory elects to concentrate on the question: Given the expectations, plans, uncertainties, hopes and fears, as well as the distribution of resources, which exist *at some moment*, where

must the price of bonds stand to equilibrate the resulting market impulses? (Shackle, 1961(a), p. 264, emphasis added.)

Here, as elsewhere[25], Shackle's position is suggestive of the need for adoption of a continuous time framework for investigation of the stock-flow issue. This is the subject matter of the next section of the article.

Continuous Time Analyses

The impact of continous time analysis has recently been explored in depth in the context of the literature concerned with beginning- and end-of-period equilibria. The "limiting form", as the time interval tends to zero, of the beginning-of-period specification is a pure-stock model in which *ex ante* flows have no role to play[26]. Since transactions requirements over a zero time interval are also zero, this result would be unaffected by modifying the specification of the discrete time model in the way suggested in the preceding section. The limiting form of the end-of-period specification of equilibrium is also a pure-stock continuous time model as, in effect, Buiter and Woglom (1977) and Turnovsky and Burmeister (1977) showed[27]. Indeed, it transpires that the "limiting forms" of *all* the discrete time models discussed in the preceding subsection above are equivalent, and preclude any influence for *ex ante* flows[28]. As Shackle had long ago suggested[29], adoption of an instantaneous impact interval generates an LP theory of interest. This is so despite the fact that, as we have seen, there is a presumption in favour of LF in period analyses except where disturbances are entirely money financed. Evidently the choice of impact interval, and especially of discrete versus continuous time, is critically important.

This position contrasts with that apparent in much of the recent literature[30]. Foley (1975, p. 310), for example, enunciated the following "methodological precept"[31].

No substantive prediction or explanation in a well-defined macroeconomic period model should depend on the real time length of the period.

Either our analysis or this precept is unacceptable, and, naturally, we prefer the latter position. The process of allowing the time interval of analysis to tend to zero in our view fundamentally alters the character of period models which cannot, in any real sense, be said to have "continuous time equivalents". The time interval in period analyses is not selected arbitrarily, at least in so far as the intention of the architects of such approaches is that the chosen interval should possess behavioural significance. Of course, this judgement is open to dispute, but the crucial point is that the time interval cannot simply be shrunk to zero without violating a basic premiss of all period analyses. In the eyes of advocates of such analyses, it is the limiting process itself, and not the choice of discrete time interval, which is arbitrary. The interval is chosen so as to permit some types of behaviour, but preclude others. This distinction is violated by the limiting process. For example, a Robertsonian period is *defined* in terms of the interval required for the money stock to change hands once and for expenditure plans to be implemented. As the time interval tends to zero the distinction between lagged and current income loses its meaning as does the entire Robertsonian analysis. But this clearly does not constitute a refutation of that analysis unless good reasons are advanced for believing that the technical limiting process results in economic behaviour which is meaningful.

Period analyses are generally founded, sometimes implicitly, on the notion that transactions costs, or some other "friction" in the system inhibits or precludes some types of behaviour over the interval. To investigate the effects of allowing these intervals to tend to zero clearly involves examining the behaviour of the world *in the absence of such frictions:* it amounts to a denial of the very foundations of period analyses. This is why, in our view, the limiting forms of the *different* discrete time models of asset behaviour collapse to a *single* model in continuous time. This pure-stock model represents the appropriate specification of asset market equilibrium in a world of negligible transactions costs: it has nothing whatsoever to do with the period models from which it can be technically derived.

No doubt, in some circumstances, the specification of discrete time models can be altered so that some vestige of their character would be apparent even after the limiting process. Foley (1975, 1977), for example, shows, in effect, that flows remain significant in continuous time, provided portfolio reallocation is subject to a partial adjustment parameter. Nevertheless, this preserves only one of the range of possible mechanisms which could conceivably afford flows some significance in real world asset markets.

The continuous time, pure-stock model seems to embody an assumption of negligible transactions costs, at least relative to the costs of being out of desired portfolio positions. Shackle's preference for such an analysis seems to stem in large part from the presumed volatility of expectations. Dramatic revisions to expectations imply that the cost of deviations from desired portfolio positions is likely to be high relative to the cost of revising the allocation of portfolios. Instantaneous adjustment of portfolios consequently makes sense. However, it should be emphasised that this is not the motivation of extant continuous time formulations, which are all far too "well-behaved" to be capable of capturing Shackle's views. We now turn to consider expectations and their bearing on bond market behaviour.

Expectations and Speculation
Both the feasibility and the nature of spot market speculation are integrally related to the stock-flow characteristics of any market. Markets for perishable or ephemeral goods/services are comparatively unaffected by speculation and merely reflect the influence of the tastes and initial endowments of transactors, in accordance with traditional value theory|32|. Markets for durable goods facilitate, and may require, the holding of inventories which can, in general, be deployed either to effect a stabilising or destabilising effect on market price, consumption and production|33|. Where the costs of holding, and adjusting, inventories are high and where flows onto the market are relatively large, Ackley (1983) argues that inventories are likely to be used to smooth production and consumption and moderate price fluctuations. The reason is that transactors expect future flows to dominate the determination of market price, and so expectations are "disciplined" by the impact of flows, and speculation is stabilising.

In contrast, in markets where holding costs are low and where new production and demands are small relative to outstanding stocks, flows over the relevant time interval may be relatively unimportant. This could be so partly simply because of the absolute size of production, but also because low holding costs are likely to be associated with lower minimum sensible expected holding periods. In this context (that which Shackle

98   Journal of Economic Studies 12,1/2

considers relevant for bond market analysis), flows are not expected to have a signifi-
cant influence on market price, and so they do not act to constrain expectations|34|.
Rather, speculation becomes concerned with "anticipating what average opinion ex-
pects the average opinion to be" (Keynes, 1936, p. 156). There is an infinite regress
of expectations about expectations|35|. Shackle's (e.g., 1972, chapter 19) pure gambler
model of the bond market captures the essence of real bond markets: interest becomes
a *psychic* phenomenon|36|.

An important element in Shackle's approach, and, indeed, in that of other "fundamentalist Keynesians"/"post-Keynesians" is the emphasis on the *heterogeneity* of
speculators' expectations|37|. The current market clearing interest rate reflects an
uneasy balance between the "bulls", who hold bonds in anticipation of capital appreciation, and the "bears", who hold money to avoid an anticipated negative return
on bonds|38|. Events must prove either all bulls or all bears wrong in their initial ex-
pectations, and this must undermine the basis of the initial equilibrium. Some bulls
must become bears or *vice versa* until a new tentative equilibrium is established. This
is the source of Shackle's view that interest is an *inherently restless* variable|39|.

Expectations, and thus the market clearing interest rate, are subject to continual
revision in response to "news". The same, of course, is true of many rational expectations models of asset markets, and of particular relevance in the present context is
the class of models based on the efficient markets hypothesis|40|. This similarity reflects
what might be described as the identical *expectational structure* of the two approaches
in the sense that the structural models imply that "only surprises matter". Here the
similarity ends, however. In rational expectations models "news" usually simply takes
the form of updated estimates of the values of the exogenous variables of the relevant, and correct, model of asset price determination that is presumed to be known
to all transactors. News permits new unbiased forecasts to be formed conditional on
the new information set|41|. In Shackle's account of LP theory "news" is fresh infor-
mation on whatever the market *psychology* deems to be relevant to price determination. Expectations are revised capriciously, and not necessarily in response to a change
in any underlying "objective reality". The future is unknowable in Shackle's view
whereas the rational expectations hypothesis assumes that foresight is perfect on
average: the hypothesis assumes that the probability distributions attached to all
possibilities are assumed to be known and used as the basis of individuals' expectations.

Shackle's vision seems to imply that in asset markets expectations are continuously
revised, that there is considerable instability and that prices are frequently subject to
dramatic changes. This is the basis of Shackle's objection to Hicks' (1935) suggestion
to marginalise the theory of money. Expectations of bond price changes can be such
that there is no margin at which the transactor is happy with his/her portfolio; the
whole of his wealth (with the exception of a reserve) may be shifted into and out of
bonds in response to news|42|.

This vision of turbulence in bond markets is also the major source of Shackle's
objection to period analyses:

> Values of assets of "lasting" type can thus be created and destroyed in a moment, without any accom-
> paniment of time-using acts of production, consumption or exchange. Not merely Say's Law but Walras'
> Law, applied to any interval of finite length, however short, must be abandoned, for between its beginning

and end a man's total wealth can increase, not by productive effort and saving, but "out of nothing"; and can likewise dissolve. (Shackle, 1967(a), p. 246)|43|.

Herein lies Shackle's motivation of an instantaneous interval analysis, and the implications for LF theory are clear in view of our earlier analysis.

Despite the inherent turbulence of bond markets, temporary intervals of stability are possible, not because of the "discipline" of factors stressed by value theory, but because of *convention*. However, such stability as does occur is extremely fragile, liable to give way to "cascading disorder" once the stability comes into doubt|44|.

We do not dispute that Shackle's vision of the bond market has, on occasion, appeared to capture the essential elements of its behaviour, but we do doubt its applicability over all time intervals. Specifically, comparative *tranquility* seems to us to be much more common than could be accommodated by Shackle's vision|45|. Within the "corridor" of comparative tranquility, expectations are not generally subject to dramatic revision (and so are not expected to be)|46|.

Within the corridor, "frictions" in real world asset markets are important relative to the costs of portfolio disequilibrium (related to the size of expected capital value changes), and the "only surprises matter" structure no longer applies. These frictions encompass transactions costs broadly defined and the predominance of institutional investors with long expected holding periods|47|. The instantaneous portfolio reshuffling envisaged in Shackle's theory would not occur|48|. Indeed, the existence of uncertainty in a world of irreversibilities somewhat paradoxically, inhibits the active portfolio management which seems central to Shackle's theory. Uncertainty, within the corridor, may actually *enhance* stability by encouraging adoption of more or less sophisticated "rules of thumb" among investors|49|.

In a world with frictions *in addition to* uncertainty (and not instead of it), period analysis may well be sensible. Furthermore, this is not despite uncertainty, but partly because of it. Nevertheless, uncertainty may well constrain the form of period analyses which are judged relevant. In particular, transactors would, more often than not, be incorrect in their conjectures and the response to undesigned income flows, for example, would have to be a central feature of the analysis. This, in our view, rules out beginning- and end-of-period concepts of asset market equilibrium. We would suggest, however, that the concept of financial buffers may provide a useful starting point in this regard|50|.

In summary, Shackle has been successful in developing a logically consistent LP theory of the bond rate out of the elements of Keynes' *Treatise*. In very turbulent times his instantaneous interval, pure-stock LP theory of the bond rate seems applicable. In comparatively tranquil times, period analysis — especially that based on the concept of financial buffers — cannot be dismissed and can be made consistent with Shackle's emphasis on uncertainty. In such intervals, an LF theory of the bond rate will be applicable for all disturbances other than those financed exclusively out of money balances.

The Significance of Interest Rate Maladjustment for Macroeconomics
Interest rate maladjustment could hardly be afforded greater significance than that attributed to it by Shackle (1967(a)) in the quotation presented in the introduction to this article, for it is therein asserted to be the source of all macroeconomic deviations

from a stable price, full-employment equilibrium. The Classical Theory, in holding that the interest rate adjusted so as to ensure pre-reconciliation of saving and investment plans, implied that disturbances to saving or investment influenced only the composition of aggregate demand without affecting its total. Rejection of the Classical Theory is thus an essential prerequisite to the development of a theory of involuntary unemployment.

The central point of Keynes' critique, according to Shackle, is that the Classical Theory neglects the impact of the existence of a (non-commodity) liquid asset in a world of uncertainty:

> If we sought to condense Keynes' whole thesis concerning employment into a single sentence, we might say that he ascribes the possibility of involuntary general unemployment to the existence of a liquid asset in a world of uncertainty. (Shackle, 1974, p. 28.)
>
> The reason why *money* destroys the full-employment nexus is that it makes possible the divergent composition of the incomes that employing enterprisers are willing to pay and the incomes that suppliers of services are willing to receive. (Shackle, 1974(a), p. 14.)

Money provides a store of generalised purchasing power. It permits *"deferment of specialised, fully detailed choice"*[51]. An increase in the propensity to save as a result of increased uncertainty is likely to be reflected in an increased desire for money balances since this provides a means of avoiding any specific commitments. However, even if desires for liquidity are met through increased supply, non-commodity money does not require an offsetting increase in the demand for labour for its production. Furthermore, there is no mechanism for communicating savers' intentions to potential investors[52] let alone for the pre-reconciliation of savings and investment plans. Indeed, there is little to communicate except that households have decided for the present and until some unspecified, indeterminate future date to avoid making specific commitments in the market for commodities or the market for loans.

The assumed circumstances, however, are precisely those in which firms are in greatest need of specific commitments from households. Production takes time, and for many products at least, occurs in advance of marketing. Firms, therefore, have to make employment and output decisions on the basis of anticipated sales. In the absence of signals to the contrary from households, firms, at times of particular uncertainty, are likely to revise their expectations of sales downwards.

The savings-consumption composition of the wage received by households has consequently shifted in exactly the opposite direction of that required by firms. This is the "divergent composition" of incomes to which Shackle refers in the above quotation, and it is clearly only possible because of the existence of a liquid asset which permits a retreat from specific commitments.

It is, of course, possible to reject both the Classical Theory of Interest and Keynes' proposed alternative. Indeed, as we have seen, Shackle rejects the account of interest rate determination of the *General Theory* in preference for that which he detects in Keynes' *Treatise*. Furthermore, the LF theory of interest rates is quite consistent with a theory of involuntary unemployment. The source of interest rate maladjustment in LF theory, however, is simply a degree of interest sensitivity of the transactions demand for money balances, although the theory would also concede the importance of the pattern of financing of the initial disturbance[53]. Nevertheless, "saving" is typically viewed as "lending" in this approach[54]. In LP theory, as interpreted by

Shackle, it is speculation concerning bond prices which is the main source of interest rate maladjustment, and, of secondary importance, the predominant source of shocks to the system is such as to lead to a presumption of all money financing of major disturbances. These differences prove to be of significance when considering the likely persistence of interest rate maladjustment.

Leijonhufvud (1981), building on one of the themes of his (1968) book, argues, in effect, that current mainstream macroecnomics has all but neglected interest rate maladjustment and mistakenly concentrated on issues of wage and price flexibility. However, given the LF account of interest rate maladjustment which Leijonhufvud (1981) prefers, and which, we have argued, may be relevant in tranquil periods, wage and price changes can, in principle, act in such a way as to correct the prices of today's goods relative to tomorrow's. An increase in planned saving, for example, exerts a deflationary impact on the economy as a whole. If wages and prices are responsive to own market excess demands in the manner conventionally assumed in general equilibrium theories, the excess supplies generated by the increased saving will reduce the transactions demand for money, and *ceteris paribus* tend to push the interest rate in the required direction. If wages and prices are ultimately perfectly flexible, the interest rate is eventually forced back to a level consistent with full employment equilibrium[55]. Price and wage flexibility can act in such a way as to compensate for interest rate maladjustment.

It is reasoning of this nature that, we suspect, has led to the concern of the recent macroeconomics literature with theories of price and wage adjustment rather than theories of interest. Mainstream Keynesian macroeconomics, for example, is now firmly rooted in the economics of multi-market quantity rationing, the proximate source of which is labour and commodity market price inflexibilities[56].

Whilst the traditional variant of monetarism admitted the possibility of involuntary unemployment, it emphasised the flexibility of wages and prices relative to the flexibility of corrective demand management policies[57]. More recent variants tend to assume perfect (instantaneous) price and wage flexibility with respect to perceived excess demands, and thereby preclude even a transitory manifestation of involuntary unemployment. In some accounts systematic misperceptions generate conventional cyclical behaviour. In Muth-rational expectations versions, however, systematic misperceptions are ruled out by assumption, and the need for an explanation of apparent cyclical behaviour has led to a search for sources of the persistence of the effects of non-persistent expectational errors.

Given a judgement that wage and price flexibility can overcome interest rate maladjustments, the emphasis of mainstream macroeconomics is defensible[58]. However, whilst Shackle recognised the possible corrective role of price and wage flexibility given that the source of interest rate maladjustment was the presence of an interest-elastic transactions demand for money, he explicitly denied its relevance to the speculative LP theory that he was, in part, responsible for developing[59].

Keynes' own major objection to wage and price flexibility as a solution to involuntary unemployment focused, as is well known, on the inability of labour as a whole to reduce its *real* wage. Furthermore, price and wage flexibility could easily, via expectations, give rise to price and wage instability. Keynes' arguments, if accepted, certainly provide a basis for a critique of mainstream macroeconomics, but it would be a critique which is not dependent on the source of interest rate maladjustment.

102 Journal of Economic Studies 12,1/2

In Shackle's view wage and price flexibility, even if Keynes' doubts of the system response to this are ignored, cannot correct interest rate maladjustment because the latter reflects speculators' expectations (which are not modified in any simple way by price and wage changes). No doubt if all other things could be held constant over an interval it would have to be conceded that price and wage flexibility (on present assumptions) would ensure that speculators would have continuously to absorb bond market flow demands and supplies. Over a sufficiently long period this might be expected to correct the maladjustment, but, in view of the comparative sizes of stocks and flows, the required interval could be very long. Shackle's perspective of the bond market, however, implies that the *ceteris paribus* assumptions could not be sustained over such long intervals: either bulls or bears would be proved wrong in their expectations for "immediate" changes in bond prices, and the conditions underlying the current, tentative bond market equilibrium would be undermined. The rate of interest is inherently restless.

For Shackle, the adverse judgement on price and wage flexibility is reinforced by consideration of the effects of uncertainty, which is at the root of liquidity preference, elsewhere in the system. Specifically, employers shoulder the risks of enterprise by having to produce in advance of the market. The value of the marginal product is thus unknown at the time at which labour is hired, and expectations of demand may be such that no reduction in the wage would stimulate firms' desired employment.

If our own view, that in tranquil, "within corridor" intervals, transactions costs lend importance to flow elements in the bond market, were to be accepted, and a stable system response to price and wage changes assumed, it would follow that in such intervals price and wage flexibility could, in principle, correct for interest rate maladjustment. Even in such circumstances, however, appropriate modification of the policy stance may permit more rapid and less costly correction of the inter-temporal price vector, an argument which has even greater force if there is any doubt (as surely there must be) concerning the stability of the system's response to wage and price deflation in particular. In turbulent periods, in contrast, the size of expected capital value changes overcomes the inertia which is otherwise imparted to asset markets by transactions costs. Consequently, stocks dominate flows, and the LP theory of the bond rate is validated. Furthermore, even if prices and wages were flexible, this could not ensure maladjustment correction, and such flexibility is unlikely to be desired: the predominance of stocks would preclude correction; the assumed conditions are such that an unstable response to price and wage changes is more likely. Whether this "hybrid" view of interest rate maladjustment is to be preferred to the universal variants of both LF and LP is ultimately an empirical issue. The lack of empirical work which seeks to discriminate among competing views must be attributed to what we consider to be the failure of mainstream macroeconomics fully to appreciate the significance of the nature of interest rate determination.

Summary and Conclusions

This article began by contrasting Professor Shackle's view of the originality and importance of the liquidity preference theory of interest with the currently dominant view that it is simply unimportant or seriously flawed. The main part of the article was devoted to a critical appraisal of the elements of Shackle's view of LP theory, and we then turned to consider its significance for macroeconomics as a whole.

The analysis serves to vindicate Shackle's position in the sense that it establishes that he assisted in the development of a logically consistent impact interval LP theory of bond interest rates[60], which, if accepted, has important implications for macroeconomics. His arguments with respect to the stock-flow issue, the nature of bond market expectations, and his preference for an instantaneous interval analysis were judged to be persuasive in the context of a theory of bond rate determination in very turbulent times. However, within the "corridor of comparative tranquility", which seems to us to be the predominant state of the world, his arguments would no longer apply. Period analyses in such a context were argued to be rendered relevant by the significance of frictions in the system additional to uncertainty, a fact which offers some support for an LF theory of bond rates. Even in such periods, though, Shackle's judgement as to the source and nature of financing of typical disturbances could form the basis of another variant of the LP theory of bond rates, although this is not a line which Shackle himself pursues.

The significance of interest theory for macroeconomics was viewed as depending largely on the likely persistence of the impact interval interest rate maladjustment (as compared to Classical Theory) which is characteristic of both LF and LP theories of interest rate determination. It was argued that price and wage flexibility could, *in principle,* correct for the source of interest rate maladjustment envisaged by LF theory, but not for that in Shackle's interpretation of LP theory. If this is accepted stabilisation policy *may* not be required to correct within corridor deviations from a full employment, stable price position, but definitely is essential to cope with turbulent intervals.

In conclusion, the current adverse assessment of the liquidity preference theory of interest rates implied by mainstream macroeconomics and monetary theory is in need of a major reappraisal, as Shackle's contributions suggest. Such a reappraisal is likely to lend approval to Professor Shackle's preferred version of liquidity preference theory, but as an important element in interest rate determination rather than the whole story.

Notes
1. If further evidence of the importance which Shackle attaches to liquidity preference theory is thought necessary, it can be found in, e.g., Shackle (1949(a); 1961(a), (d); 1967(a) chapters 12 and 15; 1972, book III; 1973(c) chapters 6, 9 and 10; 1974(a); 1980; 1983(a), (c)).
2. This is the basis of Leijonhufvud's (1981) critique of mainstream macroeconomics, which is discussed in the sixth section of this article. The "maladjustment" label is borrowed from this source.
3. The first quotation in this paper refers to the *technical* analysis of Keynes' theory. See, e.g., Shackle (1967(a), p. 209; 1983(c), p. 113).
4. These are the other areas of the macro-economy most often emphasised as being heavily influenced by uncertainty. See, e.g., Shackle (1967(a), p. 159).
5. This is the interpretation adopted by Bain and McGregor (1985).
6. Keynes' (1937(a), (b)) articles modified the position on *ex ante* investment, but we do not accept the view that the "finance motive" provides a reconciliation of LF and LP theories (McGregor, 1983).
7. See, for example, Shackle, (1961(d)).
8. This point, and the subsequent discussion, is attributable to Bain and McGregor (1985) and McGregor (1985(a)).
9. See Laidler (1984), Goodhart (1984) and Bain and McGregor (1985) for developments of this concept.
10. See, for example, Shackle (1974(a), pp. 58-59) and Shackle (1967(a), pp. 235-238).
11. One suggested to me by a reading of Rose (1957, p. 114).

12. It should be noted, however, that Kahn (1954), had proposed a very similar view of liquidity preference theory, as, indeed, had Townshend (1937) from whose work Shackle has often quoted. All of these authors, of course, view their analyses as interpretations, or developments, of Keynes' own theory.
13. Throughout this section, expectations are assumed to be given.
14. See, e.g., Shackle (1961(a), 1972, 1983(a), (c)).
15. May (1970), Foley (1975), Buiter and Woglom (1977), Turnovsky and Burmeister (1977), Buiter (1980).
16. McGregor (1985(b)) provides a more extensive analysis, on which the discussion of the text is based.
17. LP results apply in the sense that the increased saving has no immediate effect on bond rates.
18. This seems to coincide with Shackle's (1961(a), p. 241) own objection to the finance interval analysis.
19. See, e.g., Tsiang (1956, 1966, 1980, 1982), Kohn (1981(a), (b)).
20. McGregor (1983) attempts to develop this critique.
21. Appeal to an "as if" methodology does not provide a way out for LF theory here because of the "*ex ante* saving problem" — on which, see below.
22. Buiter (1980).
23. See McGregor (1985(b)). Part of the object of that paper is to show how the alternative models surmount the "*ex ante* saving problem" identified by Keynes (1937(a)) — i.e., how can mere plans to save influence market interest rates? — in very different ways.
24. Although we have expressed doubts about the theoretical basis of two of the three formulations of which this is true.
25. Numerous other references could be cited in support of our interpretation — even from the same paper (e.g., p. 246, 250, and the quotation from Clower, 1954 on p. 251 of Shackle, 1961(a)). See also Shackle (1967(a), p. 234, pp. 246-247; 1964, p. 20).
26. Foley (1975).
27. Foley (1975) had initially supposed that no such limit existed for the unmodified end-of-period equilibrium specification.
28. See McGregor (1985(b)). Recall that expectations are currently assumed to be exogenous.
29. See, e.g., Shackle (1961(a), p. 246).
30. A notable exception is Harrison (1980).
31. Whilst Foley (1975) attributed this to May (1970), Harrison (1980, footnote 14) disputes the exegetical accuracy of this attribution.
32. See, e.g., Shackle (1972, p. 157).
33. See, e.g., Ackley (1983, p. 2).
34. Ackley (1983) notes that this is an instance where rational expectations do not preclude prolonged periods of destabilising speculation.
35. See, e.g., Shackle (1972, p. 164).
36. Shackle, e.g., (1967(a), p. 247).
37. See also Kahn (1954) and Davidson (1971).
38. Underlying Shackle's view is a theory of individual portfolio selection which appears to imply a rather restrictive composition of individuals' portfolios. Ford (1983) has recently provided an exhaustive exposition and critique of Shackle's theory based on potential surprise, the ascendancy function and gambler preference map which is discussed in the preceding contributions to this volume by J. L. Ford and John Hey. It is consequently not considered in detail here.
39. e.g., Shackle (1961(a), 1972, p. 201).
40. These models actually preceded the development of more general rational expectations models, but, even in their weak form, seem to require the hypothesis of rational expectations for their validity.
41. Perhaps a weaker version suffices, which asserts that transactors can, on average, be viewed *as if* they know the relevant and correct model.
42. See, e.g., Shackle (1967(a), p. 223).
43. See also Townshend (1937) whom Shackle has often quoted with approval.
44. See, e.g., Shackle (1967(a), p. 247).
45. Econometric studies of asset markets based on conventional portfolio theory, especially when augmented to reflect the impact of transactions costs and other real world frictions, have achieved a fair measure of success.

46. The term is Leijonhufvud's (1973). We do not wish to imply, however, that there is no scope for stabilisation policy within the corridor. Stabilisation is essential, however, outwith the corridor.
47. See, e.g., Bain (1973).
48. Admittedly equilibrium can be re-established even in the absence of any actual transactions, a point which Shackle has often made. This is not costless reshuffling, however.
49. Peter Earl and Neil Kay in their contribution to this volume provide an interesting general discussion of related issues.
50. Robertsonian analysis can be interpreted as a special case of the theory of financial buffers in that it forces money to act as the sole financial shock absorber in the system. It is therefore one variant (and a particularly restrictive one) of "buffer stock monetarism" (Bain and McGregor, 1985).
51. Shackle, (1967(a), p. 91), emphasis in the original.
52. See, e.g, Shackle, (1967(a), p. 240).
53. See Johnston (1951-2). Robertson (1951-2) notes the extra deflationary effect of a money-financed increase in saving.
54. See, e.g., Chick (1983, p. 185).
55. Kohn (1981(b)) makes this point in criticism of Leijonhufvud (1981), in which context it is valid. The argument does not, however, possess the generality which Kohn attributed to it as we show below.
56. See, e.g., Barro and Grossman (1975), Hahn (1980) and Drazen (1980).
57. Laidler (1981) and Tobin (1981) provide reviews of monetarism.
58. Leijonhufvud's (1981) preferred interest theory seems inconsistent with his critique of mainstream macroeconomics.
59. See, e.g., Shackle (1961(d), as reprinted in Shackle, 1961(a), pp. 42-43).
60. We hinted that Keynes' *General Theory* contains the roots of a logically consistent, and distinct, LP theory of bill rates, but this is not a part of Shackle's theory and so it was not developed further.

References
Ackley, G., "Liquidity Preference and Loanable Funds Theories of Interest", *American Economic Review,* Vol. 47, 1957, pp. 662-73.
Ackley, G., "Commodities and Capital: Prices and Quantities", *American Economic Review,* Vol. 73, 1983, pp. 1-16.
Bain, A. D., "Flow of Funds Analysis: A Survey", *Economic Journal,* Vol. 83, 1973, pp. 1055-93.
Bain, A. D. and McGregor, P. G., "Buffer Stock Monetarism and the Theory of Financial Buffers", *The Manchester School,* (forthcoming).
Barro, R. J. and Grossman, H. I., *Money, Employment and Inflation,* Cambridge, Cambridge University Press, 1975.
Buiter, W. H., "Walras' Law and All That: Budget Constraints and Balance Sheet Constraints in Period Models and Continuous Time Models", *International Economic Review,* Vol. 21, 1980, pp. 1-16.
Buiter, W. H. and Woglom, G., "On Two Specifications of Asset Equilibrium in Macroeconomic Models: A Note", *Journal of Political Economy,* Vol. 85, 1977, pp. 395-400.
Chick, V., *Macroeconomics After Keynes: A Reconsideration of the General Theory,* Oxford, Philip Allan, 1983.
Davidson, P., *Money and the Real World,* London, Macmillan, 1972.
Drazen, A., "Recent Developments in Macroeconomic Disequilibrium Theory", *Econometrica,* Vol. 48, 1980, pp. 283-305.
Edwards, E. O., "The Interest Rate in Disequilibrium", *Southern Economic Journal,* Vol. 23, 1966, pp. 49-57.
Foley, D. K., "On Two Specifications of Asset Equilibrium in Macroeconomic Models", *Journal of Political Economy,* Vol. 83, 1975, pp. 305-324.
Foley, D. K., "Reply to Buiter and Woglom", *Journal of Political Economy,* Vol. 85, 1977, pp. 401-2.
Ford, J. L., *Choice, Expectation and Uncertainty,* Oxford, Martin Robertson, 1983.
Goodhart, C. A. E., "Disequilibrium Money — A Note", Chapter X in Goodhart's *Monetary Theory and Practice,* London, Macmillan, 1984.
Grossman, H, I., "Money, Interest and Prices in Market Disequilibrium", *Journal of Political Economy,* Vol. 79, 1971, pp. 943-61.

Hahn, F. H., "The Rate of Interest and General Equilibrium Analysis", *Economic Journal*, Vol. 65, 1955, pp. 52-66.

Hahn, F. H., "Monetarism and Economic Theory", *Economica*, Vol. 47, 1980, pp. 1-7.

Harrison, G. W., "The Stock Flow Distinction: A Suggested Interpretation", *Journal of Macroeconomics*, Vol. 2, 1980, pp. 111-128.

Johnson, H. G., "Some Cambridge Controversies in Monetary Theory", *Review of Economic Studies*, Vol. 19, 1951/2, pp. 90-104.

Kahn, R. F., "Some Notes on Liquidity Preference", *The Manchester School*, Vol. 22, 1954, pp. 229-57.

Keynes, J. M., *A Treatise on Money*, London, Macmillan, 1930.

Keynes, J. M., *The General Theory of Employment, Interest and Money*, London, Macmillan, 1936.

Keynes, J. M., "Alternative Theories of the Rate of Interest", *Economic Journal*, Vol. 47, 1937(a), pp. 241-52.

Keynes, J. M., "The Ex-Ante Theory of the Rate of Interest", *Economic Journal*, Vol. 47, 1937(b), pp. 663-669.

Kohn, M., "In Defence of the Finance Constraint", *Economic Inquiry*, Vol. 19, 1981(a), pp. 177-195.

Kohn, M., "A Loanable Funds Theory of Unemployment and Monetary Disequilibrium", *American Economic Review*, Vol. 71, 1981(b), pp. 859-879.

Laidler, D., "Monetarism: An Interpretation and Assessment", *Economic Journal*, Vol. 91, 1981, pp. 1-28.

Laidler, D., "The 'Buffer-Stock' Notion in Monetary Economics", *Economic Journal*, Vol. 94, 1984, pp. 17-34.

Leijonhufvud, A., *On Keynesian Economics and the Economics of Keynes*, Oxford, Oxford University Press, 1968.

Leijonhufvud, A., "Effective Demand Failures", *Swedish Economic Journal*, Vol. 75, 1973, pp. 27-48, reprinted as Chapter 6 in Leijonhufvud (1981).

Leijonhufvud, A., "The Wicksell Connection: Variations on a Theme", Chapter 7 in Leijonhufvud's *Information and Co-ordination*, Oxford, Oxford University Press, 1981.

May, J., "Period Analysis and Continuous Analysis in Patinkin's Macroeconomic Model", *Journal of Economic Theory*, Vol. 2, 1970, pp. 1-9.

McGregor, P. G., "Finance Constraints, Keynes' Finance Motive for Liquidity and Monetary Theory", *University of Strathclyde Discussion Papers in Economics*, No. 83/6, 1983.

McGregor, P. G., "Financial Buffers and the Liquidity Preference versus Loanable Funds Debate", University of Strathclyde, mimeo, 1985'a).

McGregor, P. G., "On the Appropriate Specification of Asset Market Equilibrium", University of Strathclyde, mimeo, 1985(b).

Robertson, D. H., "Comments on Mr Johnson's Notes", *Review of Economic Studies*, Vol. 19, 1951/2, pp. 105-110.

Robinson, J., "The Rate of Interest", *Econometrica*, Vol. 19, 1951.

Rose, H., "Liquidity Preference and Loanable Funds", *Review of Economic Studies*, Vol. 24, 1957, pp. 111-119.

Tobin, J., "The Monetarist Counter-Revolution Today — An Appraisal", *Economic Journal*, Vol. 91, 1981, pp. 29-42.

Townshend, H., "Liquidity premium and the Theory of Value", *Economic Journal*, Vol. 47, 1937, pp. 157-169.

Tsiang, S. C., "Liquidity Preference and Loanable Funds Theories, Multiplier and Velocity Analyses: A Synthesis", *American Economic Review*, Vol. 46, 1956, pp. 539-64.

Tsiang, S. C., "Walras' Law, Say's Law and Liquidity Preference in General Equilibrium Analysis", *International Economic Review*, Vol. 7, 1966, pp. 239-45.

Tsiang, S. C., "Keynes' 'Finance' Demand for Liquidity, Robertson's Loanable Funds Theory and Friedman's Monetarism", *Quarterly Journal of Economics*, Vol. 95, 1980, pp. 467-491.

Tsiang, S. C., "Stock or Portfolio Approach to Monetary Theory and the Neo-Keynesian School of James Tobin", *IHS-Journal*, Vol. 6, 1982, pp. 140-171.

Turnovsky, S. J. and Burmeister, E., "Perfect Foresight, Expectational Consistency and Macroeconomic Equilibrium", *Journal of Political Economy*, Vol. 85, 1977, pp. 379-393.

Name Index

Pioneers in Economics

19. William Whewell (1794–1866), Dionysius Lardner (1793–1859), Charles Babbage (1792–1871)

20. George Scrope (1797–1876), Thomas Attwood (1783–1856), Edwin Chadwick (1800–1890), John Cairnes (1823–1875)

21. James Mill (1773–1836), John Rae (1796–1872), Edward West (1782–1828), Thomas Joplin (1790–1847)

22. James Wilson (1805–1860), Issac Butt (1813–1879), T. E. Cliffe Leslie (1827–1882)

23. Karl Marx (1818–1883)

Section III: Neoclassical Economics and its Critics

24. Johann von Thünen (1783–1850), Augustin Cournot (1801–1877), Jules Dupuit (1804–1866)

25. Leon Walras (1834–1910)

26. Carl Menger (1840–1921)

27. Eugen von Böhm-Bawerk (1851–1914) and Friedrich von Wieser (1851–1926)

28. Knut Wicksell (1851–1926)

29. Alfred Marshall (1842–1924) and Francis Edgeworth (1845–1926)

30. Gustav Schmoller (1838–1917) and Werner Sombart (1863–1941)

31. Dissenters
    Charles Fourier (1772–1837), Henri de St Simon (1760–1825), Pierre-Joseph Proudhon (1809–1865), John A. Hobson (1858–1940)

32. Thorstein Veblen (1857–1929)

33. Wesley Mitchell (1874–1948), John Commons (1862–1945), Clarence Ayres (1891–1972)

34. Henry George (1839–1897)

35. Vilfredo Pareto (1848–1923)

Section IV: Twentieth Century Economics

36. Arthur Pigou (1877–1959)

37. Frank Knight (1885–1972), Henry Simons (1899–1946), Joseph Schumpeter (1883–1950)

38. Edward Chamberlin (1899–1967)